KINNOCK

KINNOCK

MICHAEL LEAPMAN

UNWIN HYMAN

London   Sydney

First published in Great Britain by Unwin Hyman, an imprint
of Unwin Hyman Limited, 1987

UNWIN HYMAN
Denmark House, 37-39 Queen Elizabeth Street,
London SE1 2QB
and
40 Museum Street, London WC1A 1LU

Allen & Unwin (Australia) Ltd
8 Napier Street, North Sydney, NSW 2060, Australia

Allen & Unwin New Zealand Ltd with the Port Nicholson Press,
60 Cambridge Terrace,
Wellington, New Zealand

British Library Cataloguing in Publication Data

Leapman, Michael
  Kinnock.
  1. Kinnock, Neil   2. Politicians –
Great Britain – Biography
I. Title
941.085'092'4   DA591.K5
ISBN 0-04-440006-3

Set in 11 on 12 point Plantin by Fotographics (Bedford) Ltd
and printed in Great Britain by Mackays of Chatham

Contents

Introduction

The question I was asked most often while writing this book was: 'Is it an official biography?' The answer is no on both counts – neither official nor a biography. It is not official because the initiative came from me, not from Neil Kinnock or the Labour Party. It is not a biography because it skips lightly over his life before he became Leader of the Opposition in October, 1983, a period well covered in the two 1984 biographies by G. M. F. Drower and Robert Harris, listed in the bibliography. My book effectively picks up the story from there. It is an account of how a young and relatively unknown politician was able to take an enfeebled, notoriously fractious party and, in a very short time, mould it into shape to mount a credible challenge to the Government at a general election. If at times it reads like *The Perils of Pauline* – or, as Kinnock himself calls it, 'High Noon' journalism – it is because that is what those four years have been like.

I decided that, without Kinnock's co-operation, I would not undertake the project – not just because he was clearly a crucial source, but because if my purpose was to assess his impact on the party I would have to tap party sources. I assumed that unless Kinnock gave his consent I could not expect much help from his colleagues, either.

His office took a long time to respond to my initial proposal. After all, I had never met him, nor any of his close confidants. As a journalist I had never worked at Westminster and had written about politics only obliquely – as a diplomatic reporter, a newspaper diarist and a foreign correspondent. It was some months and several phone calls after my first approach that I was able to meet first his press secretary, Patricia Hewitt, then Kinnock himself.

He was not encouraging. He pointed out that, even if he agreed, my access to him would be less frequent and less complete than I should require. He said he was not good at sitting down and analysing his own actions and motives, even if his schedule allowed it. He warned me that I should be frustrated by the limited time he could give to me and my endeavours. When that failed to deter me, he agreed to submit himself to the ordeal. I offered to show him the manuscript prior to publication and to take his observations on it into account, although this did not amount to a right of veto. Nor does it mean that the blame for any errors lies on shoulders other than mine.

In the event the process worked rather better, at least from my point of view, than Kinnock had predicted. I soon learned that the only way I could count on any sustained stretch of time with him was when he was travelling – thus beyond most other claims on his attention. So we had a series of discussions in cars, trains and, once, on a plane between Gatwick and Atlanta. This book owes an enormous amount to his consistently helpful attitude, and I am most grateful to him.

Kinnock's colleagues and friends, and his wife Glenys, were also accommodating and generous with their time. Regrettably, most of his opponents in the party were deterred when I told them that Kinnock was co-operating. Some of the discussions I had were on 'lobby terms' (if the phrase is not nowadays redundant). I have therefore decided not to identify any sources, since a partial list would be misleading. My thanks to them all.

My first – I hope not my last – exposure to Westminster has been invigorating and intriguing. It is a self-contained world with its own rituals that affect the mind-set of the men and women who work there. They choose to seek election to Parliament because of their conviction that they have the ability to put into practice political ideas which will benefit their fellow citizens. Once there, they discover that to be effective they have to master techniques that often conflict with their idealism. They must speak the language of self-righteousness while cynically practising the black art of the possible, making deals and forging alliances that may compromise their ideological purity. Just as I was finishing this book, early in 1987, John Biffen, Leader of the House, expressed it succinctly. Asked by a Liberal MP whether he had no shame, he told the Commons: 'If I had any shred of shame I would not be following this profession.' I do not think he was joking.

Kinnock found it hard to adjust to that *realpolitik* when he arrived in the House in 1970. He was frustrated by how little influence a junior backbench MP could wield. He knew, though, that if he wanted to gain the power to give effect to his beliefs, he would have to learn the rules and how to play by them. How he adopted the politics of realism and persuaded the party to accept them is the theme of this book. It is not a compendium of his ideas and attitudes in every policy area. The issues I have highlighted are those that best illustrate the nature of his leader-ship – those where he was able, by a combination of determination and political dexterity, to rally reluctant colleagues to his viewpoint. Thus there are gaps: nothing about Northern Ireland or South Africa, not much about health and education – issues on which the party is more or less united.

My induction into the mysteries of Westminster was made much easier by the help I received from Kinnock's staff. Despite the hectic pace of work in an Opposition Leader's office, they found time to respond to my pleas for assistance and do me numerous kindnesses. I thank them all, in particular Patricia Hewitt, Andrew Fox, Hilary Coffman, Chris Child, Charles Clarke, Dick Clements, Kay Andrews and the super-efficient Sue Nye. Peter Mandelson and Anna Healey, of the Labour HQ at Walworth Road, also gave valuable help.

The book owes much to Adam Sisman, the chief editor who commissioned it. While I was writing it the publishers, George Allen and Unwin, merged with Bell and Hyman to become Unwin Hyman. Robin Hyman, the new managing director, and his colleague Mary Butler, faced with the many problems of re-shaping two companies into one, at the same time inherited a book which by its nature had to be published at unusual speed. They overcame the difficulties with professionalism and good humour, as did Barbara Fuller, a skilful and understanding editor.

KINNOCK

1 *Here We Go*

At noon on the final day of the Labour Party's 1986 Blackpool conference, visitors seated on the balconies of the ornate Empress Ballroom in the Winter Garden, viewing the platform from the sides rather than the front, were treated to an intriguing spectacle. A slim young man with a pale face and a black moustache, wearing a stylish dark suit, tiptoed warily on to the platform carrying two boxes of fresh red roses. Concealed from the main body of the hall by the screen that had been put behind the rostrum for the benefit of the television cameras, he carefully placed the boxes out of sight on the floor. Then he made his way to one of the VIP seats at the back of the stage, behind those reserved for the National Executive Committee.

From the middle of the front row Larry Whitty, the Labour Party's general secretary, was making his closing remarks, cracking ritual jokes at the expense of the conference chairman, Neville Hough. When he sat down, a 65-year-old woman, a long-time party member, proposed the motion of thanks to the organizers. It was seconded by a 20-year-old man wearing a smart suit for his first party conference. The industrial correspondent of the *Star* made a surprisingly witty speech on behalf of the press and then it was time for the rousing finale – the boisterous rendering of *The Red Flag*, followed by *Auld Lang Syne*. That was the point at which the man who had brought the roses – Peter Mandelson, the party's new director of communications – handed them to Neil and Glenys Kinnock, who tossed them randomly into the congregation of around 2,000. As the delegates scrambled to gather up the blooms as souvenirs, the organist switched to the unattractive but optimistic chant that had become the unofficial theme of the conference: 'Here we go, here we go, here we go . . .'.

It was an untraditional end to an untypical conference. For once, there had been no spectacular clashes between the left and right wings of the party. The policies recommended by the National Executive Committee (NEC) had, with only minor exceptions, been adopted. The expulsion of leaders of the Trotskyist Militant tendency had been confirmed overwhelmingly. A potential embarrassment about the new non-nuclear defence policy had been nipped in the bud. Speeches from the floor had been less virulent than usual and there were few overt attacks on the leadership. As a bonus for Kinnock, his rigid old opponent Eric Heffer, who had walked out of the Bournemouth conference a year earlier as a protest against the leader's attack on Militant, had been voted off the NEC – the party's supreme authority on

1

matters of policy and organization. He had been replaced by the Scottish MP Tam Dalyell, more likely to support the leadership.

The press had contrasted this new mood of bullish confidence with the atmosphere at Brighton three years earlier. There, in the wake of a demoralizing election defeat, the 41-year-old Kinnock had been picked to replace Michael Foot as leader by a party in desperate need of fresh inspiration. The optimism at Blackpool was not simply a reflex reaction to the prospect of a general election before the next gathering of the faithful. Nor was it a result of the slicker presentation that Mandelson had masterminded, scornfully derided by traditionalists as 'stage management'. It was true that there were improved press facilities, and a better worked-out timetable, and extra thought was given to which speakers to call from the floor. The low-key pale beige platform – sporting a red stripe like an Inter-City railway carriage – made it easier on the television viewer's eye. But none of this would have been effective were it not for the firm and ever tighter grip that Kinnock had been able to impose upon the party in his three years as leader.

He had achieved it partly by dealing in person with apparently minor details that others in his position would have left to subordinates. The roses were a case in point. Kinnock had long been critical of the old logo – the party's name in the form of a billowing flag. He had suggested a new symbol with broader appeal and greater vitality. He wanted something as uncomplicated as the plain red map pin employed by the social democrats in Germany. A red rose came to mind because it is the flower of the Socialist International, which Kinnock supports enthusiastically. During the leadership campaign he had cards printed with his name and the SI rose symbol. It was also used during the European Election campaign in 1984 – the first campaign after he assumed the leadership.

In January 1986 he thought it time to make the rose the official party emblem. He discussed the change with Mandelson, a former television producer who had been appointed in October 1985, with Kinnock's keen support, to revamp the party's image. Mandelson had already been in touch with designers and advertising professionals who supported Labour and were willing to donate their services. He asked one of them to create a rose and the symbol was approved by the NEC shortly before the conference began. The anti-Labour press made predictable jokes about the thorns concealed on the stem, and left wingers feared that abandoning the flag signified a weakening of the party's campaigning tradition.

Dennis Skinner, one of the stalwart members of the hard left on the NEC, penned a song about it and sang it in front of a television camera in the Winter Garden lobby. It went to the tune of *The Red Flag* and began:

The people's rose in shades of pink
Gets up your nose and makes a stink.

But most delegates liked the new symbol. Rose lapel badges sold out at the conference bookshop before the week was half over. Carrier bags with the motif were in great demand and everyone agreed the rose draperies over the stands in the exhibition hall were strikingly effective. Kinnock had his reservations about some of the fine detail. He thought the stem was too long, it leaned too much and the flower head needed tightening up. Still, it gave him and Glenys something symbolic to hurl from the platform at the end of the conference. Delegates could leave on an up-beat note, the lucky ones clutching their cherished blooms.

*   *   *

The Friday morning of the conference is always less well attended than the previous five days. Most constituency and trade union delegates stay until the bitter end but many MPs have already left for their constituencies and some journalists have written their last assessments and returned to base. The proceedings on 3 October 1986, however, were worth waiting around for. They amounted to a microcosm of today's Labour Party, a measure of how far Kinnock had taken it in three years, pulling it from the floor to be in credible shape to fight an election.

The morning began with a short debate about the media, with the conference approving a resolution calling on the next Labour Government to pass a law preventing foreigners from owning British newspapers or broadcasting organizations. Since it was proposed by the National Graphical Association and seconded by the Society for Graphical and Allied Trades – the unions most concerned in the Wapping dispute – there were no prizes for guessing that it was aimed at Rupert Murdoch, the Australian-born citizen of the United States, with whose papers the unions were in conflict. The Wapping anti-Murdoch picket had been a principal moral crusade of the left throughout 1986, and it was fitting that the arguments, however familiar, should be aired ritually at the Labour conference: ritually because the party had already severed relations with the Murdoch press and it was hard to see what more could be done.

Next came a discussion of the youth section. For two decades the Labour Party Young Socialists have proved a fertile recruiting ground for the Militant tendency, a group Kinnock sees as incompatible with democratic socialism. He and his colleagues on the NEC had spent much of the previous 12 months in a lengthy and ultimately successful operation to expel Militant leaders. The proposal before conference

3

now was to establish an inquiry into the youth section with a view to reducing the maximum age for membership from 26 to 21 – a move that would weaken Militant's hold by weeding out the more mature and self-confident revolutionaries whose influence can be decisive. Militant supporters tried the procedural manoeuvre of referring the resolution back to the NEC but Neville Hough, the no-nonsense chairman, would not allow it. A group of young delegates rushed to the rostrum and tried to address the conference but the loud-speaker had been turned off and they gesticulated in vain, chanting 'reference back has been moved', as though it were some divine incantation. Russell Profitt, one of the six black Labour candidates likely to be in the Commons after the next election, took advantage of the confusion to renew his advocacy of a separate black section in the party, a proposal Kinnock is vehemently opposed to and one that had been rejected decisively by conference earlier in the week. The rumpus died down and a card vote was taken. It resulted in a huge majority in favour of reorganizing the youth section – 6,051,000 to 256,000.

That was Militant's final attempt to salvage something out of Blackpool 1986. On the Monday, the day after the conference opened, delegates at a secret session had confirmed by a similarly overwhelming majority the NEC's decision, reached after lengthy disciplinary hearings, to expel eight leading Liverpool Militants, including Derek Hatton and Tony Mulhearn. The eight had decided not to make their anticipated final plea to delegates: they complained about the press being excluded and added that their allotted five minutes each was not enough time to make their case properly.

It would have been over-optimistic to assume that, with the expulsions ratified, the Militant problem had now been solved; but there was a distinct feeling that the Trotskyists were in retreat. Most members appreciated that this was largely due to Kinnock's personal determination to stamp out 'entryist' groups using the party as a recruiting ground for sects whose philosophy is essentially in conflict with mainstream politics as practised in Britain. It is only through the conventional political system that Labour can regain power. The activities of Militant have been an obstacle on the path to this objective.

Neil and Glenys were not on the platform that Friday mid-morning to watch the final futile attempt by Militant adherents to make their mark. Instead, the couple were visiting the crèche established in the Winter Garden for delegates' children, posing for winsome photographs that appeared on the front pages of many of the next morning's newspapers. As they held babies and fed them their bottles, they were very deliberately personifying the 'cuddly left' – radicalism with a gentler face than that presented by far left activists.

They returned to the hall in time for the debate on shipbuilding

4

where Dennis Skinner, having stayed silent on the platform until now, was given the opportunity to put the NEC's case and condemn the Government's record. It was a rousing, popular speech, proving that Skinner was not daunted by the loss from the NEC of his hard-left ally Heffer, or by the other setbacks suffered by his wing of the party during the conference:

'The next Labour Government will see to it that the Red Duster is flying throughout the shipping lanes of the world,' he declaimed. Labour would build a ship to send American nuclear missiles back, one to take food mountains from the European Community to the Third World, and another to defend Nicaragua against American incursions. Kinnock joined in the appreciative applause. He has less antipathy towards Skinner than to the other left-wingers on (and off) the NEC, especially Heffer and Tony Benn. A blunt man who does not know how to be devious, Skinner's views are unshakeable and he has no truck with compromise. He boasts that he has not changed his position on any fundamental political issue for 30 years.

Being silenced until the dying moments of the conference was not the only tactical defeat Skinner had to endure during the week. More significant was his failure to be elected vice-chairman of the party – a post that comes around on the 'Buggins' turn' principle, leading to the chairmanship of the party, and thus of the conference, the following year. Skinner and Kinnock had equal seniority on the NEC but it is not usual for the party leader to take up such a post. Anxious to avoid the damage to the image of the party that could be caused by having Skinner running a conference, Kinnock broke with precedent and offered himself for the post, adding that he was going to propose a change in the rules so that he would not in fact succeed to the chairmanship. He was elected – another small but significant victory over the left.

There was more for Kinnock to smile about in the speech by Larry Whitty, whose appointment he had secured a year earlier to head the party organization at Walworth Road, South London. Under Whitty, Labour HQ is better administered than ever before to give constructive support to the leadership in the election. In his closing speech, Whitty said:

'This has been a very effective conference. It has been serious, unified and self-confident. We managed to introduce pretty radical policies with the minimum of fuss.'

*   *   *

Yet in many superficial respects, Blackpool 1986 was little different from Labour conferences for the last decade and more. While the far left may have been muted in the conference hall itself, all shades of

5

socialist opinion and most of the causes that concern party members were reflected in the rich variety of the fringe meetings held during lunch breaks and in the evenings. In the official conference guide book – redesigned by Mandelson and his team to give it the feel of a Sunday colour supplement – a fringe diary listed 169 meetings and gatherings between the Saturday before the conference and Thursday, the penultimate day. Many others were not listed: either arranged too late for inclusion or too far from party orthodoxy to be acceptable in the official guide.

Anyone who made a selective tour of the fringe on Monday, after the first full day of the conference, could have been forgiven for thinking that the hard left was alive and well and about to take over the party. The circuit could have started at the Imperial, the headquarters' hotel, at a meeting of the Campaign Forum, the latest of the periodic attempts to link groups of the far left under a single banner. It advertised itself as a tripartite alliance of grassroots campaigns, already linked in Labour Left Liaison, with the Campaign Group of MPs (formed in 1982 as a far left alternative to the more moderate Tribune Group) and left trade unionists. Labour Left Liaison includes the Campaign for Labour Party Democracy, black section activists, Labour CND (Campaign for Nuclear Disarmament), LWAC (Labour Women's Action Committee) and some journals. Ann Pettifer of LWAC was in the chair and as it happened she had something to crow about: the left's first – and by some reckoning its last – victory at the 1986 conference.

On the previous day, Sunday 28 September, the opening debate had resulted in a defeat for the NEC. It was about women's rights. One of the resolutions called on the next Labour Government to create a Ministry for Women with a Minister in the Cabinet. This had been among the most controversial matters discussed by the NEC at their pre-conference session earlier in the day. Kinnock, though in favour of a women's ministry, did not want to commit himself to putting the minister in the Cabinet, as there were other special interests that could be regarded as worthy of that status; among them science, the arts and overseas development. The danger was that he would find himself bound to expand the Cabinet to an unworkable size. With some reluctance the NEC bowed to his wishes and agreed not to endorse that resolution but to ask for its reference back. When it came to a vote, the conference approved the resolution by 3,335,000 to 2,905,000, probably because Jo Richardson, deputed to make the case on behalf of the NEC, began by saying that she was personally in favour of the minister being in the Cabinet. Kinnock put a brave face on this minor setback, stressing that he himself supported the principle, although he would have preferred to keep his options open in practice.

The incident allowed Ann Pettifer to speak of a 'magnificent victory' when she opened the Campaign Forum meeting. In a general statement of the principles of the group, she stressed their opposition to the singling out of particular left organizations (i.e. Militant) for persecution. But she laid emphasis, as did many left speakers throughout the week, on the paramount need to secure a Labour Government.

She introduced Marc Wadsworth, the chair of the black sections movement. He denounced the Black and Asian Advisory Committee which the NEC had set up as a way of diverting pressure for the establishment of black sections. The demand of black people in the Labour Party to 'self-organize' was non-negotiable, he declared, adding that the six black MPs likely to be elected for Labour would all join the Campaign Group. And he referred to the case of Amir Khan and Kevin Scally, expelled from the party in the Sparkbrook, Birmingham constituency where Roy Hattersley, the deputy party leader, is the sitting MP. Hattersley is a favourite target for left-wingers. Many had hoped to make the campaign to reinstate the two men a focal point for agitation at the conference, but the NEC outflanked them by announcing that the cases were being reviewed anyway.

Tony Benn spoke next, for the Campaign Group. Invariably the most sought-after fringe speaker, he addresses three or four meetings on most days of a conference. At this one he gave a straightforward account of the Campaign Group's record on contentious issues: support for the miners' and teachers' strikes, for the Wapping pickets, for black sections, against expulsions. He renewed his call for an electoral college to elect both the Shadow Cabinet and the Cabinet itself when Labour achieves power, similar to the college of trade unions, constituency parties and MPs that now elects the leader. At present the Shadow Cabinet is elected by the Parliamentary Party. Under new party rules a Labour Prime Minister is obliged to include all elected Shadow Cabinet members in his first actual Cabinet, but is free to make subsequent changes and new appointments on his own initiative – a prerogative Kinnock would be unwilling to forfeit.

Benn characterized the conference as an eve-of-poll rally designed to make Kinnock and the party look good. 'But we're also trying to re-found the Labour Party. Neil Kinnock in power will need a strong Labour Party.' The kind of strong party Benn envisages, however, is precisely the kind of party Kinnock would find an embarrassment both in the process of achieving power and of exercising it.

Tony Benn was also in the cast list for the main far left event of Monday evening, the *Labour Herald* rally at the Spanish Hall in the Winter Garden. *Labour Herald* is a London-based journal founded by Ted Knight, former leader of Lambeth Council, and Ken Livingstone, former leader of the Greater London Council. Knight was in the forefront of the campaign by Labour local authorities against the

Conservatives' ratecapping legislation and he led Lambeth councillors in their refusal to set a rate to accord with the Government guidelines. The result was that he and the other rebel councillors incurred heavy personal surcharges and were disqualified from office. Livingstone had broken ranks with Knight by approving a legal rate for the GLC, in its last months of life before abolition.

Livingstone then resigned as a joint editor of *Labour Herald* and was replaced by his former deputy leader on the GLC, John McDonnell. The personable Livingstone, a popular performer on radio and television discussion programmes, became a leading figure in the Labour Co-ordinating Committee (LCC), the so-called 'soft left', whose views correspond broadly with those of the Tribune Group. To McDonnell fell the task of chairing the Blackpool fringe meeting. Several hundred people, paying £1 each, packed the hall – a neo-baroque extravaganza with crude tableaux beneath the ceiling at each corner, depicting idyllic Iberian landscapes of cottages with lighted windows under electric blue skies.

McDonnell speaks softly but with a passion laced with vitriol. He called for commitments from Labour to reinstate striking miners who had been sacked, to pardon those convicted of picket line violence and to repay councillors' surcharges. He demanded dates for withdrawing British troops from Northern Ireland, for closing the South African embassy and getting rid of nuclear bases. 'As Neil Kinnock jumps out of his jacuzzi and Roy Hattersley slaps on the make-up for *Newsnight*,' they should remember that people were suffering – such as those on the picket line at Wapping.

The audience cheered wildly, as they did for Diane Abbott, one of the new black candidates. She complained that 'to make the party acceptable to the great and the good', it was being purged of its left wing. 'We don't want a party that places a higher premium on packaging than content. ... We can't settle for anything less than a radical transformation of society.'

Tony Benn, dashing in from another meeting, was clearly not going to settle for anything less, either. 'Labour is a funny party,' he confided, pointing to the enthusiasm shown at the conference that day when tribute had been paid to the Jarrow unemployment marchers of 1936. Where, though, was the leadership's support for today's heroes, the miners and the Lambeth councillors? And he warned Abbott, a relative newcomer to the platforms of the left: 'First they'll say you're dangerous, then they'll say you're mad.'

Arthur Scargill, President of the National Union of Mineworkers, arrived even later, to a tumultuous welcome. His target was the politics of 'consensus' – a word Kinnock had used the previous month at the Trades Union Congress at Brighton. 'I believe in socialism, not consensus. If the people in Nicaragua and Zimbabwe had sought consensus it wouldn't have worked. They were revolutionaries.' Scargill was responsible for the débâcle of the miners' strike of 1984–5 but he insisted that, despite setbacks, he would continue to fight. 'I'm not downhearted. I know we're on a winning trail.'

The meeting had started at 7.30 and by the time Scargill sat down it was past 10 pm. The audience began to break up as a speaker from Sinn Fein took the floor, and by the time Ted Knight stood up to make the final speech the hall was barely half full. That was not, however, what he was referring to when he complained about the attempt to marginalize the far left at the conference: the surcharged councillors had not even been allowed to occupy a stand in the exhibition hall to raise money. Nevertheless, the working class would continue fighting imperialism on all fronts: 'I want a Labour Government elected in the wake of a struggle to keep the Labour Party firm.'

From the noise and fervour of the *Labour Herald* rally, and from the variety of choice every evening of meetings of a like persuasion, you would not guess that the far left was being marginalized. Among other fringe events to choose from during the week were a discussion of witch-hunts between Eric Heffer and a member of the Independent Labour Party; 'No retreat from socialism – halt the drift to the right', organized by the Campaign for Labour Party Democracy; 'Organizing for a Labour Victory' by the Militant-backed Labour Party Young Socialists; meetings on gay and lesbian rights, nuclear weapons, Palestine, Northern Ireland, Nicaragua, Namibia, Iran, Eritrea, Chile, Vietnam – virtually every foreign and domestic issue of concern to the far left.

Yet while the opportunities for left-wingers to express themselves outside the conference chamber were not noticeably fewer in 1986 than in previous years, there were a number of subtle differences. To begin with, press and television reporters took less interest in fringe events than anyone could remember. The party organization had grabbed the initiative and was setting the agenda for the week, rather than let the extremists make the running in terms of publicity. Another change was a growing number of fringe meetings not sponsored by the left. The Parliamentary Labour Party has its own groups and committees dealing with specific policy areas and some of these organized meetings – the foreign affairs group, the home affairs group and the environment committee, for example. And while the noisy left could not get the coverage it was accustomed to, some hitherto obscure organizations managed to attract attention by having Glenys Kinnock on the panel. Since she is clearly an electoral asset, media interest in her is encouraged: so when she appeared at meetings talking about overseas food aid or child care for the under fives, the cameras would often be there. And if they were with her, they could not at the same time be filming revolutionary gatherings elsewhere.

Glenys's opportunities to perform on the fringe were limited by her obligation to accompany Neil on his compulsory rounds of that other form of conference night life, the parties and receptions. They are invited to more than they can possibly attend. The ones they must not miss are hosted by the trade union leaders whose support is so vital in Neil's battle for majorities in the NEC and on the conference floor. So on Monday, after the first full day of the conference, he called in at nine receptions before returning to his hotel room to write his speech for the following day.

Wednesday 1 October was a less busy night but included some of the Kinnocks' most important social obligations of the week. Glenys arrived ahead of Neil at the first of them, a party hosted by Robert Maxwell at the Imperial Hotel. Maxwell's Mirror Group newspapers are sometimes erratic in their support for Labour but, in the context of an otherwise hostile press, they are invaluable. Neil was late because he had been at the meeting of the National Executive Committee where he successfully proposed himself for party vice-chairman to stop the job passing to Dennis Skinner. He did not have to stay with Maxwell long because he had earlier lunched with the tycoon and been presented with a cheque for £10,000 for the election fund.

After only 15 minutes he was ushered into his car for the short drive to the Savoy Hotel, further up the promenade, and a party given by the shop workers' union USDAW. Before all such union gatherings he is reminded by experts on his staff about the names of the principals and the union's current chief concerns, for he is expected to deliver a little speech. It is invariably safe to mention the political fund ballot, where the Conservative Government legislated to force unions to ballot their members about whether they wanted to continue paying a levy to the Labour Party. If the ballots had been lost the effect on the party's funding would have been disastrous, but all the unions voted in favour, most by large majorities.

With so many speeches for Kinnock to make, it is scarcely surprising that passages recur. One of his favourites concerns idealism and realism. 'Idealism is the energy of socialism and realism the means to carry it out.' But there are always, too, segments tailor-made for the particular audience: in the case of USDAW he congratulated them on the Parliamentary defeat of legislation to allow Sunday opening, which the union opposed. Neil and Glenys posed cheerfully for seemingly endless group photographs and signed dozens of autographs before the staff tactfully eased them back to the car.

Next stop was the upstairs room of the Raikes Hall, a pub near the town centre, for a hot and crowded meeting of the National Union of

10

Labour and Socialist Clubs. Men sweating in open-neck shirts pushed to get close to where Kinnock stood making appropriate remarks and a few raucous jokes. Even in the crush, space was cleared for more group pictures.

His next function was the most significant – a cabaret evening for Trade Unions for Labour (TUFL), a body established before the 1983 election as a response to the Conservatives' moves since 1979 to curb the power of the unions. Recognizing that the only sure way to reverse this trend is to elect a Labour Government, TUFL raises funds for the election campaign. Kinnock's first meeting after arriving in Blackpool was with the two most influential officials in TUFL – Ron Todd, the general secretary of the TGWU (Transport and General Workers Union) and Bill Keys, formerly general secretary of SOGAT. It was a measure of the importance he places on their support.

The cabaret was in progress when the Kinnock party arrived at the Winter Gardens' Spanish Hall. A 'socialist magician' told variable political jokes and made blue handkerchiefs turn red. Kinnock enjoyed it and generously bounded over to congratulate the magician. Then Todd and Keys got down to the main business of the evening: they handed Kinnock a cheque for £500,000 to launch the election campaign. He bubbled with gratitude. Pointing out that the sum came to 25p for each person unemployed, he suggested calling it the Norman Tebbit memorial fund. It was an important boost for the party and, by chance, it was announced in a room that had meant a lot to him at past conferences. It was in the Spanish Hall, at a Tribune rally in 1975, that Kinnock first caught the eye of the party when he made a wickedly funny fund-raising speech. (But the headlines were stolen from him then by Jack Jones, Todd's predecessor but one at the TGWU, who stormed on to the stage a few minutes later and tried to grab the microphone from Ian Mikardo in the middle of one of his characteristically pungent speeches. It was the sort of damaging row that, ten years later, party managers have learned to deflect.)

Kinnock handed the cheque to an aide and moved off for his last engagement of the night. Press photographers and television crews had been briefed by Andrew Fox, his acting press officer, and were milling round the stage in the Washington Suite at the Imperial Hotel, making the room as hot and crowded as at the last party but one, in that upstairs room of a pub. It was Welsh Night, which the Kinnocks have made something of a tradition at party conferences since he became leader. His advance guard (senior aide Richard Clements) had warned the organizers from the Welsh Labour Party of the leader's impending arrival and the all-male choir was on stage singing *Men of Harlech*. Neil climbed up amongst them and the cameras turned. Glenys joined them a bit later. The confined space meant that photographers had to be brought to the front in relays, so there were several retakes before the press was asked to leave. The singing continued but Neil and Glenys descended from the stage and moved round the room, shaking hands and posing for more private pictures. After an hour or so they were back on stage again, this time singing political material: *The Red Flag, Avanti Populo* – an Italian socialist song that is one of their favourites – *We Shall Overcome* and, inevitably, *Here we go, here we go, here we go.* It was past midnight when, after yet more pictures and autographs, they were allowed to go to bed.

*   *   *

That random panorama of the Labour Party, as displayed at the annual conference, gives an idea of the complex strands that make up this extraordinary political movement. For any leader, to pull those strands together and weave them into a credible electoral force represents a formidable challenge. How did the party come to embrace all those contrasting radical philosophies in a coalition so turbulent that from time to time it becomes virtually untenable?

In 1867 the franchise was broadened beyond the property-owning class. Before that there had been no point in forming a democratic political party to represent the interests of people who did not have a vote. In 1891 Keir Hardie, a Scottish miner, became the first Independent Labour MP but the Independent Labour Party (ILP) itself was not founded for another two years. In 1900, as a result of an initiative by the Trades Union Congress, the Labour Representation Committee was formed at a meeting in a hall near London's Ludgate Circus. Its member bodies were trade unions (mainly representing unskilled workers) and three recently-formed societies espousing variations on the new egalitarian creed of socialism: the ILP, the Fabian Society and the Marxist Social-Democratic Federation. So from the very outset the committee was a coalition spanning a broad range of left-wing views.

After some encouraging victories in by-elections, the committee won 29 seats in the 1906 general election and changed its name to the Labour Party. Three years later the Miners' Federation, until then allied to the Liberal party, switched its allegiance, bringing the total of MPs to 42 after the second election of 1910.

There were splits and rows from the very beginning. In the very first ballot in the Parliamentary party, for the post of leader (then called chairman), there was a tie between Keir Hardie and David Shackleton, secretary of the Amalgamated Cotton Weavers. Hardie was elected but the post rotated, with the result that Parliamentary leadership was weak and there were frequent disputes between the 'political' MPs and the generally less radical union representatives. Ideological schisms abounded. Even then there were elements in the party impatient with democratic politics, seeking to take control of the economy through the more direct method of strike action. When the First World War began there was a split between the pacifists and those who supported the war effort. Ramsay MacDonald, a pacifist like most of his ILP colleagues, resigned his chairmanship of the Parliamentary party and was replaced by Arthur Henderson from the union side. In 1915 Henderson joined the wartime coalition Cabinet.

In 1918, shortly before the end of the war, the party formally adopted for the first time a socialist constitution, including the historic Clause Four, committing Labour to common ownership of the means of production 'to secure for the producers by hand and brain the full fruits of their industry'. In the election at the end of that year Labour won 57 seats.

Two years later the National Executive took a decision representing the first of many attempts to define for Labour a more precise position in the spectrum of left-wing groups. The newly-formed British Communist Party applied for affiliation as a socialist society but was rejected on the ground that its aims and methods conflicted with those of Labour. In his *Short History of the Labour Party*, Henry Pelling wrote: 'The decision was an indication of the hardening discipline of the party as well as of its hostility to extreme revolutionary tactics.' At the 1922 election Labour won 142 seats, overtaking the Liberals as the second largest party in the Commons, and Ramsay MacDonald became leader again.

At the end of the following year the Prime Minister, Stanley Baldwin, called a snap election on the issue of tariff reform. Although the Conservatives won most seats they had no overall majority. Labour now had 191 seats and, as the leader of the larger opposition party, MacDonald was invited to form a coalition government. It lasted only nine months until he fell out with the Liberals and was forced to call an election, which the Conservatives won outright. All the same the interlude established Labour as a potential party of government.

The abject failure of the General Strike of 1926, provoked by a cut in miners' pay, was a temporary embarrassment for the Labour movement. The long-term effect of the débâcle on the trade unions was to discredit the concept of industrial action for political ends. Despite the setback, Labour emerged as the largest single party after the 1929 election and MacDonald became Prime Minister again. Yet the party did not unite behind him. During the financial crisis of 1931, union leaders, notably Ernest Bevin of the Transport and General Workers (TGWU), refused to agree to the cuts in service pay and unemployment benefit that were being demanded by international bankers. The Government were forced to resign and MacDonald was invited to form a coalition with the Liberals and Conservatives. This was regarded as a sellout by a majority in the party. They disowned MacDonald and the Labour ministers who had gone into the new Cabinet with him. The veteran Henderson took over the leadership again. In the election that year, Labour was reduced to a rump of 46 seats, with five for the ILP, who had campaigned separately and broke completely with the party a year later.

Defence was the subject of the next party split. George Lansbury, who had succeeded Henderson as leader, was a pacifist who opposed rearmament. With the growing menace of the Fascists in Germany, the trade union element in the party did not share this view and in 1935 Lansbury was replaced by Clement Attlee. In that year's election Labour began to restore its position, winning 154 seats.

In the late 1930s Communism grew in strength, especially among intellectuals. Stafford Cripps, a Winchester-educated barrister, led the Socialist League, a left-wing group affiliated to the Labour Party. He advocated a popular front linking Labour with the Communists, the Socialist League and the ILP. The union leaders would have none of it and Cripps was expelled from the party along with a handful of supporters including the young Welsh MP, Aneurin Bevan. Cripps stayed out until 1945 but Bevan was readmitted a few months after his expulsion, having given assurances of good behaviour.

Meanwhile the party in Parliament was piling up credit for the future by opposing Neville Chamberlain's policy of appeasing Hitler. When calls began for a coalition, Attlee said he would participate only if Chamberlain resigned. Thus he exerted an important influence on the appointment of Winston Churchill as Prime Minister. Despite the MacDonald precedent, the coalition was approved by the party.

The 1945 election, fought immediately after the defeat of Germany but while the Pacific war continued, resulted in a bigger Parliamentary majority for Labour than it has achieved before or since. With 393 seats, it had a lead of 146 over the other parties, a comfortable base for the launch of its radical programme of nationalization and development of social services. While there was unanimity on these aims within the party, there was division over foreign policy. Many on the left criticized Britain's membership of NATO and the alliance with the United States, masterminded by Bevan as Foreign Secretary. They would have preferred a Labour Britain to take a neutral stance between the Americans and the Russians.

The election in 1950, after five years of rigid post-war austerity, left Labour with an overall majority of only six. Its prospects for surviving in Government were further reduced by a damaging split in the Cabinet the following year. Hugh Gaitskell, succeeding Stafford Cripps as Chancellor, had imposed charges on false teeth and spectacles prescribed under the National Health Service. This infuriated Bevan, who as Minister of Health had introduced the service, and he resigned from the Government, along with Harold Wilson, President of the Board of Trade, and John Freeman, a junior minister. Attlee called another general election and Labour lost it narrowly, even though it polled more votes than the Conservatives – indeed at 13,948,605 more than any British party has polled before or since.

In opposition, Labour MPs felt free to squabble among themselves with a clearer conscience. Some 50 supporters of Bevan's stand on the health service formed a group under the banner of *Tribune*, the left-wing journal, edited by Michael Foot. (Until it was outflanked on the left by the Campaign Group in the 1980s, the Tribune Group was the keeper of the radical conscience in the Parliamentary party.) Bevan had been appointed to the Shadow Cabinet but resigned in 1954 to campaign against the party's support for rearming Germany. Wilson had no reservations about agreeing to replace him in the Shadow Cabinet. At the 1954 conference Gaitskell defeated Bevan for the post of party treasurer, and at a fringe meeting Bevan characterized him as a 'desiccated calculating machine'. Labour politicians have seldom had qualms about engaging in personal abuse to dramatize their differences on policies.

The following year Bevan led a group of 62 MPs abstaining from a Commons vote on the hydrogen bomb, the devastating new weapon developed from the atomic bombs used on Japan at the end of the war in the Pacific. Party policy was to support British development of the weapon, but Bevan and the others, horrified by the effects of the Japanese bombs, could not stomach it. For that, he was punished by having the party whip withdrawn and narrowly avoided being expelled for a second time.

Against this background of dissension, small wonder that Labour fared even worse in the 1955 election than in 1951, attracting 1½ million fewer votes. Attlee resigned soon afterwards and Gaitskell easily defeated Bevan for the leadership, with Herbert Morrison a poor third. Bevan, though, was elected treasurer, and it seemed that the two poles of the party might be coming together. In 1957 Bevan changed his mind about the British H-bomb, saying that without it a Labour Government would be going 'naked into the conference chamber'. But a development of longer-term significance was the election as General Secretary of the Transport and General Workers Union of Frank Cousins, a left-winger and a supporter of unilateral nuclear disarmament.

The large unions, through their block votes, control decisions at the annual conference and elect the majority of members of the NEC.

(Apart from the 12 members the unions elect among themselves, they are the dominant influence in choosing the five women members, giving them a clear majority of the 30 places.) Hitherto the unions had with few exceptions been reliable allies of the right. The left had drawn its strength from the activists in the constituency parties, many of them middle class intellectuals, who commanded comparatively few conference votes. When the party lost its third successive election in 1959, by an even greater margin than the other two, the scene was set for a round of still fiercer left/right in-fighting.

Gaitskell was convinced that the electorate perceived the party as being too closely bound by class-war dogma and campaigned for a revision of the constitution, in particular the repeal of Clause Four and its commitment to nationalization. This was more than the unions could take and his proposal was defeated, encouraging the left to challenge the leadership on the more emotional issue of defence. The party's commitment to a nuclear defence strategy was narrowly reversed at the 1960 Scarborough conference, because of the opposition of the TGWU under its unilateralist general secretary Frank Cousins. Gaitskell responded with the declaration for which he is best remembered: 'There are some of us who will fight and fight and fight again to save the party we love.' He fought and won: at the following year's conference the unilateralists were defeated.

The dispute had produced casualties – among them Michael Foot, one of five MPs who had the whip withdrawn after defiantly voting against the defence estimates. (Bevan had died in 1960 and Foot had taken over his seat at Ebbw Vale.) In 1962 the rift between left and right began to heal again with a unanimous rejection of Conservative plans for Britain to join the European Community. Thus when Gaitskell died the following year he bequeathed to his successor a party more united than had seemed likely four years earlier.

In 1964 Harold Wilson led Labour to its first election victory for 14 years, albeit by only four seats. The slimness of the majority and the unfamiliar taste of power put a damper on dissension. There were murmurs of discontent in the trade unions about plans to limit wage increases but the appointment of Frank Cousins to the Cabinet helped soften them. At a new election in 1966 the majority was increased to a healthy 96, but that marked a high point in Wilson's fortunes. Economic difficulties and more troubles with the unions led to a steady erosion of support. After a long rearguard action, the pound had to be devalued in 1967. A year later, following a series of deplorable by-election results, divisions began to re-emerge at the party conference. With the support of the large unions, a resolution was passed criticizing the continued statutory control of wage increases.

The following year, union anger boiled over when the Government introduced proposals to regulate industrial relations, set out in a leaflet called *In Place of Strife*. They included a ballot of members and a month-long 'cooling off period' before strike action was permitted. Many left-wing MPs threatened not to vote for such legislation and the plan was withdrawn.

An even more emotional issue for many Labour supporters was the Vietnam war. The Americans were pouring men and equipment into Vietnam and launching deadly bombing raids in their attempt to prevent the Communist north over-running the non-Communist south. Wilson infuriated the left of his party by giving moral support to the United States President, Lyndon Johnson. Protests against the war, in Britain as in America, took the form of numerous street demonstrations, sometimes ending in violence. They became characteristic of radical politics in the 1960s. Strong anti-war movements were formed, especially on university campuses. Through them, young people on the left expressed a disillusion with conventional Parliamentary politics, which did not seem to be addressing their real concerns.

In 1970 the Conservatives regained power under Edward Heath. That was when Neil Kinnock, a 28-year-old lecturer with the Workers' Educational Association, entered Parliament as MP for the South Wales mining constituency of Bedwellty. Born in Tredegar, in Bevan's former constituency, Kinnock counted himself on what used to be called the Bevanite wing of the party; but he did not subscribe to the growing fashion for street politics. He believed that Parliament was and would remain the centre of effective political power in Britain and that to influence events you had to work through the conventional methods of democracy. His selection as candidate had been surprising, for previous MPs in this area had generally been elderly retired miners, like his predecessor Harold Finch. To win the nomination he had to fight a vigorous campaign against the candidate of the National Union of Mineworkers and was eventually chosen by a mere two votes (76 to 74) after a dead heat in the previous ballot. His arrival at Westminster so young helped strengthen the commitment to Parliamentary as against extra-Parliamentary politics that was to characterize his battles against the far left in later years.

Heath's term as Prime Minister lasted less than four years, although it included Britain's entry into Europe in 1973. The Conservatives' own industrial relations legislation provoked unrest in the unions leading to a number of strikes, culminating in the miners' strike at the beginning of 1974. Heath imposed a three-day working week and called an election specifically on the issue of 'Who governs Britain?' – the unions or Parliament. That question did not provoke the response he expected. The Labour manifesto, promising to negotiate a 'social contract' with the unions to regulate industrial relations, proved more seductive.

Labour won only four more seats than the Conservatives and returned to office with the support of the 14 Liberals, although it was not a coalition. At a further election later in the year, the party strengthened its position.

Membership of the European Community had by now become one of the most contentious issues inside the party. Wilson achieved a slight improvement in the terms and fulfilled his election pledge to hold a referendum on continuing membership. Against the opposition of the left wing, the referendum resulted in a 'yes' vote, as recommended by the Government, by 67% to 33%. Eric Heffer, a left-wing junior minister, was dismissed by Wilson for speaking against the Government line in the Commons. (The rule was that ministers could express opposing views only on the hustings.) Tony Benn had switched from a pro-Europe to an anti-Europe position and Wilson demoted him from the Industry Department to be Minister for Energy. Kinnock, on the back benches, was also against membership, partly because he felt Welsh interests would best be served by withdrawing.

But it was another Welsh issue on which Kinnock, for the first time in his political career, found himself at odds with people he would normally have regarded as his allies. Labour had committed itself to holding referendums on the devolution of legislative powers for Wales and Scotland. A Welsh assembly was favoured by most Welsh Labour MPs, including Michael Foot, who represented the neighbouring constituency of Ebbw Vale and was one of Kinnock's closest personal and political friends. Kinnock, though, felt strongly that devolution would be in the interests neither of the party nor the principality, and that there was no strong call for it in Wales. He campaigned vigorously for a 'no' vote and as a result was subject to much local abuse, including hate mail.

Wilson's resignation in 1976 brought a clear right-left division over the choice of a successor, represented by James Callaghan and Michael Foot. Kinnock campaigned hard for Foot, despite their differences over devolution. Callaghan won by 176 votes to 137 – a better showing for Foot than anyone had expected. Foot was put in charge of the devolution plans but they were abandoned, to Kinnock's delight, after negative referendum votes in Wales and, more surprisingly, Scotland. Kinnock was offered a junior Government post but, detecting an attempt to muzzle him as a spokesman of the left, he declined.

Fresh pressure on the pound in 1976 forced the Government to seek a further loan from the International Monetary Fund, granted only on stringent conditions. Public spending had to be cut, which was bound to worsen the accelerating rate of unemployment. The left protested and 26 Labour MPs voted against the cuts. After suffering losses in by-elections Callaghan could not command an automatic majority in the

Commons, so he negotiated a pact for Parliamentary support from the Liberals. At the PLP meeting where this proposal was discussed, Kinnock's was a lone voice raised against it. He said it would provide a lifeline for the ailing Liberals without producing any long-term advantage for Labour. But when he sought to move a motion opposing the deal, he could not find a seconder.

When David Steel, the Liberal leader, announced that the pact would end in the summer of 1978, it was expected that Callaghan would call an election in the autumn. He decided not to – misguidedly, as it turned out, for there began a bout of industrial troubles dubbed 'the winter of discontent'. The Government were seeking to impose a 'norm' of pay increases of only 5% – not enough for most unions. There were strikes by lorry drivers, car workers, municipal employees and other groups. At the end of March, 1979, Callaghan lost a motion of confidence in the Commons and was obliged to call an election for May. The Conservatives won with a comfortable majority of 59 and Margaret Thatcher became Britain's first woman Prime Minister.

The Callaghan Government had leaned substantially to the right. Many members blamed the defeat on this and were frustrated by how little control they could exert over a Labour government once it gained office. The left sought to use the defeat to swing the party in their direction. They began with two campaigns to introduce greater democracy into the party and to reduce the power of MPs, who as a group tended to line up to the right of the opinions expressed by constituency delegates at conference. The NEC generally veered to the left, strongly influenced by Tony Benn, who invariably won the largest number of votes among the seven members elected by the constituency parties. Kinnock had been elected to the NEC in 1978 and in his first years was regarded as a reliable ally of the left.

The first success for the democratization campaign came at the 1979 conference, which approved the compulsory reselection of all MPs by their constituency parties between general elections, forcing them to take more account of the views of constituency activists. Kinnock supported that, as he did the second rule change, approved the following year, under which the leader would be chosen by an electoral college representing all sections of the party, rather than by MPs alone.

There was to be one more leadership election before the new rules came into effect. Callaghan resigned at the end of 1980 and Michael Foot was chosen to succeed him, defeating Denis Healey by just ten votes. Healey was elected his deputy. Kinnock, who had been appointed shadow education spokesman by Callaghan a year earlier, was a powerful influence in Foot's campaign.

Their success was a sign that the left was now more powerful in the Parliamentary party than for many years. Choice of candidates was in the hands of constituency parties, dominated by general management committees composed of enthusiastic and often idealistic 'conscience' politicians who believed that the socialist Utopia could be attained by adhering rigidly to egalitarian principles which commanded scarcely any support beyond their own limited circle. They selected candidates who agreed with them. Despairing MPs on the right of the party could see no prospect of this changing. At the beginning of 1981 four former ministers – Roy Jenkins, Shirley Williams, David Owen and William Rodgers – announced the formation of a breakaway party, the Social Democrats (SDP) and were joined by another 11 sitting Labour MPs, with ten more recruited by the end of the year. They hoped to persuade other senior Labour right-wingers to join them, such as Denis Healey and Roy Hattersley, the Shadow Home Secretary; but they resisted, clinging to the hope that 'sensible' policies might still prevail. In his long talks with the Gang of Four, Healey was avuncular, drawing on his many years of international experience.

'All you're doing,' he told them, 'is making control of the party more difficult to restore. In Europe, right-wing breakaways from left-wing parties have always weakened the "goodies" in the party without coming to anything on their own. It will take a few years to change the Labour Party but it can be done.'

That process of change began only a few months after the breakaway in 1981. In a crucial trial of strength between left and right Tony Benn, against Foot's wishes, decided to oppose Healey for the deputy leadership. Some of Kinnock's friends had been urging him to run but he was opposed to widening the inter-party conflict still further. Although hitherto an ally of the left, he decided to abstain, after painful discussions with Glenys and against her advice not to cause himself trouble. He gave his reasons publicly in *Tribune*. Like Foot, he was outraged that Benn had chosen this time to establish himself as the standard-bearer of the constituency left. He wrote that the already weak party had been seriously damaged by the campaign for the deputy leadership, which had lasted several months. If Labour was to regain power it had to discipline itself to stop wrangling in public, to present instead a united front to the electorate. The bitter and uncompromising article concluded thus:

'I believe that, through an inaccurate analysis of the position and power of the Labour movement and by a tactically mistaken decision to contest the deputy leadership in 1981, Tony has significantly harmed the current standing and electoral opportunities of the Labour Party.'

Some of his very closest friends were not altogether surprised at Kinnock's stand. Since soon after his election to the NEC in 1978 he had been expressing to them privately his reservations about Tony Benn, who had been a loyal member of Wilson's Cabinet during the Vietnam era and whose emergence as the guru of the left had come quite late in his political life. Kinnock found something peculiar about this born-again radicalism and was put off by Benn's messianic approach. Far from regarding him as the keeper of the party conscience, he foresaw a time when Benn could become a positive menace.

Healey won the deputy leadership by the narrowest of margins and, in doing so, certainly prevented more defections to the SDP. When the result of the ballot was known Kinnock was hailed by *The Observer* as 'the man who saved the Labour Party' but was abused by many former allies. He had now become distinctly identified with the 'soft left', represented in Parliament by the Tribune Group, as against the 'hard left' led by Benn, who briefly allied himself with Tribune but later helped form the Campaign Group. Kinnock was heckled at meetings and even faced criticism in his constituency party. He lost a number of old friends and someone picked a fight with him in the lavatory at the party conference.

Unpopularity was an unfamiliar and unhappy experience for him, although in the long term the break with his former allies did much to enhance his reputation. Those who had written him off as a Welsh charmer with an ebullient oratorical style, essentially a lightweight, now had to reconsider. He had twice chosen the tough option – over devolution and now over the deputy leadership. Maybe he had been under-rated. When the time came for his reselection at Bedwellty he won a comfortable victory. He was also re-elected to the NEC (though with a reduced vote) despite a determined attempt by Benn's supporters to unseat him.

The division between the hard and soft left was now clearly definable. The Bennites thought it a priority to get the party unalterably committed to truly radical policies, insisting on strict accountability to ensure that there was no backsliding on principle in the name of pragmatism – as had happened, in their view, under Wilson and Callaghan. The moderates of the Tribune Group do not like being called soft. They believe they are harder than the extremists, at least in the head and the nose. Although intellectually sympathetic with many of Benn's beliefs, they are convinced that it is more important to devise a realistic strategy for winning power than to construct a straitjacket for the leadership after the election. Every constitutional reform proposed by the hard left provided scope for a hostile press to portray a Labour leader imprisoned by his extremists. It was no use dismissing the capitalist press as unworthy of consideration: however much the left disapproved, it was still a powerful instrument for constructing images and perceptions that, once established, are hard to eradicate.

In retrospect Benn's failure to win the deputy leadership was the beginning of the decline of his power in the party; but he was still

21

capable of making life difficult for Foot at the monthly meetings of the NEC. These are held in a large L-shaped room on the third floor of the Walworth Road headquarters, a haphazard jumble of modern offices built behind an elegant late Georgian façade. Up to 50 people can attend the meetings – the 25 elected members plus officials and office-holders. They sit on modern wooden chairs around a rectangle formed of 14 wood and metal tables, 6 on each side and 1 at each end. This occupies the stem of the L, while the spur is quite empty. For those, including the leader and deputy leader, who sit facing this empty expanse, it is like being in a disused warehouse. The party secretary sits on the chairman's left in the middle of one of the long sides of the rectangle, with the leader and the chairman a few places to his left, near the corner. The left-wingers sit together in the diametrically opposite corner, as far as they can be from the leader. This geographical factor encourages raised voices when one group is addressing the other, simply to be sure of being heard.

Under Foot, NEC meetings turned into long theoretical wrangles, with harangues from Benn and his followers provoking counterblasts from the hard right, led by the formidable John Golding. Foot had no idea how to deal with this rancour and harassment, which caused meetings to run a whole day and sometimes into the evening. His qualities and experience did not include a gift for stamping his authority over his colleagues. Because he could never be sure of commanding a majority on crucial issues, he would be obliged to sit through the whole meeting so as to be on hand for the votes. An appalled Kinnock now saw clearly that for any party leader to be effective he had first to ensure for himself a virtually automatic majority on the NEC.

Despite Foot's lifelong reputation as a figure on the left of the party, he found himself increasingly relying on support from the right. It was clear to all except the Bennites that action would have to be taken to prevent the growth of the Militant tendency inside the party. The constitution forbids members to belong to any other political party but Militant got round that by asserting that they were not a party at all, merely supporters of a newspaper. After bitter discussions in the NEC, the five members of the editorial board of the *Militant* newspaper were expelled from party membership in 1982. Most people regarded that as only a preliminary to more radical action against the group, especially in places (such as Liverpool) where they were in control of entire local parties.

Foot's worst humiliation came over the 1983 Bermondsey by-election. Bob Mellish, the right-wing MP for the constituency in what used to be London's dockland, resigned his apparently safe seat after disputes with the left-wing constituency party. The local choice as candidate was Peter Tatchell, a young Australian homosexual who had written an article in *London Labour Briefing* advocating 'extra-parliamentary opposition' as a way of defeating Conservative legislation unpalatable to the Labour movement. Foot initially made a ringing declaration that Tatchell could not be the candidate. The NEC (by a majority of only one) ordered the Bermondsey party to repeat its selection process. When they chose Tatchell again, Foot was obliged to endorse him. Partly as a result of the controversy the formerly safe seat was lost to Simon Hughes, an attractive Liberal, and has yet to be won back for Labour.

The Falklands War in 1982 set the stage for Margaret Thatcher's overwhelming win in the general election on 10 June, 1983. Labour won only 209 of the 633 seats and 8,457,124 votes – its lowest total since the Second World War by more than three million. It amounted to a mere 27.6% of the electorate. This was only 2% more than voted for the SDP/ Liberal Alliance; and within weeks the Alliance had actually overtaken Labour in the polls. The Falklands factor certainly played its part in the Conservative victory; but the most significant cause of the Labour disaster, as Kinnock had predicted in his *Tribune* article, was the debilitating division in the party. The manifesto reflected it. A compilation of numerous half-digested ideas originated by policy departments at party headquarters, it was wordy and unclear. Nobody had imposed any rigorous political discipline on it. For instance, the vital issue of defence policy was fudged and during the campaign spokesmen had made conflicting statements about it.

Although Michael Foot was a popular figure in the party, the general election result had confirmed that he was an ineffective leader. It was clear to everyone, including him, that he would have to go. Roy Hattersley, after Healey the leading figure on the right, had already indicated that he would be a candidate for the succession; but many feared that he would exacerbate the doctrinal divisions.

The first move to get Kinnock nominated as leader was made by Clive Jenkins, the influential general secretary of the Association of Scientific, Technical and Managerial Staffs (ASTMS). On the day after the election he telephoned his fellow Welshman, Moss Evans of the TGWU. Both agreed that, out of respect, they should support Foot if he wanted to stay on; but assuming he did not they would, in Jenkins's words, 'have to jump a generation'.

'Are we both thinking of the same person?' Evans asked. They were. Jenkins said he would determine Foot's view. He telephoned the leader, who invited Jenkins and his wife Moira to dinner at his Hampstead home.

Foot had already all but decided that he would not seek re-election as leader at the October party conference but he had not planned to make an immediate announcement. Over dinner he asked Jenkins what he had in mind should he decline the nomination.

'I know who he's going to suggest,' declared Jill Craigie, Foot's wife.

'That's only because I know who you want next as well,' Jenkins replied. He added that he believed Kinnock's and the party's interest would be best served by an immediate announcement, giving Kinnock the chance to establish himself during a lengthy campaign. He knew too that Hattersley would receive powerful support, most importantly from the largest right-wing union, the Amalgamated Union of Engineering Workers (AUEW, later AEU). It would be to Kinnock's advantage to get his hat into the ring first.

Foot delayed his formal decision only until the end of the meal, when he was sipping whisky from a little silver cup.

'I've decided not to accept the nomination,' he told Jenkins. 'I appreciate it, but no. And I'm going to tell Neil now.'

He brought a telephone to the table, but Kinnock was out and the baby sitter forgot to pass the message on. Kinnock heard of the move first of all from Clive Jenkins the following lunchtime whilst waiting to be interviewed at Broadcasting House. Jenkins was at a meeting of the executive committee of the ASTMS which had unanimously decided to nominate Kinnock.

The suggestion came as no surprise to Kinnock. As the general election approached and the prospect of a Labour victory diminished to nothing, he became increasingly certain that there would be a contest for the leadership and that he would be a candidate. By mid-May, a fortnight before the election, he was fairly certain he could win it, but he was still not anxious to hurry the process. In a talk with John Evans, Foot's Parliamentary Private Secretary, Kinnock advised that the leader should stay in place for a while after the election, however grave the defeat, so that the party could decide a successor carefully, not on the rebound from electoral disaster. Foot, however, did not agree. Once Jenkins had assured him that Foot would not be standing, Kinnock did not hesitate.

* * *

Denis Healey, the deputy leader, had decided not to stand, leaving the field clear for Hattersley as the candidate of the right. The two other declared contenders were Peter Shore on the centre right and Eric Heffer on the far left. Heffer had hoped to carry the standard of the Bennites in the absence of Benn himself who, fortunately for Kinnock's prospects, had lost his Bristol seat. As a result of redistribution, one of Labour's two seats in the city had become marginal. Michael Cocks, the right-wing Chief Whip, had maintained his hold on the safe Bristol South, leaving Benn to lose Bristol East by nearly 2,000 votes.

Heffer, although admired for the sincerity of his convictions, lacks the charisma for leadership and few rallied to him – nor to Shore as the anti-European alternative to Hattersley. It was a two-man contest. To prevent too acrimonious a campaign that could sharpen ideological differences in the party, Kinnock and Hattersley agreed to be candidates for deputy leader should the other win the main event. Kinnock calculated that, assuming he won, it would be to his advantage to have Hattersley visibly committed to his leadership, to prevent his becoming a focal point for right-wing factionalism. Hattersley felt he had no alternative but to make a reciprocal gesture, though he did so with reluctance.

It was the first leadership election to be held under the new 'electoral college' system. Votes were weighted to give the unions 40%, the constituencies and the Parliamentary party 30% each. The backing of some of the powerful unions was therefore essential and it was here that Kinnock reaped an advantage from the way he had operated as an MP. Until he joined the Opposition front bench, he had been an irregular attender at the Commons. He preferred to range the country talking to union branches and constituency parties. So before the campaign started he had already made useful grass-roots contacts with people who could deliver votes.

All the same, he knew he had to work hard between June, after Foot's announcement of his departure, and October, when the final decision would be taken at the party conference. An enthusiast for professional campaigning, he borrowed a computer and tabulated expected levels of support from all three sections of the electoral college. He distributed separate manifestoes to the main trade unions, customized to address the individual concerns of each. He asked Robin Cook, MP for Livingston and a member of the Tribune Group, to co-ordinate the campaign, with emphasis on garnering support from MPs. With Heffer the only rival on his left, Kinnock had no doubt that he could gain a sufficient majority among the unions and constituencies to win, but he wanted to maximize his vote in the Parliamentary Party to make it easier to exert his authority on his colleagues. Hattersley, who had not truly taken on board the implications of the new voting system, was concentrating on securing MPs' votes – the old style of campaigning for the leadership – and did comparatively little in the constituencies or with the unions.

Hampered by trouble with his voice, strained during the general election, Kinnock still undertook a vigorous schedule of rallies around the country, making speeches on all the main policy areas – including one, significantly, that included a detailed programme for reform of the party organization. He was setting out his stall even before his formal election. An intriguing innovation in the campaign was to accept an offer of help from the Red Review, a group of Glasgow students who put on politically committed satirical shows. They organized a benefit at London University to help pay the costs of the campaign. He has remained friendly with them since and always has a walk-on part in their annual performance at the party conference.

Within weeks after Foot announced his retirement in June, the certainty of a Kinnock victory had spread beyond his followers to the party and country at large. Hattersley had calculated that his one remaining hope lay in attracting the votes of the largest union, the TGWU. While the executive would be certain to plump for Kinnock, given the right to choose for themselves, Hattersley thought he would have a chance if there was a ballot of the membership. One evening in July he went to see the American musical *Mr Cinders* in London's West End. On the way out he was met by Julia Somerville and a BBC television camera crew, working on a profile of him. Somerville told him the TGWU had decided not to ballot its membership. She sought his reaction.

'I have a little motto,' he said, the strains of the musical still running through his head. 'I use it whenever I'm feeling blue. Even when the darkest clouds are in the sky, you mustn't cry and you mustn't sigh . . .' At that point, although he formally stayed in the leadership contest, he knew he would have to settle for the number two position.

He did not have a clear run even for the deputy's post. His main rival was Michael Meacher, a former Bennite in the process of shifting to a softer left position. The result was expected to be close; but some of the large unions, worried that a Kinnock/Meacher partnership would isolate the right and further divide the party, switched their votes to Hattersley at a late stage and he won 67% – not far behind Kinnock's winning total of 71% for the leadership itself.

The 'dream ticket' of Kinnock and Hattersley was thus elected at the 1983 Brighton party conference. The two men beamed, clasped hands and raised their linked fists to the sky. In his acceptance speech, Kinnock stressed that the prime object of the party must be to gain power to achieve a 'patriotism that does not count its greatness in the number of warheads it has got.' The word 'win' was dotted through the speech – 'We have to win . . . we can win . . . we will win . . .' – and was greeted every time with loud applause. If anyone wondered why winning was the priority, 'just remember how you felt on that dreadful morning of June 10th, just remember how you felt then and think to yourselves, June 9th, 1983, never, ever again.'

He addressed the same theme in his main conference speech later that week:

Those who prate about Blimpish patriotism in the mode of Margaret Thatcher are also the ones who will take millions off the caring services of this country. I wonder they don't choke on the very word patriotism. They are the enemy, they must be defeated and we must defeat them together. If we try by groups and factions we won't do it. If we give greater attention to arguments between ourselves than our enmity against them we won't do it ... We must defeat them together. That is our purpose. There must be no activity in this Labour movement that is superior to that purpose.

There was wild applause. Over the next four years some of the people in the hall on that day, sharing in the excitement and enthusiasm, were to discover to their cost that he not only meant what he said but, to a greater extent than any other Labour leader in recent memory, he had the strength, skill and determination to act on it.

2 *The Lost Year*

Kinnock sought a suitably symbolic gesture to begin his leadership. It had to involve an issue bearing on his central philosophy about the role of Labour as the party committed to alleviating hardship and addressing the problems of humble people. That, after all, was what set it apart from the Conservatives, whose concern for the national prosperity and well-being was, in his view, restricted to those at the top of the social scale.

There were, too, more personal reasons for choosing the National Health Service as the subject of his inaugural campaign, just as it had been the topic of his maiden speech in the Commons in 1970. He had said then:

> Compassion is not a sloppy, sentimental feeling for people who are under-privileged or sick, to be used as a tear-jerker or as an expedient at the time of an election. It is an absolutely practical belief that, regardless of a person's background, ability or ability to pay, he should be provided with the best that society has to offer.

Health is a preoccupation of coal mining families and Kinnock's was no exception. As he pointed out in that Commons speech, he was the only adult male member of his close family free from any physical disability. His father Gordon contracted severe dermatitis from working in the pits and many of his uncles had suffered industrial injuries. His mother Mary was a nurse. When he was growing up in the 1950s his idol, in common with nearly every other committed socialist in South Wales, had been Aneurin Bevan, the eloquent and passionate MP for the Ebbw Vale constituency, which included Kinnock's home town of Tredegar. Bevan had made the nation's health the topic of his own maiden speech in 1929. As Minister of Health he had introduced the NHS in 1946 and resigned from the Government five years later when Hugh Gaitskell, the Chancellor of the Exchequer, insisted on charges for some services. Charges for prescriptions and other items had long since come to be accepted, but the service itself survived and Kinnock wanted to make sure it was not too seriously damaged by spending cuts.

So at the end of the Brighton conference he announced that he was sending a letter to Margaret Thatcher, the Prime Minister, demanding a debate in Government time, as soon as Parliament resumed, on how the cuts were affecting the service 'so that we can expose the extent of their harm and the contempt of their attitude.' Not surprisingly, Mrs Thatcher did not feel obliged to comply with the request, so Kinnock used the first available Opposition day for the debate. Nor did the Prime Minister see any reason why she should personally adorn her brash new rival's big occasion, fighting on ground of his choosing: Norman Fowler, the Social Services Secretary, replied on the Government's behalf.

Kinnock's speech did not rock the Commons rafters but it was a suitable enough start to his new role. The issue, he said, was of paramount importance on the national agenda. The Health Service was not an 'exclusive bauble' that the Conservatives could let decay at will but was above partisan politics, something that was cherished and fought for by people of all political views.

Four days later, health was the subject of the first of the campaigns on social issues that were to be a feature of his leadership. An ambulance toured the country carrying leaflets and stickers, and there was intensified activity in Parliament. At the launching ceremony he quoted Bevan as saying that free health care had become part of the national life and no government would seek to destroy it. Labour had to ensure that held good.

*   *   *

The new system for electing the leader had given Kinnock a more solid base of support than any of his predecessors. Even many who had backed other candidates were impressed by the patent good sense of his call for unity as a precondition for electoral recovery: they vowed to sink their differences and rally round the leadership. Yet like all politicians he had, over his years in Parliament, established a few enmities so acrimonious as to be beyond repair. With Benn mercifully sidelined for the moment, his greatest difficulty was always likely to be with Eric Varley, the former Secretary of State for Industry, just elected party Treasurer at the annual conference.

A year earlier Kinnock and Varley had been the combatants in a clash unwittingly provoked by Michael Foot. Labour's Shadow Cabinet is elected every autumn by the Parliamentary Labour Party (PLP) at the start of the new session. The leader is free only to decide what responsibilities to assign them. Following the PLP's 1982 selection Foot, encouraged by the leaders of some of the left-inclined unions, decided to make Kinnock the spokesman for employment, replacing the dour Varley. He would appease Varley by giving him an ill-defined supervisory role covering both employment and industry.

Kinnock was keen on the move and responded enthusiastically when it was put to him before the Shadow Cabinet balloting. Although education was important, he had held the portfolio for three years and a change would be welcome. With the jobless total going up remorselessly, employment had become a burning issue in Parliament. He would be at centre stage. But Foot was never strong on the niceties of political leadership. After having secured Kinnock's agreement he allowed the plan to be leaked to lobby correspondents before Varley had been officially informed. Varley felt ill-used and would not accede meekly. He threatened to resign rather than accept the switch and rallied his senior colleagues on the right to press for the reversal of the decision. To avoid a still more public split, including possible resignations from the Shadow Cabinet, Kinnock agreed to forgo the promotion. But he remained resentful of Varley, not just for depriving him of the post he wanted but for publicly exposing his friend Michael Foot as an ineffectual leader.

Varley would certainly not have kept the employment post in Kinnock's new front-bench team. Few were altogether surprised when, before the 1983 Shadow Cabinet elections, he declared he would not be a candidate for any position. Kinnock, rid of a potentially embarrassing problem, was relieved. He was less pleased three weeks later when Varley announced that he was resigning from Parliament altogether to assume a senior post in private industry. At 51, it was a premature end to Varley's once promising political career – he had been a Cabinet minister in his early forties and was once seen as a leadership contender.

As far as Kinnock was concerned, the most important consequence of the resignation was an impending by-election in the safe seat of Chesterfield. It provided an opportunity for a return to Parliament for one of the former MPs defeated in the general election. The most prominent was Tony Benn. He duly won the nomination, then the by-election, and returned to provide a figurehead for the left in the Parliamentary party. The sequence of events that had rid Kinnock of one rival had strengthened another, potentially more dangerous.

*　　*　　*

The first thing a new party leader needs is protection. Suddenly he is in tremendous demand as MPs seek to petition him for guidance, for possible advancement or to engage his interest in a cause dear to them. He may genuinely wish to make himself accessible, but as a practical matter he must be surrounded by a wall of aides to filter the petitioners and ensure that he spends his time effectively. It is also important to recruit a retinue of advisers who are not elected politicians. However loyal a fellow MP might appear, his first loyalties are to the constituents who elected him, to the advancement of his own career and possibly to the particular party faction he has allied himself with. It is necessary for any political leader to be served by people who owe their chief loyalty – and their position – to him alone. That need has been recognized for a long time in Washington, where congressmen and senators employ a substantial personal staff. It has come comparatively recently to Westminster, a consequence of the growing complexity of political issues, requiring ever more specialized technical advice. A Labour leader needs his own people, because he does not have the privilege of choosing the members of his Shadow Cabinet.

As education spokesman Kinnock had been allotted a cramped office off the Shadow Cabinet corridor at the House of Lords end of the Palace of Westminster. It was scarcely big enough for himself, his secretary Maureen Willis (whose husband Norman was to become general secretary of the TUC) and Charles Clarke, the sole research assistant he was entitled to. Now, as leader, he inherited from Michael Foot an inconveniently laid out suite of offices on two floors at the other end of the building, immediately north of the Commons chamber. The capacity of these offices effectively limited the size of the team of advisers who formed his personal cabinet.

Clarke was chief among them. A former President of the National Union of Students, he had begun working with Kinnock as a part-time education researcher in 1981. They soon found they shared views on broader issues than education, in particular on what had to be done to reconstitute Labour as a credible party of government. Before long Clarke was tendering advice to Kinnock in all political areas, including the bid for the leadership. Tall, bearded and burly, he is a more subtle man than he looks. He quickly recognized that Kinnock was not going to be the sort of leader to soak up advice from a number of sources and then magisterially select the right course. Kinnock is not a natural committee man but an instinctive politician who can decide quickly and with clarity whether a particular proposal does or does not accord with his priorities. Clarke saw that the most useful role he could play was to feed Kinnock with suggestions for solving problems or initiating policies, stimulating discussion, rather than present him with formal sets of options. He also took it upon himself to develop contacts in the unions and other seats of party power, providing a rudimentary intelligence service to prevent the leadership being taken by surprise at developments in party opinion.

Because he was young (in his thirties), came from outside Parliament and clearly had better access to Kinnock's ear than anyone, Clarke was initially resented by those Labour MPs who found it hard to gain their leader's attention. They would maintain that so inexperienced a leader needed people around him with more political weight, and the complaints seeped into political gossip columns. Their grievances grew when Kinnock appointed another outsider, roughly Clarke's age, as his chief press officer. Patricia Hewitt, an Australian, had been general secretary of the National Council for Civil Liberties (NCCL) for nine years, a vociferous campaigner for radical causes. She wrote to both Kinnock and Hattersley during the leadership tussle, offering to work for whichever became leader. She knew Hattersley the better because he had been Shadow Home Secretary while she was at NCCL. Kinnock asked her to become his press officer. He knew he was destined, like all Labour leaders, to have a bumpy ride from the predominantly Conservative press. At the NCCL Hewitt had gained a reputation for toughness and attracting publicity – qualities his press officer would need.

To provide a ballast of experience, Kinnock asked Richard Clements, one of Michael Foot's advisers, to stay on. Clements, a veteran of the left, had been editor of *Tribune* for more than 20 years when Foot, on becoming Opposition leader, invited him to join his personal staff. He was also a friend of Kinnock's, having published several of his articles and invited him to speak at *Tribune* rallies. Although his role in the office is less central than Clarke's, his value is that he knows most Labour MPs and provides a channel of communication with them. That is also the function of the Parliamentary Private Secretary, an unpaid post usually given to an ambitious MP. Kinnock chose Derek Foster, an early supporter of his leadership claim and one of the campaign team, as well as being a devoted member of the Salvation Army. (In 1985 he was elected Chief Whip.)

In truth, politics was a subject Kinnock needed less advice about than most others. A man who has been elected leader of the Labour Party at the age of 41 can be assumed to have a fund of expertise in the craft and its mysteries. More urgently, he required in-house experts in policy areas that he was unfamiliar with. He is not a natural delegator of authority. When a crisis blows up in any area his instinct is to get to grips with it himself: but he can be persuaded to let members of his staff get on with things if he has confidence in their ability. Shadow ministers have their own specialist advisers but he was keen to employ independent experts to help him evaluate their proposals, to ensure that nothing slipped past him that he would have opposed had he understood it better. It did not take him long to acquire them. Soon, the warren of alcoves immediately outside his comfortable office, with its side-on view of Westminster Bridge, were crammed with specialists on the economy, foreign affairs, industrial matters and the like. They were young, ambitious and had impeccable academic credentials. If they were poorly paid, the reward would come later, assuming they had judged correctly that they were joining a winning team.

*   *   *

The first step towards winning the next election, Kinnock saw, was to identify how the last one had been lost. It was hard to know where to start. The campaign itself had been a shambles, and there would clearly have to be radical changes at party headquarters in Walworth Road (near the Elephant and Castle in South London). The biggest single mistake had been the manifesto, a cumbersome, non-selective document of 40 tightly-packed pages containing – or so it seemed – almost every notion that anyone in the party had ever had on any issue. It was rather like the Bible, an unco-ordinated text from many different hands. And like the Bible, once committed to paper it was regarded by the faithful as holy writ. After the election Gerald Kaufman, the Shadow Home Secretary, dubbed it 'the longest suicide note in history'. Some sections appeared to have been devised to patch up internecine quarrels by giving every side's views an airing. On disarmament, for instance, it contained the magnificently meaningless sentence: 'Unilateralism and multilateralism must go hand in hand if either is to succeed.' It was essentially a Walworth Road production, with too little input from the political leadership at Westminster. If Labour had managed to achieve power in 1983, its leaders would have been confronted with a bewildering task in trying to interpret the manifesto so as to put its provisions into effect.

The reason for its great length was that in 1979 Callaghan had drawn the wrath of many in the party by simply excluding from the manifesto any policy he found objectionable. Foot did not favour such high-handed action, so he let it all go in with the minimum of amendment. Kinnock did not want to have to use Callaghan's blunt instrument either. Better, he thought, to act at an earlier stage, to adjust the method of making policy, so when the manifesto reached its final stages it would already have been cleared of its clutter.

It was essential, he saw, to involve the Parliamentary party in the first phase of the procedure. They, after all, would be charged with implementing the policies. Their analysis of the political possibilities was at least as relevant to building the programme as the technical expertise – and sometimes the rigid theoretical dogma – of officials at Walworth Road. Before long, he knew, the whole structure of head office would have to be reorganized, but it was important to create new machinery for making and promoting policies before that. He devised two new sets of committees to bridge the gap between the party's officials and its politicians, who had in the past often found themselves working (and speaking) at cross purposes.

Joint policy committees were set up, with equal representation from the NEC and the PLP, to make policy on specific priority areas, such as housing and defence. Once the policy was agreed, the new committees would cease to exist. They replaced a sprawling network of sub-committees of the NEC's Home Policy Committee, where party officials and outside experts had greatly outnumbered politicians. These used to produce policy documents that took no account of electoral strategy or, as it sometimes seemed, of political reality. On the key question of defence, for instance, Denis Healey and Denzil Davies, Shadow Foreign and Defence Secretaries, could now play a role in deciding the policy. They had been excluded before – one reason why the presentation of the policy in the 1983 election had been so chaotic.

The second innovation was the establishment of a Campaigns Strategy Committee, chaired by Kinnock, with representatives from the PLP, the NEC and the trade unions. It meets every six weeks or so to decide the issues the party should be campaigning about, the timing and the tactics. One of the techniques recommended in the Committee's terms of reference was opinion polling. It was planned to commission private polls to gauge popular reaction to policies and their presentation. This was regarded with great suspicion by the left, who despise anything that smacks of slick public relations rather than the gritty business of getting down to hard issues. If you are constantly monitoring public opinion, they believe, then you will inevitably trim your policies towards the lowest common denominator, souring the pure milk of socialism. They also felt that the proposal threatened the sovereignty of the NEC. Since the left is generally stronger on the NEC than on any other party body, its representatives are quick to react to any scheme that might reduce its power.

At the November NEC meeting Dennis Skinner moved an amendment to abandon opinion polling, but it was heavily defeated. Tony Benn suggested that more research be done before the polling was approved, but that was rejected as well. Today the private polls play a major role in Labour's strategic decisions.

By common consent, the immediate priority that autumn was to agree a workable defence policy that could be sustained consistently in opposition and realistically adopted when the party achieved power. Disarray over defence had proved a crippling handicap in the election. The manifesto committed Labour to abandoning nuclear weapons within the lifetime of the next Parliament. This need not in itself have lost votes, since feeling against all forms of nuclear power was growing, especially amongst the young. But senior members of the Shadow Cabinet, who had serious reservations about the policy, made speeches and statements that threw open the question of how long it would take to implement, especially scrapping the Polaris missile. Callaghan infuriated the left by saying that no weapons should be withdrawn without concessions from the eastern bloc – the multilateralist line. He was still fighting Gaitskell's battle of 1960; but it was a losing battle in a party that had been moving steadily towards unilateral nuclear disarmament since Callaghan gave up the leadership in 1980. The Conservatives had been able to exploit the obvious confusion.

One of the new joint policy committees was given the task of formulating a defence policy. It included Denis Healey and Denzil Davies, front-bench spokesmen on foreign affairs and defence, as well as representatives of the NEC and the unions. Given decisions of conference and the overall mood of the party and its leader, there was no question: the policy had to be unilateralist. The committee hammered out a document called *Defence and Security of Britain*, containing a firm commitment to remove all nuclear weapons, British and American, from British soil, but at the same time to increase spending on conventional forces and to remain committed members of NATO. The policy was approved overwhelmingly at the 1984 conference. Right wingers – notably Peter Shore – still had the gravest doubts about the wisdom of unilateralism, but suppressed them for the sake of unity. Nor was the document a total victory for the far left, who would have preferred to leave open the possibility of quitting NATO. But Kinnock's consistent record on defence persuaded the party to accept from him compromises that they would have regarded with deep suspicion had they originated from any other quarter.

He had always been a unilateralist. At university, both he and Glenys were members of CND and for a time he belonged to the more extreme Committee of 100. They had maintained their opposition to nuclear weapons ever since. In September 1983 he made his position clear in an article in *New Socialist*. 'There are no circumstances,' he wrote, 'in which I would order or permit the firing of nuclear weapons. Nothing could justify a first strike and retaliation would be the supremely useless act of all history.'

The issue had been dramatized since 1982 by the women's protest outside Greenham Common, the US air base near Newbury in Berkshire, where cruise missiles were due to arrive at the end of 1983. The women had received wide publicity as the focus for anti-nuclear demonstrations and as a target of hostility from local residents. They had been stigmatized by their opponents as unclean, feckless, uncaring about their families and in some cases lesbians. There were clashes with police, leading to arrests. As the anticipated delivery of the missiles at the end of 1983 drew nearer, the protests intensified. In October, Kinnock addressed a march in London of 200,000 people demonstrating against cruise. He said the Trident and cruise missiles made Britain a launching platform, the first line of American defence, and he called for a freeze on the testing, deployment and use of all nuclear weapons. In the Commons a week later, Thatcher labelled him 'a total unilateralist whose object is to undermine NATO and the defence of the free world'.

In mid-November the missiles arrived and the Labour Party issued a statement: 'The British people will not forgive the Prime Minister for allowing first-use nuclear weapons to be deployed in the United

Kingdom, especially when the United States Government which owns those weapons shows contempt for the views of the British Government.' Addressing the Socialist International in Brussels ten days later, Kinnock said Europe was in danger of becoming a 'nuclear minefield'.

Because the Conservatives thought defence a vulnerable area for Labour, they would continue to make as much as they could of it throughout the lifetime of the newly-elected Parliament. A second major news event of the dying weeks of 1983 also raised issues that would dominate public debate for the ensuing years, although its significance was not then as apparent. For most of the year an industrial dispute had been simmering at the *Stockport Messenger* group of free newspapers in the Manchester area, fuelled by the 1980 and 1982 Employment Acts that restricted the right of trade unionists to picket premises owned by companies with which they were in dispute.

A stubborn young entrepreneur named Eddy Shah ran the group. He was seeking to introduce new printing technology and to end the closed shop enforced by the National Graphical Association (NGA). The original disagreement concerned only eight men but because it involved issues that were coming to the fore nationally, and because the NGA suspected Shah of deliberate union-busting, they escalated it. Pickets arrived from all over the country, including members of other unions and supporters of extreme left groups whose presence often means trouble. Violence erupted outside Shah's printing works at Warrington. As customarily occurs in such situations, allegations of improper conduct were made against the police. Shah obtained injunctions against the unions under the new laws and the courts imposed substantial fines on the NGA for disobeying them. At the end of November the ramifications spread to Fleet Street, where the national newspapers were off the streets for four days.

Attitudes to the industrial relations legislation are among the many issues that divide left from right in the Labour movement. Both factions deplore the laws but only the extremists believe that because they disapprove they should fight back by flouting them or encouraging others to do so. They dub them 'Tory laws', applied by Tory courts as means of crushing the working class. They must be resisted at all costs until they prove unworkable.

On the other hand, Kinnock and the moderates insist that the letter of all laws must be obeyed, even if their motivation is clearly political. They argue that respect for the law is one of the necessary bastions of socialism: to condone law-breaking by Labour supporters in opposition would encourage the party's opponents to take the law into their own hands when confronted with Labour legislation that might disadvantage them. The one way Conservative Acts of Parliament can effectively be fought is through repeal by a Labour government: and violent law-breaking by activists damages the prospect of Labour being elected.

On 28 November 1983, while the Fleet Street papers were still on strike, Kinnock made that point in a speech to the executive council of the Transport and General Workers Union. He blamed the dispute on the new laws, which put judges in the role of 'assistant personnel managers' and challenged the very principle of trade union membership and organization.

Next day, at Prime Minister's question time in the Commons, Kinnock called for Government intervention. John Biffen, the Leader of the House, was standing in for Margaret Thatcher, away at a Commonwealth Prime Ministers' Conference. There were calls from Conservative and Alliance MPs for Kinnock to denounce violence on the picket lines – a cry that was to become familiar in other disputes over the next 18 months. Kinnock speaks out consistently against violence, but never unequivocally enough for his critics. He is inhibited by two considerations, first the desire to express support for the demonstrators' cause although without condoning their tactics, and secondly the need to take into account charges of police misbehaviour. Thus the following day, after he and some Shadow Cabinet members held a meeting with NGA leaders, he issued a statement saying: 'I condemn without reservation the violence at Warrington whoever uses it and the union have already made it plain that they share this view.'

By 1 December Thatcher was back and taking Question Time herself. The twice-weekly verbal duels between the Prime Minister and the Opposition leader, on Tuesdays and Thursdays, are eagerly awaited by MPs, who regard them as crucial tests of the leaders' mettle. Kinnock has never enjoyed them much. It has taken him time to learn the technique of asking incisive and potentially damaging questions. His talent is for passionate oratory, preferably delivered to large and enthusiastic audiences, rather than cut-and-thrust debate. He likes to take up points and embroider them, to indulge in flights of rhetoric; but the short, sharp sallies of Question Time give him no scope for exhibiting those qualities. The respective performances of their champions are judged by MPs not on the basis of the quality of their reasoning but on who comes closest to making the other squirm. Kinnock is certainly better at it than Foot, but Thatcher does not squirm easily.

On this occasion Kinnock started well by producing at the despatch box a newspaper showing Thatcher talking to Shah on the very October day that he applied for his first injunction against the NGA. Had there been collusion? Thatcher cleverly extricated herself by saying she had advised Shah to stick to the law, and she hoped Kinnock was giving the same advice to the unions. The exchanges continued in that form on successive Tuesdays and Thursdays; but through December the demonstrations were losing their steam. The TUC withdrew its support for the illegal picketing and the NGA accepted defeat.

In its comparatively small way, Warrington provided Kinnock with a lesson about the problems such industrial disputes pose for Labour leaders. It was a lesson he would need to draw on in the coming months, as the two sides limbered up for a massive industrial confrontation that would provoke an appalling crisis both for him personally and for the party he led.

*   *   *

Arthur Scargill had been spoiling for a fight since he was elected president of the National Union of Mineworkers (NUM) in December 1981, gaining nearly three quarters of the vote. A man of the extreme left, formerly a member of the Young Communist League but now in the Labour Party, he had come to prominence in the union as the organizer of a crucial mass picket at the Saltley coke works in the West Midlands during the successful strike of 1972. The Government had been anxious to keep the works open and 1,000 policemen were on hand to curb the pickets. In the end they had to concede victory to more than ten times that number of pickets, in an operation Scargill co-ordinated.

For years the miners had picked their leaders from the right of the Labour movement. In 1981 they chose a left-wing activist because they were convinced that the Government intended to impose large-scale cuts on the industry: and if anyone could stop it, Scargill, the hero of Saltley, would. He had warned them repeatedly that the National Coal Board (NCB) had a 'hit list' of pits for closure. In 1982 he had tried to persuade the union to strike on the issues of pay and pit closures, but the proposal was defeated in a ballot of the membership. His warnings on closures were reinforced when in March 1983 Thatcher announced the appointment of Ian MacGregor, the 71-year-old Scottish-American industrialist, as head of the NCB. Coming from the United States in 1980 with a reputation for union-busting, he had been made chairman of British Steel and imposed slashing cuts on the industry.

MacGregor's appointment was a clear sign that the Government too were spoiling for a fight. The miners' victories in 1972 and 1974 – the second had resulted in Edward Heath's Government losing office – still weighed heavily on Conservative consciences. They had to be exorcized. Plans for doing so, by preparing thoroughly for a strike and then provoking it, were outlined in a report to Conservative policy-makers by the MP Nicholas Ridley, leaked to *The Economist* in 1976. At the time nobody had taken it especially seriously but by the end of 1983 all the suggested preparations had been made, notably the stockpiling of coal to avoid the necessity for the power cuts Heath had to impose almost as soon as the 1973–4 strike began.

In October 1983, the month Kinnock became leader, the miners began an overtime ban in another protest against pay and pit closures. Before the end of the year MacGregor announced his target of slimming the industry to a production of 100 million tonnes from its level then of 118 million tonnes. There would be improved terms for miners made redundant – an estimated 20,000 in the first year. Scargill called the plan 'catastrophic' and 'a recipe for disaster'. Over the winter, a series of meetings between the board and the union served only to highlight their differences. Scargill refused to discuss pit closures. The NCB refused to take them off the agenda. Meanwhile, the overtime ban continued with no noticeable effect.

On 1 March 1984, the NCB area director for South Yorkshire said that Cortonwood pit, employing 830 men, was to be closed. Five days later, coincidentally as Kinnock was visiting the Coal Board's Yorkshire showpiece mine at Selby, the Board announced more closures and job losses. Yorkshire miners were called out on strike in protest and were joined by their colleagues in Scotland, who had been taking sporadic action against local closures since the autumn. According to the constitution of the NUM, a national strike may not be called without a majority of members voting for it in a ballot: it was the rule that had thwarted Scargill in 1982. However, local strikes may be called with the approval of the National Executive and this was the procedure used by Scargill. The executive approved a series of local strikes that would, he hoped, halt the entire industry, while avoiding another possible ballot defeat.

The absence of a national ballot was the most important factor in persuading Nottinghamshire miners not to support the strike. It also presented Kinnock and the Labour Party with their most intractable difficulty in deciding how to deal with the issue that dominated British politics for a year and cast a pall over Kinnock's leadership. It came at a time when he ought to have been making his initial impact on the party and the country as a potential Prime Minister. Instead, he spent much of the year dodging arrows both from the Conservatives, who accused him of not speaking out against the miners and their picketing tactics, and from members of his own party, who said he had not committed himself to the strike with sufficient fervour. Kinnock's supporters had a wry name for 1984–5: the lost year.

*   *   *

It is hard to imagine a more painful blooding for Kinnock than the personal as well as political dilemma posed by the coal dispute. It should, on the face of it, have been an easy one to handle. This was the industry in which he had grown up and where many of his constituents worked, the industry that had formed the backbone of the British Labour movement for nearly a century. Although he now lives in London, he looks forward eagerly to those weekends – at least one a month, usually more – when he can bowl along the M4, cross the Severn Bridge and turn north into the scrubby hills and valleys, through ribbons of grey mining towns that are still welcoming, despite the growing desolation caused by the contraction of the coal and steel industries.

He likes to wake up in the modest terraced house he uses as a *pied à terre* at Pontllanfraith, just south of Blackwood, the main town in his Islwyn constituency. Friends going to keep an early morning appointment might find him buttoning a clean shirt, then gesturing towards the back window with its view south-east towards Abercarn and Ebbw Vale. 'Look at that,' he will enthuse. 'Marvellous, isn't it?' To a stranger it is as scarred as most South Wales valleys; but to Kinnock it is home.

Perhaps his constituency agent, Doreen Moore, will have arranged a meeting with local union officials at Oakdale, the only remaining pit in Islwyn. Just north-east of Blackwood, it employs 1,300 miners but there are geological problems about reaching a seam of coal to its south. The men are worried that the NCB might pull out rather than make the investment needed to mine there, Kinnock keeps in close touch with developments. Or he might be visiting owners and tenants of the Coal Board houses on the ridge above an old pit, to talk about maintenance problems. They will offer him tea and Welsh griddle cakes and the conversation will turn to local matters, not the intractable issues he has left behind at Westminster. Like any other MP, he holds constituents' surgeries once a month. And there is generally time for a pint or two at one of the working men's clubs at the end of the day.

Kinnock enjoys talking to the miners and their families. He shares their background, their assumptions, their grasp on reality and their boisterous, teasing sense of humour; and he admires their tenacity. South Wales miners have traditionally been among the most united and determined in Britain. Indeed, they had sought to call a national strike on the issue of closures before 1983, but received scant support from colleagues elsewhere. Certainly, nobody has anything to teach Kinnock and his constituents about the case for coal and for the men who mine it.

Now, in his first year as party leader, the industry that nurtured him was fighting for its survival against a ruthless administration prepared to sacrifice whole communities in the name of an arguable concept of efficiency. Kinnock was convinced that the Government had seriously under-estimated the future demand for coal as an energy source for industry. Moreover, he saw their action as part of a concerted offensive against the trade union movement. Only weeks before the strike began, they had taken the extraordinary step of banning all union membership at GCHQ in Cheltenham, a high security listening post that plays an important role in the intelligence services.

Viewed against that background, the coal dispute amounted to the most clear-cut class conflict Britain had seen since 1926. Protecting jobs and safeguarding communities were at the very core of the Labour Party's reason for existing. If the party could not unite wholeheartedly behind the miners and their cause, what had it come to?

Two factors prevented the argument from being that simple: the absence of a pre-strike ballot and the rapidly developing violence on the picket lines. The first threw doubt on the legitimacy of the action. The second gave the miners' opponents a permanent means of diverting the argument away from the issues behind the strike and towards the tactics employed in pursuing it. Both factors could be attributed to the dominance of the NUM leadership by one man, Arthur Scargill.

Scargill is the kind of socialist that Kinnock instinctively mistrusts, the 'impossibilist' who will not give an inch on ideology, who will lead his followers to defeat rather than compromise on any one of his demands. The accepted technique of labour negotiation is, in the event of winning one concession, to use it as a basis for a negotiated settlement. That is not Scargill's way: instead, he will instantly and intractably move on to the next, more improbable demand. He is of the breed that entertains no doubt about the rectitude of his philosophy. He seeks the support of others on the left as a matter of moral duty. The simple certainties of his speeches prove seductive to young radicals in search of a cause. He convinces them that the politics of the streets and the picket lines are more likely to bring victory in the class struggle than the (to his mind) discredited methods of Parliamentary democracy.

Kinnock has never concealed his mistrust of Scargill. They quarrelled publicly over the 1981 deputy party leadership campaign. And in 1983, Kinnock said of the miners' leader: 'He's destroying the coal industry single handed. He's the Labour movement's nearest equivalent to a First World War general.' In his speech to the 1984 party conference in Blackpool, Kinnock stated unambiguously his opposition to any kind of socialism not based on popular consent:

We see industries decimated, communities deprived, liberties lost . . . and we ask ourselves what we can do. For socialists that is the question of the ages. Because it is in our very nature and conviction that we want to do something, especially when it is injustice. It was a question faced by our movement in the 1930s and they came back with the answer that the democratic road was the only route for British socialism. All other options, they said, were closed since

41

socialism by insurrection was a fantasy and socialism without the ballot box would simply never secure the understanding and support of the British people ... Democracy is the first premise of our socialism. It is a matter of principle, not of convenience. It is a matter of common sense, not of tactics ... We are upholding the only system which can give us power. The only system that we want to give us power. And the only system that we are prepared to wield when we have that power.

Scargill believed the miners could inflict defeat on the Government in 1984 as they had done ten and twelve years earlier. Because he could not count on winning a ballot, he manipulated his Executive Committee into approving a strike without one. The end justified the means. The miners would be led to the high ground of victory whether they liked it or not. But in choosing that path Scargill forfeited the automatic backing of the Labour Party. While the natural instinct of Labour supporters is to side with workers engaged in disputes, many found it hard to accept Scargill's tactics. Support was far from wholehearted and there was a sharp split in the party between those who went all the way with Scargill and those who had their doubts. Kinnock was decidedly in the second category. He was not prepared to give an open-ended commitment to support a union over whose tactics he could have no control.

The failure to hold a ballot therefore had two disastrous consequences: it made defeat for the miners virtually inevitable and provoked a division in Labour's ranks that did not heal until the strike was over.

Kinnock has regular meetings with the major union leaders. As it happened, Scargill was the very first of them to go to his new Westminster office in October 1983. He warned Kinnock that a clash was in the offing. Kinnock said *he* needed no convincing of the case against pit closures; but Scargill had to persuade his men to go along with him and convince the public of the merits of the argument. That had been the secret of the victories of 1972 and 1974. Scargill seemed to agree. Because of that, Kinnock was able to convince himself, despite his suspicion of Scargill, that there would be a national ballot. From the moment it became clear there would not be, he did not feel bound to support the strike as wholeheartedly as it was his instinct to do.

After the October meeting, Scargill sought no further contact with Kinnock or other Shadow Cabinet members until the strike was under way. He was to say later that the miners had been let down by the Labour Party and the TUC over the General Strike in 1926 and this time they would go it alone. He had been expected to attend a meeting in February with the group of MPs sponsored by the NUM. Stan Orme, the Opposition energy spokesman, had been invited and was keen to discuss the prospects of avoiding a strike: but Scargill sent a deputy.

Because there had been no national ballot, the strike was never solid. In Nottinghamshire, where the local leadership had been deeply mistrustful of Scargill, work continued. Almost as soon as the strike began, teams of flying pickets were dispatched from Yorkshire, Kent and other striking coalfields to the working pits. Squads of police from forces around the country were sent to protect the miners going to work and the lorries departing with their loads. In the first few days, they even prevented miners driving north from Kent to join the picketing, by turning their cars back at the Dartford Tunnel. With passions getting hotter, violence was not long coming. On 15 March came the first fatality, when a picket died at Ollerton, Notts., following a blow to the chest.

In the House of Commons, exchanges on the strike soon fell into a pattern. The Opposition accused the Government of provoking it deliberately, through the agency of Ian MacGregor, and of being unwilling to compromise. Government supporters self-righteously called on Kinnock and his colleagues to condemn the picket line violence. When they did so, the stakes were raised and condemnation was demanded in still more explicit terms.

On 28 March the party's NEC agreed a unanimous resolution – a rare event indeed – proposed by Eric Heffer, party chairman for that year. It expressed support for 'all miners in their struggle to save the coal mining industry' and expressed concern at the police operation, which seemed designed to prevent peaceful picketing, an activity still allowable under the law. The statement maintained that the picketing had been peaceful. 'However, the NEC deplores all forms of violence to which, in this instance, the massive police presence has contributed.' It went on to condemn the interference with pickets on their way to pits as 'a move towards the ending of free movement in Britain.'

It was a firm declaration of support for the miners and a victory for the left on the NEC, in that it blamed violence on the presence of the police and made no reference to the need for a ballot. Kinnock still believed that a ballot was possible, but thought that to call for it publicly might encourage Scargill to dig his heels in. Later he was to regret not making his view clear from the very beginning.

In numerous speeches on the dispute, Kinnock attacked the Government for the policy that led to the strike. 'They are going to try to starve the miners into submission,' he told the Scottish TUC in Aberdeen, setting out the financial position of the strikers (no benefits for a striker without dependants, £24.75 a week for a man with a wife and two children). But they fought on because 'many miners know that if they relinquish jobs now they will simply not work again'. Then he called for a development plan for the coal industry that recognized that the cost of keeping 70,000 miners out of work was greater than the cost of the investment and subsidy needed to keep most of them at work producing coal.

Opinion polls showed that if he had taken a ballot of his members, Scargill could have expected a majority of around 60–40 for the strike. Kinnock had real hopes that he might call one when, during one of their rare telephone discussions in April, Scargill told him that his executive planned to alter the constitution to make a bare majority of members sufficient to authorize strike action, instead of the 55% that then ruled. It was on the strength of that discussion that Kinnock maintained in the Commons that a ballot was nearer. Yet although the rule change was approved at a special delegate conference of the union, it was decided not to call a ballot. Kinnock became increasingly impatient. On 1 May, in a BBC Television interview, he said that until there was a national ballot the strike would not be effective and the industry could not be properly defended.

Two weeks later the Labour Party became involved, almost by chance, in the first real attempt to resolve the dispute by negotiation, two months after it had begun. During an angry exchange in the Commons Peter Walker, as Secretary of State for Energy the Cabinet Minister responsible for the coal industry, clashed with Stan Orme, Labour's shadow spokesman. Orme, pursuing his party's theme, urged Walker to intervene to get negotiations under way. Walker snapped back at him. Why didn't *he*, Orme, do something? Why didn't he use his influence to get the miners to the negotiating table?

It was no more than a routine Commons jibe. Nine times out of ten Orme would have brushed it aside and forgotten about it. But when he arrived home late that night he turned the prospect over in his mind. Why shouldn't he do something about it? It was true that Scargill had made no move to get the Labour Party involved – except in demanding its unequivocal support – but then neither had the party taken any initiative. Next morning, from his office on the Shadow Cabinet corridor, Orme put a call in to Scargill at NUM headquarters in Sheffield. The miners' leader came on the line immediately. Orme said he wanted to explore ways in which the party might help negotiate a settlement. Could they meet?

'Anything wrong with tomorrow?' Scargill asked. Nothing was wrong with tomorrow. Scargill and two of his colleagues turned up at Westminster and had a 90-minute talk with Orme in the Shadow Cabinet room, a large, high-windowed conference room that forms part of Kinnock's suite of offices. Orme stressed that he was not going to make proposals, just seeing if he could facilitate contact between the two sides. Scargill had been there primarily to explain the miners' case. Kinnock supported the initiative but thought it best not to risk raising artificial hopes by getting involved personally, although Orme kept him closely informed as the negotiations progressed.

Next morning MacGregor was on the phone to Orme, asking to be allowed to put the Coal Board's case. Orme checked with Kinnock, who agreed the meeting should go ahead. After it, Orme went back and explained MacGregor's points to Scargill and for some weeks engaged in shuttle diplomacy between the two sides. He was the only person they would both talk to. And it was through his intervention that, on 23 May 1984, the protagonists met for the first time since the strike began.

The date had been set long in advance for one of the regular consultative meetings between the NCB and the NUM. Scargill had not planned to attend it but on the previous day Orme invited him to the Commons to try to persuade him to go. Kinnock was there too – his first face-to-face meeting with Scargill since the previous October. Scargill said he would go to the meeting with the NCB but he had nothing fresh to offer and he did not think MacGregor had either. Kinnock tried to get him to look ahead to a possible solution.

'What's the strategy, Arthur?' he asked, more than once. 'What's the game plan? Tell me and I'll see what we can do.'

Scargill gave no answer. The strategy was not one he wanted to discuss with Kinnock, nor did he think the Labour Party could help much in carrying it out. He did agree to attend the next day's meeting, but only for the sake of appearances. It lasted scarcely more than an hour.

Orme helped set up further meetings between the protagonists in Edinburgh on 8 June and again at the beginning of July. Yet the central, intractable difficulty remained. Scargill would not concede the Coal Board's right to close any pit on the grounds that it was economically unviable. MacGregor would not accept a deal that did not give him that right. No matter how they juggled with forms of words, no compromise was possible unless one of the immovable objects moved.

Three days after Scargill met Kinnock at the Commons, several weeks of violent clashes began outside the Orgreave coke depot, a few miles from NUM headquarters in Sheffield. The pickets wanted to stop the production of coke for British Steel and tried to prevent lorries leaving. Police on foot and horseback kept the road clear for the lorries but the violent scenes were shown night after night on the television news, provoking criticism of the tactics of the police as well as the pickets.

On 1 June Kinnock, under pressure from the Conservatives to denounce the violence, issued a statement.

There is no place in any industrial dispute in Britain for missiles, battering rams or any other implement or act of violence. The miners, like all other British trade unionists, realize that their strength comes from peaceful organization, peaceful protest and peaceful picketing.

Other methods give succour and advantage to the enemies of the trade union movement and do nothing to advance the cause of the workers in dispute.

At the same time he was accusing the Prime Minister of keeping the dispute going as a deliberate act of policy – a point he made forcefully to a delegation of miners who lobbied Parliament on 7 June.

The television cameras were busy not only on the picket lines but in the towns and villages of the coalfields, reporting how the families of striking miners were managing, uncovering bitter feuds between old friends and even inside families, where some were crossing the picket lines to go to work and others were not. Angry strikers attacked working miners and stoned their houses. The one area where this did not happen was South Wales, Kinnock's territory. There, the strike remained solid until the final weeks.

One part of Scargill's strategy was working: the dispute had become the central issue in British politics and the miners quickly became the heroes of the Labour Party and all left-wing groups. Public meetings were held across the country. (Tony Benn was among the most popular speakers at them.) Scores of miners and their wives were sent on speaking tours to Labour Party and trade union branches, explaining the hardships being suffered by strikers and their families and taking collections for the fund. Striking miners set up offices in London and regional centres to co-ordinate the activity.

'Everyone's got mineritis,' Kinnock was told by a bemused constituent who had been on one of the speaking tours. The miners returned from the cities with wry tales, some probably apocryphal. One told how delegations from two local Labour parties had gone to Paddington Station to meet NUM groups off the same train: there were petulant scenes as one lot accused the other of filching their miners from under their noses.

Kinnock joined the laughter, but uneasily. All this smacked of what he called gesture politics, lending automatic support to a fashionable cause without thinking it through. He had never believed in that – hence his refusal to support Welsh devolution and the deputy leadership campaign of Tony Benn. It was all very well to turn the miners into the darlings of the left, but he knew they were undergoing real hardship. A Blackwood bank manager told him of one couple in their mid-fifties who had been meticulous about staying out of debt all their lives. But now they had gone through their savings of £4,500 and had an overdraft of £1,200. They were shattered and ashamed by the thought. There were scores of such stories. Despite the efforts of the support groups, some families were going hungry. What if, as he increasingly feared, all this sacrifice was to prove fruitless? What if his childhood friends and compatriots were suffering simply to feed the unattainable ambition of a revolutionary?

In many of the crises a Labour leader confronts, the problem is how to keep the party united. Not this time. There was no question but that Labour supporters would back the miners' cause. He was worried, though, that this quite proper sense of obligation would be exploited, and the party persuaded to endorse Scargill's most extreme positions because of their over-riding emotional loyalty to workers in conflict. This would cause immeasurable damage to his prospects of gaining the middle-ground support he needed to win a general election.

He was not himself immune from the obligation to lend verbal support to the miners' leader. On 1 July he spoke at a rally marking the 150th anniversary of the Tolpuddle martyrs. He asked:

When will they ever learn that working people will not be starved into submission or browbeaten into silence? Do they still believe that miners will be coerced back to work by cutting benefits? People will endure any hardship to protect their families, their future and their principles.

Two weeks later he underlined the message when he shared a platform with Scargill at the annual Durham Miners' Gala:

Here in this mining industry you have said: No more obedience, no more compliance, no more acceptance. No more rip-off, no more rundown. Here in this mining industry you have said you won't take the bribes and you will not take bullying. People who do not know this industry, people who do not know miners and miners' families and communities ask why you put up such a fight. The answer is a single phrase. There is no alternative.

He had borrowed the saying from Thatcher, who used it to justify her Government's rigid economic policy. Kinnock developed it further:

When your backs are against the wall of unemployment, there is no alternative but to fight for jobs. All other options are empty. All other roads are blocked. This is a fight for survival. That is what all of the comfortable people, the complacent people must understand . . . You can't sell your futures. You can't sell the future of your children and your communities. There is no price high enough to pay for these things. That is the truth that Margaret Thatcher won't understand.

He ended with a rousing warning to the Prime Minister:

She has broken records of ruin. She has broken records of arms spending. She has broken records of unemployment. She has broken families. She has broken hearts. But she has not, she cannot and she will not break the coalmining people of Britain, now or ever.

The truth was that, despite such rhetoric, the prospects of victory for the miners grew more slender the longer the strike dragged on. Sporadic negotiations produced no sign of a breakthrough and the Government were confident that the level of coal stocks, added to that being produced by working miners, was high enough to prevent power cuts. Continuing violence on the picket lines ate into public sympathy for the miners, giving the Government no incentive to settle quickly.

Scargill, having spurned the help of the TUC and the Labour Party earlier, now sought to maximize his support. He went to the Trades Union Congress in Brighton on 3 September and delivered a powerful appeal for practical help from other unions. He wanted them to refuse to handle 'scab' coal and he called on the power station workers and electricians not to agree to produce power from substitute sources such as oil. He was given a tremendous ovation and the resolution calling for support and co-operation was passed by a large and enthusiastic majority – although it had no effect on the subsequent actions of trade unionists.

Kinnock addressed the Brighton Congress the following day, and responded to the call from much of the press and many of his Shadow Cabinet colleagues to make a further denunciation of the persistent picket line violence. After making the economic case for a thriving coal industry, he declared:

> We must put that case without violence. Our asset is reason. Our strength is the rationality of the case for coal. Violence distracts attention from the central issues of the dispute. It obscures the justice and validity of the miners' case. Violence has given the Government its only bone of excuse to gnaw on. It has enabled them to evade their central responsibility for promoting a settlement of the dispute. It has provided them with the opportunity which they have long sought to introduce politically motivated change in the methods of British policing. Violence . . . provides opportunities to our enemies, whose lurid imaginations are bigger than their brains, to pretend that trade unionists are trying to secure power by means other than those of Parliamentary democracy.

In the afterglow of Scargill's potent address the previous day, there was some heckling at Kinnock's references to violence. For many of the miners' most committed supporters, a person's attitude to the picket-line excesses was a kind of virility test of loyalty to the cause – and by denouncing violence Kinnock was deemed to have failed it. 'Whose side are you on?' was the cry. To be on the miners' side meant accepting the way the dispute was being conducted and laying the blame for all the clashes at the door of the police. Kinnock could not do that. Nor were the miners and their supporters too pleased with the next segment of the party leader's speech, about the underlying motive for the strike. Scargill had repeated his theme that it was as much against the Government's anti-union legislation as about pit closures, a crusade for the entire working-class movement. To the extent that this implied ousting the Government by extra-Parliamentary means, Kinnock felt obliged to state his position:

> This Congress and its affiliated unions, its leadership and its rank and file, have repeatedly demonstrated and asserted the abiding belief that trade unionism is for changing conditions. General elections – and only general elections – are for changing governments. This Congress and British trade unionism has *never* in its 116 years of history preached or practised any other creed. And it never will.

A month later, at the party conference at Blackpool, Scargill repeated his Brighton performance and provoked a still more ecstatic response. The miners, he asserted, were entitled to seek Labour's support. They were

> not fighting for the NUM, not fighting for jobs for miners but fighting against the whole concept of this Government's economic policy which is designed to destroy jobs and wreak havoc amongst the British Labour and trade union movement.

Conference passed a resolution offering support as wholeheartedly as the TUC had, blaming all the violence on the police. In his speech next day, Kinnock reacted with a powerful attack on the pit closures policy, combined with a denunciation of violence from either side:

> The Government creates the climate of confrontation, the conditions of conflict. It speaks only the language of conquest. And in the midst of all that chaos, in the midst of all that assault on the essentials of civilized life in this country and of the values of this country, they call for condemnation of violence. I do not respond to that because it is a taunt, a call to forswear intimidation from a Government that bases its whole policy on intimidation. I do condemn violence. I condemn the violence of despair . . . of long-term unemployment . . . of loneliness, decay and ugliness. I condemn the violence done to hope . . . to

talent . . . to family security and family unity. I condemn the violence done to civil and personal rights in this country. I condemn the violence too of the stone-throwers and the battering-ram carriers. I condemn the violence of the cavalry charges, the truncheon groups and the shield bangers. I condemn violence . . . all violence, without fear or favour. That is what makes me different from Margaret Thatcher. I don't have her double standards. I do not take her selective and blinkered view of conflict.

He was given a standing ovation longer than the one bestowed on Scargill but, according to those who monitor such things, not quite as loud.

Standing ovations could not assuage Kinnock's growing conviction that the strike was now doomed to fail. The NUM had been taken to court and fined £200,000 for defying the law demanding a union-wide ballot before a strike. The union responded by moving its funds overseas; beyond, as it hoped, the reach of court officials. Kinnock grew more and more dismayed. He finally became convinced that there was virtually no chance of a negotiated settlement when Scargill refused to consider a peace formula on the lines of that accepted by NACODS (the National Association of Colliery Overmen, Deputies and Shotfirers). This had contained concessions on the machinery for deciding on pit closures. Kinnock declared publicly that he thought this could have been used as a basis for a settlement with the NUM. But he was careful never to say outright that the miners could not win, or to make a direct appeal to them to settle. That, he thought, was what Scargill wanted: then he could pin responsibility for the defeat on him. It was important not to give him the chance.

Scargill, encouraged by his reception at the autumn conferences, thought the time propitious to attempt to widen the dispute, to put flesh on the supportive resolutions passed by the Labour Party and the TUC. In particular, he wanted a firmer commitment from the Labour leadership. The hard left began criticizing Kinnock for not doing more. Why, the strike was more than seven months old and he had not even visited a picket line. This was to become a growing criticism as the dreadful year drew to a close. He could – and probably should – have visited pickets in his own constituency quite early in the dispute. There had been scarcely any serious trouble around the Welsh pits and he could have made that gesture of solidarity without seeming to endorse the violence. That, indeed, was what he eventually did. But he resisted until the very end of the strike – too late to escape criticism. The reason for his reluctance was precisely that his presence could never be anything more than a fairly meaningless gesture. He could offer no practical help or comfort to strikers led by a man whose motives and methods he so deeply mistrusted. In other contexts he denounces 'gesture politicians' with genuine passion and is wary – perhaps too wary for a Labour politician – of adopting the soft option.

His critics maintained that he had not been persistent enough in raising the issue in the Commons – more gesturing, he felt. He was sometimes heckled on public platforms. In mid-October he went to talk to students at Ealing College, close to his West London home. The questions were nearly all about the strike and a few in the audience jeered him. He exploded: 'It's a damned cheek to ask me to support the miners. I've been supporting the miners since I was 15.' But he insisted on condemning the hooliganism that harmed the cause. A further meeting with Scargill late in October did nothing to improve their relations or find a basis for a settlement.

The miners' cause was harmed further – and Kinnock's patience tried to its outer limits – when *The Sunday Times* disclosed that Scargill had been to Paris to talk to representatives of Col. Gaddafi, the Libyan leader. They had been discussing possible financial help to the NUM. Kinnock could see that this ill-judged affair would hasten the decline of public sympathy for the strikers and sought to ensure that none of the opprobrium stuck to him or his party. Without consulting Scargill, he made a statement criticizing the Libyan adventure.

The miners' leader played his most powerful card against Kinnock at the beginning of November. At a meeting of the union executive on 2 November, he announced a series of four rallies to drum up fresh support for the strikers' case; and he invited the Labour leader to address all of them. Kinnock was not going to succumb to this tactic, patently meant to put him on the spot. If he agreed to address some or all of the rallies, he could be represented as Scargill's poodle, running to heel at the imperious snap of the Yorkshireman's fingers. If he declined there would be a fresh chorus from the left, accusing him of abandoning the miners at their time of need. Many of his advisers – among them Stan Orme and his PPS Derek Foster – urged him to go to just one rally, the one scheduled to be held at Aberavon in South Wales, his home territory. Kinnock considered that option but rejected it. The Labour leadership, he believed, must not put itself at the beck and call of a union leader, particularly one whose motives were palpably sinister. He would resign himself instead to suffering the wrath of the left. Pleading a full engagement diary, he turned down all four invitations but said the Labour Party would hold its own rally at Stoke-on-Trent on 30 November. He would be there and he hoped Scargill would be too.

The wrath of the left duly and speedily came to the boil. The Campaign Group met in the Commons and issued a statement calling on MPs to make supporting the NUM a priority over other activities. In one of his regular meetings with the PLP, Kinnock said he would have no part in leading the miners to glorious defeat. 'There doesn't have to be a Gallipoli,' he said; but Dennis Skinner warned him darkly: 'Your absence will be remembered.' Kinnock asked them to work out how many meetings he had attended to try to gain a settlement. 'Posturing is not the way to win the next election,' he insisted. 'Nor do you box by leading with your chin.' He instructed his staff to compile a file of speeches he had made on the dispute during the year and issue it as a press pack.

More hurtful than the predictable anger of Skinner and his allies was criticism from miners in his own constituency. They would have liked to see him at the Aberavon rally and on one of their picket lines. Meeting them in mid-November, he promised to make a picket line visit as soon as he had the time. As it turned out, he did well to miss Aberavon. One of the speakers at the rally was Norman Willis, who had just succeeded Len Murray as general secretary of the TUC. He denounced the violence clearly and bravely: 'I speak for millions of trade unionists whose instinct to support the miners is as strong as their opposition to violence, and that includes me.' He was jeered by the audience and a noose was dangled from the ceiling above his head. Next day Kinnock defended him at a lunch of lobby correspondents: 'Norman Willis gave strong and truthful advice last night,' he said. Denouncing violence was 'not a test of courage but a test of truth'. But it was increasingly hard to sustain that position in a climate where opposing violence was regarded as tantamount to opposing the strikers' cause.

Scenting a victory, the Conservatives in the Commons were exploiting with relish the difficulties Kinnock was having with the miners and their supporters. They took their cue from a front-page lead story in the *Daily Mail* on 15 November headed STAND BACK – HE'S LOSING. It reported that Labour leaders were distancing themselves from the dispute because Kinnock believed Scargill was leading his men to oblivion. At Question Time in the Commons that day, Thatcher declared that Kinnock did not have the guts to face striking miners and condemn violence. She praised Norman Willis's Aberavon speech and added scornfully: 'You echoed it from a safe distance.' Dr David Owen, leader of the SDP, joined in, accusing the Labour leadership of making 'squeaks reminiscent of rats leaving a sinking ship'.

As the date of the Stoke rally approached, the hard left began to pile more pressure on Kinnock and the party leadership to come down more firmly on the side of the miners. Eric Heffer announced that the Campaign Group would use disruptive methods in the Commons to put over the strikers' case. 'We will use every sort of Parliamentary harassment permitted by the rules of the House to focus on the Government's actions, which are mean, vicious and heartless.' Scargill, in a radio interview, said he expected Kinnock to affirm at Stoke that he would stick by the conference decision to support the miners.

The morning of the rally saw the most appalling act of violence in the whole dispute. A Welsh taxi driver taking a strike-breaking miner to work was killed when two men dropped a concrete slab on to his cab from a bridge over the road. Kinnock began his speech with reference to the killing: 'We meet tonight under the shadow of an atrocity.' He went on to repeat his condemnation of violence in the strongest terms: 'Violence will not bring victory. Violence is the main barrier to victory.'

The significance of the Labour Party organizing the rally rather than the NUM was that, unlike at Aberavon, the Stoke audience was overwhelmingly in favour of Kinnock. Packing meetings is a traditional Labour skill, although a few members of the Revolutionary Communist Party had found their way in. Shouting 'scab' and 'traitor', they were dragged out by stewards as he began to speak, allowing him to exercise his skill with hecklers. They were 'parasites on the miners . . . members of a lunatic fringe . . . play actors who don't know the difference between a coal miner and a snooker cue.' Theirs was 'hobby politics'. The audience roared approval.

There is a telling anecdote about the rally. Police had received a warning that someone was planning to throw a hand grenade on to the platform. They were unsure whether it was a hoax. When Kinnock was told, he refused to have the meeting halted but suggested that people on the platform should be discreetly asked to step down from it, starting with the women. One by one they retreated, until only Kinnock, Scargill and a handful of others were left. A police officer pleaded with Kinnock to leave for the sake of his safety, but he refused. As he looked at Scargill, he was heard to joke: 'Just at this moment, I can think of worse last glimpses of this earth than Arthur going with me.'

*   *   *

With Christmas approaching, the Coal Board began an offensive to lure individual strikers back to work. Each Monday morning figures were published showing that financial hardship and the colder weather were sapping morale. The number returning to work was significantly higher each week. The far left, faced with the formerly unthinkable prospect of defeat by attrition, raised the stakes further with a call for a general strike. Tony Benn, in a speech in Cambridgeshire, said such a strike might become necessary to protect trade unions and political freedom. He repeated the suggestion in his Chesterfield constituency, where he discussed the possibility that Scargill might be sent to jail as a result of the union's continuing difficulties with the law. Were we prepared to sit back and watch him being led away on television, or was it time to start thinking about it seriously? Two other members of the NEC, Dennis Skinner and Audrey Wise, supported his strike call.

Kinnock reacted swiftly to curb these suggestions. A week after his Stoke speech he attended a meeting between the miners' leaders and members of the NEC. He said that there was no chance of a general strike succeeding and that to call for one would terminally damage the chance of arguing the case for coal successfully. Turning to Scargill, he said the Labour Party wanted to go on defending the miners' case but their success was being prevented by violence. Scargill did not respond and said nothing about a general strike, either; but in that week's *Labour Weekly* he called for 'the most massive organization of industrial action our movement has ever known,' adding: 'We must have it now. There is no other way to stop the courts' attempt to destroy the NUM.' Kinnock repudiated these calls in an interview with Central Television:

I think it is a rather romantic view of affairs, rather exaggerated, but in many ways much more important is that it gives you people in the media something to talk and write about. Talk of a general strike that will not take place is a distraction from the main issue.

That weekend, in his Islwyn constituency, he received a standing ovation from 200 striking miners. He said reports of a rift between him and Scargill were 'somewhat exaggerated'. Dan Canniff, chairman of the Oakdale miners' lodge, said of Kinnock afterwards: 'Because we have a difference of opinion it doesn't mean we don't like him in general.'

If he could usually rely on being with friends in Wales, that was far from the case at Walworth Road, where the following week the NEC held what some members described as the most bitterly contentious meeting they could recall. Seeing that most of them were on hand for the shouting matches during Michael Foot's time as leader, that suggested a high degree of bitterness indeed. The meeting began with a row not connected with the miners' dispute. It was about whether Michael Cocks, the Chief Whip, should be allowed to stay at the meeting, since the NEC had received a letter from his solicitor threatening legal action in connection with the troubles Cocks was having with his constituency party. The chairman, Alan Hadden, ruled that he could stay but would be asked to withdraw while his case was being discussed. Cocks is a *bête noir* of the left and Eric Heffer, incensed by Hadden's decision, moved that he be asked to leave the chair. The proposal was voted down by 18 votes to 8.

That put everyone in a sour mood when it was time to discuss the strike. First, with deceptive unanimity, the Committee approved a motion by Tony Benn calling on the party to organize a further rally on behalf of the strikers. Next a motion from Dennis Skinner urging 'all sections of the Labour and trade union movement to respond with all-out industrial action' was defeated by 18 to 9. Most heat was generated by a third motion moved by Frances Curran, the Militant supporter representing the Labour Party Young Socialists, and seconded by Skinner. It called on the next Labour Government to repeal all Conservative trade union legislation and to reimburse all unions that had incurred fines for breaches of it. She had the miners and their £200,000 fine much in mind.

Discussion was long and passionate. 'We'll never *get* to Government the way you're behaving,' said Kinnock testily, looking towards the Benn/Skinner corner of the table. Heffer moved an amendment pointing out that the resolution was in line with a decision by conference in 1982. Then Charles Turnock from the National Union of Railwaymen, a reliable ally of Kinnock, proposed that the resolution should be referred to the NEC's Home Policy Committee – a procedural device for shelving it. It was a knife-edge vote. By 15 votes to 13, the Turnock version was passed and the resolution effectively killed. Of those members whose position on these matters is difficult to forecast, Michael Meacher, formerly a loyal supporter of Benn, voted with the Kinnock camp. And David Blunkett, leader of Sheffield City Council, cast his vote with the left, although before long he became another firm supporter of the leadership.

The Christmas and New Year break did nothing to engender goodwill in the party. Nor did Kinnock's eventual visit to the picket line at Celynen South, near Newbridge, in his constituency. He drove in the small hours from Ealing and arrived at 5 am to join 40 pickets, as they watched 33 strike-breakers going in to work. Three were going back for the first time – out of the 618 that had returned to the pits in Britain since New Year's Day. Wearing a mac and stout boots to keep out the cold, Kinnock spent 90 minutes there and said afterwards: 'At 5 am the repertoire of jokes was astounding.'

The visit did not silence his critics, as he knew it would not. The principle of the extreme left is that as soon as one demand is met, another is made. Martin Flannery, one of the most vociferous MPs in the Campaign Group, said it was disgraceful that it had taken Kinnock ten months to make the visit. 'He's looking at it the wrong way round,' he commented. 'He says if we're all very quiet we'll win the next election. He fails to see that the whole Labour movement will sustain a frightful defeat if the miners are defeated.'

Kinnock responded belligerently. A few days later, leaving Heathrow for a visit to Nicaragua, he was asked about critics who were trying to make him the scapegoat for the collapse of the strike, which seemed imminent. He warned that he would give them the 'short-arm stop' – an aggressive retaliatory tactic in rugby. 'The public believes that there is some power in the Labour Party capable of starting and stopping strikes,' he observed. 'That is profound nonsense.'

Emotions ran high at the regular Commons meetings of the PLP. Left-wingers suspected that Kinnock was deliberately not raising the issue of the strike in the House because he was embarrassed by it. That was partially true. He believed that, with the strike disintegrating, he was bound to come off worse in any Commons exchange with the Conservatives, who could justifiably count the return to work as a victory. Since he was not prepared to raise the stakes in the way his critics would have liked, he would be in an impossibly weak position.

In their anger, the Campaign Group fulfilled Heffer's pre-Christmas threat and began disrupting the business of Parliament. Fifteen of them, led by Heffer and Benn, refused to resume their seats when the Government rejected their calls for an emergency debate on the strike. The Speaker suspended the sitting. Dennis Skinner said: 'You ain't seen nothing yet. Just keep watching us. We shall organize a campaign next week for as long as is necessary.'

Kinnock knew that it was time to spike the Campaign Group's guns. He stormed into a meeting of the PLP and said:

If you actually persuade yourselves that activities like today's enhance the miners' case, then there's nothing I can do in the world to prevent you. But remember as you talk of people in the coalfields and as you look into the newspapers tomorrow and search your consciences, it doesn't help their case by half a millimetre, or our prospects of getting into power. If you think it does, you don't live in the real world . . . What happened this afternoon obscures everything that is going on. It betrays an utter lack of self-discipline and was an utter act of self-indulgence.

He spoke in that vein for nearly quarter of an hour. Some of the Left-wingers interrupted with cries of 'Rubbish' but the majority gave him a standing ovation. Roy Hattersley said on television later that week: 'It was brave, right, acclaimed by the rest of the Parliamentary party and improved his standing.'

The press, too, largely approved of Kinnock's severe line with the left. He decided to capitalize on it further by agreeing to be interviewed on *The World This Weekend* on Radio 4. He said MPs who broke the rules of the House should be suspended, no matter what party they belonged to. In any collective activity, such as sport, you had to face collective discipline based on self-discipline, or you shouldn't be on the field. A Commons debate would not help the miners. It would turn into a debate on the condition of the NUM and that would be an easy target for the Conservatives. The Government would get off the hook.

In the average bus queue or picket line they don't understand these sideshows ... We're not talking about children. We're not talking about people who have got to be scourged into line. I am saying to them: 'I am prepared to treat you as adults, as people who are conscientious, as people who want to win. Now you must accept the responsibilities involved in the strategy of winning the next election.' Without such strategy, without such desire to put our policies into effect, then all is indulgence, all is entertainment, all is a hobby for which people are fortunate enough to get paid. I don't think that's a sufficient justification for being engaged in democratic politics.

Finally, when the centre-left Tribune Group added their voice to the Campaign Group's call for a debate, Kinnock agreed to allot one of the Opposition's days to it at the beginning of February. Broadcast live on the radio, it confirmed that his initial reluctance to seek a debate was well-judged. He was catcalled by Conservative MPs and had no convincing response to Thatcher's proposal that he should pressurize the NUM into accepting the deal agreed by NACODS. He and she both knew that it was impossible for him to put pressure on the NUM about anything.

The drift back to work gained pace after Christmas and by the end of February it was clear that the strike was petering out. After a final flurry of negotiation attempts, the miners returned to work on 5 March, 1985, without an agreement.

Kinnock knew that there would be an aftermath, that it could take him up to a year to repair the damage the strike had inflicted on his party and his leadership. In the event it took a lot less than that. Just a few days after it ended Mick McGahey, Scargill's deputy, a veteran Scots Communist, was on the phone inviting Kinnock to a miners' gala in Scotland. Despite their political differences, he had always got on well with McGahey. After a ballot among miners' representatives, he was also invited to speak at the Durham Miners' Gala, the showpiece of them all, in July. As for his quarrels with the Campaign Group, Kinnock had already decided that it was important for the long-term success of his leadership to set out his stall as an opponent of the far left. The year had not been an entire write-off if it had seen the beginning of that process.

His chief regret was that it had taken him so long to define his differences with Scargill and to make it clear that he opposed the way the strike was being conducted. He could see now that the electorate were more impressed by a tough line with ideologues than by attempts to come to terms with them. He was not going to make the same mistake again.

3   *To the Aid of the Party*

The coal dispute was not the only political event of 1984, although there were times when, to Kinnock, it seemed like it. A timely early test of the party's capacity to recover its electoral fortunes, after the débâcle of 1983, came with the European elections in June. The Labour leadership had generally been ambivalent about British membership of the European Economic Community. The left were consistently hostile to it and Kinnock had counted himself with them. He campaigned for a 'no' vote in the 1975 referendum, when the official party line was to endorse membership. He had supported the policy of the 1983 manifesto, which committed a Labour Government to taking Britain out of the Community within the lifetime of the next Parliament. However, the elections to the European Parliament in Strasbourg provided the first nationwide test since Kinnock became leader. The party decided to contest them wholeheartedly. Even fervent anti-marketeers such as Tony Benn joined in with a will.

In terms of electoral strategy, the single most important objective was to re-establish Labour in Britain as the only feasible alternative to the Conservatives. In the last months of Michael Foot's leadership there had been a real danger that the Liberal/SDP Alliance could take over that role. In the 1983 election Labour had polled 28% of the vote and the Alliance 26%. This close margin had not been translated into seats because the quirks of the first-past-the-post electoral system mean that the centre party is under-represented. In a Gallup poll published in *The Daily Telegraph* on 15 September 1983, three months after the election, the Labour share was down to $24\frac{1}{2}$% with the Conservatives at $45\frac{1}{2}$% and the Alliance 29% – or $4\frac{1}{2}$ points ahead of Labour. There was an obvious danger that, like the Liberals in the 1920s, the party was heading fast for eclipse, its natural constituency eroded. Kinnock and his advisers used a boxing metaphor. By the autumn of 1983 Labour had been effectively knocked out of the ring. The Euro-elections gave it a chance to climb back in; then the next few years could be spent patiently trying to change the course of the fight, Labour keeping up its guard while delivering some judicious jabs to the Tories' head and body.

Labour had done badly in the first European elections in 1979; a performance that presaged the still darker days to come. In a low poll it had won only 33% of the votes, giving it 17 of the 81 seats. Although its fortunes had sunk lower since, the opinion polls in the early months of 1984 indicated a dramatic recovery and it was clearly possible to improve on 1979. The object was to turn the European election into a national vote of no-confidence in the Thatcher Government, while at the same time cutting into the Alliance vote. The second objective was rendered easier by the size of the constituencies, which operated against third parties: no Liberal had been elected in 1979.

Robin Cook had proved his campaigning skills in the leadership battle and was given overall charge of strategy. It was an ideal chance to revive the party's electoral machinery, because funds for the campaign were available from the European Community. Kinnock and Cook decided that there should be a centrally co-ordinated programme of speeches from party leaders across the country, mostly in large, well-organized rallies; plus a handful of pop concerts. That was part of a particular effort to appeal to young voters, contrasting the new leader with Foot, whose walking stick had been exploited cleverly by the Conservative press during the general election to suggest an ageing eccentric out of touch with the modern world. Billy Bragg, the pop singer, allied himself with the campaign team and was featured prominently.

Kinnock and Hattersley appeared on several platforms together as well as at the regular morning press conferences, developing the 'dream ticket' theme from the Brighton conference. The manifesto was crisp, to the point and, with only ten pages, a quarter of the length of the rambling general election document of the previous year. Many aspects of it had been agreed with the Europe-wide Socialist group of MPs at Strasbourg.

The party's campaign speakers made only token attempts to discuss European matters, mostly the Community budget and the threat to impose VAT on books and food. For the rest they attacked the Conservatives on the domestic issues where they were most vulnerable. 'On June 14 we can vote for the miners,' said Benn at Bethnal Green a week before polling day. He predicted victory for the strikers, the return of MacGregor to America and the eventual resignation of the Prime Minister. In his press conferences in the week of the poll, Kinnock concentrated exclusively on national issues. He called on voters to inflict a major defeat on the Conservatives, to deliver a protest vote against unemployment, the run-down of the economy, cuts in the Health Service, manipulation of the coal dispute and the attack on local democracy.

The energetic and professional campaigning paid off. Labour nearly doubled its number of seats at Strasbourg from 17 to 32, making 15 straight gains from the Conservatives. In a turnout of 32.4% (marginally up on 1979) the Labour share of the poll rose from 33% to 36.4%, while the Conservatives went down from 50.6% to 41.3%. The Alliance increased their share from 13.1% to 19.1% but, to their strongly expressed indignation, failed to win a seat.

Labour was indisputably back in the fight. Yet any excessive jubilation was tempered the following week, which saw some of the most violent scenes of the two-month-old miners' strike – the single issue that was to prevent any significant long-lasting gains for another nine months at least.

*   *   *

Re-establishing Labour as a credible electoral force was clearly a priority for the new leader; but almost equally important was to entrench his position in the party. As the first to be chosen by the electoral college he began with a significant advantage over his predecessors, but he knew how quickly such things could change. As Michael Foot had discovered, neither the left nor the right could be wholly relied upon. The votes of left-wing MPs had taken Foot to the leadership, yet in office he had expended much of his energy in staving off assaults from the left, particularly in the NEC. He also had to spend time commiserating with MPs, many with years of dedicated service behind them, who were now threatened with 'deselection' – an ugly euphemism for being thrown out by their constituency parties.

The 1979 party conference, held in the wake of Thatcher's first election victory, had decided that all sitting Labour MPs would have to be reselected by their local parties between general elections, as was already the custom with prospective candidates not in the House. Previously MPs, once elected, could expect to hold on to their right to contest their seat for as long as they wanted it, provided they had committed no spectacular act of disloyalty or malfeasance. But while the MPs had hung on, the complexion of their local support had very often changed. Throughout the 1960s scores of the old-fashioned constituency parties, many largely moribund, had been taken over by young activists of the left who found that their MP took positions some way to the right of their own. Bob Mellish in Bermondsey was the best publicized instance, but there were many others.

The left sought a way of ensuring that MPs stayed in line with the thinking of local party members, by obliging them to face regular reselection. Kinnock supported the move, seeing it as an extension of democracy, and it was duly adopted. Several MPs now felt highly vulnerable. As the date of the reselections approached, some took their troubles to Foot. 'You're the leader,' they would declare. 'Do something.'

There was very little he could do. Constituency Labour Parties enjoy a wide degree of autonomy in the selection of candidates. As far as the central HQ is concerned, virtually the only criterion candidates have to fulfil is that of party membership. Still less are the CLPs subject to influence from the leader's office, except on the rare occasions when he or a member of his staff happens to have personal contacts. Any attempt by the leadership to put pressure on a local party could prove counter-productive.

So Foot could do nothing but cluck in sympathy. Kinnock, who had observed this going on for the best part of three years, made it clear to MPs early in his leadership that he would not be receptive to such pleas for help. It was up to members to mend their own fences with their parties. But he did offer them one slender safety line: he would use his influence at party conference to have the reselection procedure made more democratic.

Constituency parties are run, and candidates selected, by their General Management Committees (GMCs) – now customarily known, in the interest of anti-élitism, as General Committees (GCs). These are composed of delegates from each branch of the constituency party; the branches usually coinciding with the wards from which local councillors are elected. The number of GC delegates is proportionate to the number of members in each branch. In addition, trade unions affiliated to the party are entitled to send delegates to the GC according to the number of members of the union living in the constituency: an exceptionally hard figure to check. Socialist societies, such as the Fabians, are also entitled to GC representation, as are Young Socialists and the women's section.

GC delegates from the wards are elected at branch meetings some-times attended by as few as a dozen members. Only the most enthusiastic and committed turn up with any regularity and it is these who elect each other to the GCs. Because they are prepared to perform the tedious chores of canvassing and organizing fund-raising events, as well as sitting for hours at dreary meetings, they call themselves activists. Politics dominates every area of their lives. The intense level of their activity means that they have no time for any other hobbies or social relationships. Mixing only with like-minded people, they become ever more convinced that their own attitudes are correct and everyone else's uninformed and mistaken, not to say malign.

In recent years activists have overwhelmingly sprung from the left of the party. Since belonging to a trade union is a condition of party membership for people in relevant occupations, it is not hard for the activists to boost their strength on GCs by getting political allies nominated for the union seats. This explains how GCs are often controlled by the left, even if that does not reflect the views of the bulk of party members in the constituency, who may turn up to ward meetings only once or twice a year, if at all. And since GCs and ward parties choose candidates for local council elections as well as for Parliament, it also explains why so many councils are run by people whose views are far to the left of mainstream party opinion.

Kinnock proposed to counter this by taking the power to select and reselect Parliamentary candidates out of the hands of GCs and spreading it among all members of the constituency parties. Under his proposed constitutional change, GCs would be given the option of holding a ballot among the membership instead of reserving decisions on these questions to themselves – something akin to the primary system in the United States. It was called the one-person-one-vote proposal (the more familiar one-*man*-one-vote having been jettisoned as sexist).

The plan sprang from Kinnock's deeply-felt view that political legitimacy derives from the widest possible extension of the franchise. He does not believe that politicians show weakness or lack of vigorous commitment by seeking a secure mandate – rather the opposite. His own climb to the top had been based on his ability to command majorities on relevant representative bodies, rather than on patronage. He won selection for the safe Bedwellty seat in 1969 by campaigning for support in the GC against a candidate sponsored by the locally powerful NUM. He rose to prominence in the party by being elected first to the NEC and then to the Shadow Cabinet.

He had always supported widening the party franchise to increase accountability. He had been advocating mandatory reselection since the mid-seventies and had consistently linked it with one-person-one-vote. In nearly every democracy where candidates are popularly selected, there is some kind of primary system. The party had in 1979 given itself the advantage of a procedure allowing for the recall of MPs and candidates, but not the instrument that would make it fully representative. Quite aside from the democratic arguments, Kinnock believed his reform would help recruitment by allowing members to participate in the selection process. While reluctant to admit that anything beneficial can be learned from the Conservatives, he had seen a television documentary about their selection procedure. It involves holding a meeting at which any member can turn up. He saw nothing wrong with that.

Although one-person-one-vote seems an unexceptional premise for a democratic party, many did take exception. Activists feel they deserve to be rewarded for the hours of unpaid work they do for the party, by being allowed to influence its affairs. They argue that they are more familiar than the rank-and-file with the personalities and issues involved, that less-informed people might be prone to persuasion by foul means (including the despised media), through their political naïvety. Kinnock regards that as élitist and wrong. He is also worried about its practical consequence: the selection as candidates of men and women of the left, giving voters an unbalanced and probably off-putting impression of the party's true nature.

He decided that his plan to widen the selection franchise would be a suitable start to creating a party that could win elections. He asked his advisers to draw up proposals and in July 1984 wrote a letter to Labour MPs explaining what he was going to put to the conference that October. He pointed out that 206 candidates had already been reselected and that the average number of GC members voting had been 37. 'Those who oppose the change have to explain how in the name of democracy they can deny the chance to vote to people in the party,' he wrote. The issue had already been projected in the press as a vote of confidence in his leadership. He challenged this. 'It is not a vote of confidence in me but in the people who make up the Labour Party.' Did the opponents of the move have no confidence in the judgment of ordinary party members? Swayed by those arguments, the NEC narrowly endorsed the plan at their July meeting.

The difficulty about the proposal was that it would negate the influence of the trade union GC delegates in the selection of candidates. Some union leaders who favoured the plan philosophically could not persuade their executives to sacrifice that element of power without any trade-off: it went against all their bargaining traditions. Had Kinnock and his advisers given themselves more time they might have devised a formula to take account of these objections, but Kinnock would not agree to putting it off for a year. He wanted the new voting system in place in time to influence those reselections – the majority – that remained to be carried out in the months after the conference.

Some of his advisers believed he would not win and that it would be a blow to his prestige to suffer a defeat on such an issue at his first full conference as leader. They tried to talk him out of it, pointing out that even under his plan it would not be *compulsory* for GCs to adopt the new procedure. The change would simply give them the *option* of holding a ballot of members instead of keeping the decision inside the committee. If they declined to do so they would not be forced. Kinnock responded by saying he knew of few GCs that would want to be seen deliberately eschewing a formula that quite patently strengthened democracy. Many in the unions and constituencies did not agree with that judgment. And it did not seem to them quite fair to apply the new scheme only to those seats that had not selected early.

An advance sign that Kinnock would have a struggle to get one-person-one-vote approved by conference came when the agenda was published in September. It contained 30 proposals from constituency parties to amend the plan in ways that would make it ineffective. Later that month the NEC came within a hair's breadth of repudiating the idea. Although they had approved it two months earlier, the NUM had written asking them to consider a postponement in putting the proposal to conference. After a long debate the Committee divided 12–12, with four of Kinnock's regular supporters absent. Eric Heffer, chairman for that year, declined to use his casting vote but left the matter to be decided at a special NEC meeting at the weekend. There, with Kinnock's people back in place, it was agreed the motion would go to conference.

Kinnock's advisers had calculated that the TGWU's vote at Blackpool would be critical. They were assured by the union's leaders that it would be cast in favour of the plan but not all of them quite believed it, because it is the union's executive committee who make the decision and they do not necessarily follow the advice of their senior officials. In the event the TGWU voted against the proposal and it was narrowly defeated on the first full day of the conference. It was a setback for Kinnock caused, as he later came to realize, by his failure to do enough groundwork. In particular, he had not discussed in detail with the unions how they could be brought into the new selection procedure. But he is determined that the issue will not be allowed to die.

'It is an idea that is not going to go away,' he said in an interview with *Tribune* in September 1985. 'People recognize that there is not a very good democratic argument against the extension of the franchise to the rank and file of the Labour Party.' In February 1987 it became clear that there was, too, a pragmatic argument for the changes. Deirdre Wood, a highly unsuitable candidate chosen by the GC, lost what should have been a safe seat at the Greenwich by-election.

*　　*　　*

In strategic discussions between Kinnock, Charles Clarke and his other advisers during his first months as leader, the phrase 'ideological baggage' kept recurring. They were unanimous that the party was over-burdened with it. Not that they were opposed to ideology as such: they recognized that it was the wellspring of the Labour movement and the party could not survive without it. But in some areas policy was constricted by ancient shibboleths that had outlasted their relevance. Socialism was not meant to be an unalterable dogma, like a strict religion, but a practical means of protecting the interests of working people and the well-being of society as a whole. Kinnock did not plan a repeat of the heated but essentially arid debate of 1960, when Hugh Gaitskell tried to push through the repeal of Clause Four of the party constitution – the clause relating to public ownership.

Kinnock was not concerned with constitutional niggling. His approach was to retain Clause Four and adapt it to the present day as a concept that would later be called 'social ownership' – a phrase inherited from early socialists. What needed fresh thought, to his mind, was not the language of the constitution but specific items of policy that had remained untouched over the years, immutable articles of faith based on conditions that no longer existed.

He believes the weight of the party's ideological baggage stems partly from a lack of confidence in the ideology itself. Party members are required, almost unthinkingly, to accept a code of beliefs about public ownership, sales of council houses, relations with Europe and the United States (hostile in both cases) and other articles of faith. These are never argued through but accepted as essential dogma. In discussions with colleagues, he would liken Labour to a football supporters' club rather than a political party, waving rattles and chanting slogans when triggered by key phrases.

Still more emotive than nationalization was the sale of council houses. With its commitment to publicly-owned services, Labour had always fervently opposed the Conservative policy of selling the housing stock of local authorities to individual tenants. The 1983 manifesto had pledged to end enforced council house sales and give councils power to buy back homes sold by the Conservatives. But it was clear from opinion polls and from simple observation that the house-sale policy was popular. Many people wanted to buy their homes and those who had done so were, in the main, pleased with their purchase. Two-thirds of homes in Britain were now owner-occupied. Kinnock felt that to end the sales for ideological reasons was perverse. It reinforced the image of Labour as the party of the dispossessed, which in modern Britain is electorally harmful. Concern for the underprivileged has always been the main reason for the party's existence and will remain so, but in so far as it succeeds in improving conditions for the worst off, that natural constituency dwindles. If council house tenants wish to become home owners they should be able to do so without thinking they have to leave the Labour Party as soon as they get hold of the title deeds. To insist on representing the lowliest to the exclusion of anyone else would condemn Labour to being a permanent minority party.

Kinnock was to articulate this in January 1986, when he gave a pep talk to an election strategy conference:

> The idea that there is a model Labour voter, a blue-collar council house tenant who belongs to a union and has 2.4 children, a five-year-old car and a holiday in Blackpool, is patronizing and politically immature . . . The idea that a vague coalition of have-nots can be built as an adequate base for Labour support and that therefore no effort is needed to secure the backing of the 'haves' and the 'haven't-got-enoughs' is a betrayal of the very people that we most want to help by gaining and using democratic power.

In 1984 a sub-committee under Jeff Rooker, the front-bench housing spokesman, began working on an alternative policy for council house sales. In May, 1985, it was announced that under a Labour government tenants would keep the right to buy their houses, except in inner-city areas where housing is scarce.

Michael Foot could never have counted on forcing such a radical change of policy through the NEC. Kinnock has, with only a few exceptions, managed to win majorities on the Executive for what he wants to do. He has achieved this both by his persuasive interventions at meetings and, as a longer-term undertaking, by ensuring as far as he can that the people elected to the NEC are likely to be favourably disposed to his policies.

It is never possible to be sure of a permanent majority in the NEC, regardless of the issue. It does not split into straight factions: unlike, say, the House of Commons, where MPs customarily vote their party ticket come what may. In the committee room at Walworth Road, the tickets are for one performance only. Alliances are made and broken on single issues. To gain most of his important victories – for instance the expulsion of Militant supporters – Kinnock has relied on the backing of the right wing and some of the soft left. This is not because he feels he has much in common with the right but because he sees the hard left as a barrier to his aim of making Labour electable. As for the soft left, he keeps their support on most occasions by standing firm for radical positions on one or two issues they regard as of crucial importance, notably defence. With all sections of the party, the essential strength of his position is that he is the only leader who can conceivably take Labour to an election victory. The price for his services is acquiescence in his most important policies and strategies.

*   *   *

The retreat from old-style nationalization proved less painful and contentious than would have seemed possible only a few years earlier. Since 1979 the Conservative Government had undertaken a more extensive programme of privatization – selling nationalized industries back to private shareholders – than had ever been attempted before. It began with Cable and Wireless, then Britoil and some smaller parts of the oil industry, followed by British Telecom, British Gas and British Airways, with proposals outstanding for the water supply industry. The Britoil sale was a comparative failure but, with the others, expensive publicity campaigns and bonuses for buyers meant a colossal demand for the shares, an instant market premium on the offer price and a quick profit for those who sold shares as soon as they had bought them.

The Government sought to turn the sales into moral crusades for universal share ownership, 'people's capitalism'. In fact they taught people little about the ups and downs of the stock exchange, affording them instead the untypical chance of making quick money almost without risk. A year after the sale of Telecom, many of the shares had found their way back into the hands of the large institutions that have always controlled the market. The biggest instant profits of all came with the sale of the Trustee Savings Bank in 1986, although this was in a different category since it was not technically owned by the Government.

Labour attacked the sell-offs vigorously, accusing the Conservatives of melting down the family silver to raise the money for tax-cutting bribes at election time. But their very scale made it practically impossible to propose reversing the process by buying back the industries for the state, as a strict doctrinal approach would have demanded. To do it without adequate compensation would antagonize the millions of shareholders in the industries and be seen as unfair even by those who did not own shares. To pay for the shares at the market rate would cost too much, leaving a Labour Government with no money to carry through urgent measures for reversing unemployment and improving the social services.

Yet British Telecom and British Gas are monopolistic utilities of the kind Labour thinks it essential to return to public control. A policy statement, issued at the 1986 party conference in Blackpool, described in detail how it would be done. At its head it quoted Clause Four, committing the party:

> to secure for the workers by hand or by brain the full fruits of their industry and the most equitable distribution thereof that may be possible upon the basis of the common ownership of the means of production, distribution and exchange and the best obtainable system of popular administration and control of each industry or service.

There is flexibility inherent in the reference to 'the best obtainable system'. Under the proposed scheme all shareholders would be obliged to exchange their present voting shares for non-voting securities of equivalent value. They could choose to be paid regular interest on these securities or let their capital value increase, like National Savings Certificates. Investors not wanting to exchange their shares for the new securities could sell them back at the original issue price, sustaining a loss on their previous market value. Control of the industries would be vested in Government-appointed boards, but they would be made accountable to their customers and their work force. Members of the boards would be asked to state their commitment to the aims of social ownership.

A British Investment Bank and a new holding company called British Enterprise would be created to provide capital for socially owned and private industries. A British Savings Bank would be formed from existing savings institutions to compete with the High Street banks.

The statement was drawn up by a committee chaired by John Smith, the shadow industry spokesman and one of Kinnock's most trusted colleagues (despite his having been Roy Hattersley's campaign manager during the leadership contest). The other most active member of the committee was David Blunkett, leader of Sheffield City Council and a key 'soft left' figure on the NEC. The endorsement of both men ensured that it would receive majority backing. In its most significant section, the statement recognized that the old form of nationalization had given social ownership a bad name:

> Current disenchantment with social ownership is above all rooted in the failure of past Labour governments to adapt to new demands. The Morrisonian model, perhaps appropriate to the immediate needs of war-torn Britain, became outdated, leaving behind it a legacy of unresponsive monoliths . . . Partly because of this, social ownership has not in itself been able to bring about any major redistribution of wealth.

In that paragraph, Kinnock's Labour Party had discarded one of its bulkiest, most battered and most cherished bits of ideological baggage. The young leader had, through his devotion to consensus, achieved what Hugh Gaitskell had sought and failed to do by fiat. When the 1986 conference approved the social ownership policy, almost on the nod, it was a genuinely historic moment, even if scarcely anyone recognized it as such.

*   *   *

Gaining control of the party machinery had to be a priority for Kinnock, but it would be of only limited value unless the machinery itself was running sweetly. It was the principal means by which his power within the party could be translated into real power in the country. His early moves to give MPs a louder voice in policy-making had proved successful in the short term but they had essentially been emergency actions at the start of his tenure of office. In one respect, by increasing the burgeoning number of committees and sub-committees, he had compounded the unwieldiness that was at the heart of many of the party's problems. Much remained to be done to convert Walworth Road into a powerful instrument and reliable ally.

He and his team decided that 1984–5 was to be the year of the party. There were, as they saw it, three vital battles to be fought and won. The first was in many ways the most important, because it involved the wherewithal to fight the others. The Conservatives' industrial relations legislation had included a requirement that trades unions could raise a political levy on their members only if the membership had voted for it in a secret ballot. Since union contributions account for two-thirds of the party's revenue, any significant shortfall would have a calamitous effect on its finances. So campaigns had to be organized for a 'yes' vote in all the affiliated unions. Secondly, they sought to ensure that the reselection of Parliamentary candidates before the next general election did not result in a preponderance of candidates from the far left, particularly Militant supporters. Finally, there must be organizational changes at Walworth Road itself.

The ballots on the union political funds were to take place during 1985. Kinnock was anxious that the party should give the unions every possible support in their campaigns for a favourable outcome. Walworth Road was keen to provide literature, workers and speakers at meetings – as though it were a by-election in a highly specialized national constituency. Many union leaders, though, believed they could campaign more effectively on their own, appealing to their members' loyalty to the union rather than to the Labour Party. They feared that too close an involvement with the party in the campaign could prove counter-productive. Most unions decided to go it alone.

The press was full of foreboding as the campaigning began. The conventional wisdom was that while the manual unions were likely to vote in favour of keeping the levy, many white-collar workers would vote against it. Clive Jenkins' ASTMS was thought one of the most likely to vote 'no', along with the Amalgamated Union of Engineering Workers (AUEW), the second largest in the country. *The Guardian* published a survey on 2 March that showed most of the major unions likely to vote against the political fund.

But their leaders campaigned with great determination, using their periodical publications and leaflets targeted at specific groups of their membership. Although they often quarrel with Labour governments in power, the unions habitually snuggle closer in opposition, especially when the government of the day shows itself, as the Thatcher administration had done, to be hostile to organized labour. The Government's decision to ban unions at GCHQ, the high-security communications centre at Cheltenham, had persuaded union leaders how vital it was to close ranks. The first result was declared on 8 May, when the print union SOGAT 82 voted by three to one in favour of keeping the levy. In the ensuing weeks the rest of the results dribbled in, all just as convincing. By the time the last votes were counted, not only had every union with a political fund decided to maintain it but two that had not previously made a contribution to the party's coffers voted to do so. As he spoke at union conferences during 1986, Kinnock was able to report this gloatingly and add: 'Thank you very much, Norman Tebbit.' It was guaranteed to raise a cheer.

He had been happy to stand aside from these campaigns and let the union leaders do the work, when he discovered that was what they wanted. The matter of reselections demanded his fuller involvement, although it had to be discreet. Under the constitution, the party nationally can have no direct involvement in the selection of candidates by constituencies, unless asked to intervene to resolve disputes. With conference having rejected his one-member-one-vote proposal, his supporters had to exert influence where they could to keep out the extremists, whose selection would have been seized on by the press as an illustration of a party veering uncontrollably to the left.

Militant had targeted half a dozen seats where it sought to get its supporters selected as candidates. Charles Clarke, Kinnock's chief political aide, busied himself rallying opponents of the tendency to concentrate their efforts on promoting a single rival candidate, to ensure that the Militants did not slip in as a result of split votes for the other contenders. The efforts paid off. In Glasgow Provan the Militant nominee was defeated by 78 to 77 votes, while in nearby Pollok it was almost as close. The Militant was beaten by two votes in Gateshead East. In Brighton Kemp Town and the Isle of Wight, where Militant candidates fought and lost in 1983, they were replaced by people of more conventional views. Apart from Dave Nellist and Terry Fields, sitting members for Coventry South East and Liverpool Broadgreen, only one Militant sympathizer was chosen – Pat Wall in Bradford North. Kinnock's decisive move against Militant was to be launched at the party conference in 1985; but in the meantime the bridgehead had been held against any significant advance.

As for Walworth Road, the third target in his year of the party, the first change had to come at the top. The senior official is the general secretary, elected by conference and thus not dependent on the leader's patronage. (This is a contrast to the Conservatives, whose chairman is appointed by the leader.) Too often the general secretary had acted as an alternative power base in the party, a focal point for opposition to the leadership. Kinnock had never enjoyed especially warm relations with Jim Mortimer, who had been appointed general secretary in 1982. Like many senior Labour figures, Kinnock had been stung by a damaging remark Mortimer made at a press conference during the 1983 election campaign, when he revealed that Foot's position as leader had been discussed by the NEC. Mortimer had never been in favour of expelling Militant supporters and he did not back Kinnock's campaign for one-member-one-vote at candidate reselections.

He agreed that he would retire as general secretary in 1985. The previous autumn Kinnock began scouting for someone he could sponsor as a replacement. He lighted on Larry Whitty, a former civil servant and a research officer with the General, Municipal, Boiler-makers and Allied Trade Union (GMBATU). At 41, nearly Kinnock's age, he had youth in his favour by comparison with the 64-year-old Mortimer. Kinnock was quite easily able to find allies on the NEC to support his nomination.

Before he took over, Whitty made a study of the organization with a view to finding ways of streamlining it. Among the many documents presented to him was a note from Mortimer to the review committee, calculated to fill him with depression. It began uncompromisingly, as it would continue:

> The basic organizational problem at Walworth Road is that there are insufficient resources to fulfil adequately and efficiently the tasks that the national headquarters are expected to discharge. In my nearly 50 years of employment, I have never worked in an organization . . . where there is such a mismatch between commitments and resources.

Mortimer went on to list 23 tasks that the head office staff of 130 were required to carry out, from upholding the party rules and discipline to maintaining liaison with the public and the PLP. His note continued:

> The mismatch between commitments and resources has become worse during my period of office. New responsibilities have been accepted . . . Simultaneously the total number of staff employed has been reduced. The number of duplicated pieces of paper passing through our general office grows year by year and now exceeds eight million copies annually.

The note mentioned suggestions that the number of heads of department – 11 – was too many. But Mortimer warned the NEC that any attempt to reduce that number could be met with resistance from the staff and involve heavy compensation payments. The party 'has no alternative but to proceed with goodwill,' he concluded.

Whitty agreed that there were too many autonomous departments. He proposed whittling them down to just three large sections, dealing respectively with organization, policy development and projection (campaigning and publicity). Since the 1983 election there had been a decision by the party to put more resources into campaigning but this had achieved only limited success because of a shortage of funds and people and a lack of coherent direction. In putting his suggestions to the NEC, Whitty made some scathing criticisms of the head office set-up. The management lacked any kind of strategic approach, he maintained.

Managers felt unable to take routine trivial decisions, which consequently had to be taken at meetings of heads of department.

There was plenty of opposition to Whitty's plan, especially from the heads of those departments that were to be subsumed into the three major directorates. It is never a painless matter to initiate reforms in an organization steeped in decades of lethargy. The left faction on the NEC were opposed to it also, on the grounds that the rationalization of Walworth Road could lead to the party seeking greater autonomy from the NEC, by whose influence the left sets great store. At the NEC meeting in June, Tony Benn suggested that implementation of the plan should be delayed pending approval by the party conference in October. Eric Heffer and Dennis Skinner supported him, complaining that the new proposal was concerned more with management than with politics. But by a majority of 16 to 6 the NEC accepted Whitty's and Kinnock's argument that, with an election perhaps only two years away, every day would count.

The key new appointment was Peter Mandelson as director of campaigns and communications. A grandson of Herbert Morrison, Home Secretary in the post-war Labour Government, Mandelson had grown up with Charles Clarke in Hampstead Garden Suburb – where one of their neighbours was Harold Wilson, the former Prime Minister. Mandelson had offered his services to Kinnock as education spokesman in 1980, but Clarke had won preferment and Mandelson, by now a Labour councillor in Lambeth, went along the Shadow Cabinet corridor to work for Albert Booth, spokesman on employment. In 1982 he left politics and joined London Weekend Television, but applied for the new post at Walworth Road in 1985. It was hotly contested. Kinnock's endorsement was crucial and it was not until the Sunday before his Tuesday interview with the NEC that he received a call from the leader's office indicating his support. The left-wingers on the NEC favoured Nita Clarke, formerly press officer to Ken Livingstone, leader of the Greater London Council. A defeated internal candidate was Joyce Gould, who became Director of Organization instead.

Mandelson, although not universally popular at Walworth Road, had an almost instant effect. Where before the image of the party had been irredeemably dowdy, he brought flair, energy and professionalism to its public face – qualities previously thought of as the monopoly of the Conservatives. Kinnock had in fact started the process as soon as he became leader, taking a grip on party political broadcasts. Previously their content and style had been decided by the NEC. On Kinnock's initiative the responsibility was passed to the Campaigns Strategy Committee, which set up a sub-committee, with him as chairman, to oversee the broadcasts. Kinnock recruited John Gau, formerly head of current affairs with BBC Television, to produce them.

Now Kinnock and Mandelson could work together to ensure that in his public appearances the leader looked as well as sounded good. Mandelson knew about the importance of details – the colour of backdrops at press conferences, publicity material that conveyed a message visually as well as textually, the proper timing of policy initiatives. In the past the party had scorned the niceties of presentation. Like it or not, in an age when the electorate is bombarded daily with sophisticated advertising, anyone who fails to exploit these techniques risks not getting the message across.

*   *   *

An issue that surfaced in 1984, and irritatingly would not go away, was the campaign to create separate black sections in the constituencies and the party nationally. It was the idea of young black party members in the large cities, who believed that having their own section would encourage recruitment among ethnic minorities. In London the Vauxhall party, which includes part of the Brixton area, established a black section in November 1983. The constitutional position is that, while groups of any kind may be established by party members, they are not allowed formal representation at the GC; nor may any national movements be set up within the party. In April Vauxhall defied that ruling and allowed delegates from its black section on to the GC, with full voting rights. Lewisham East did the same and four other constituency parties – three in London and one in Nottingham – followed their example.

Kinnock was instinctively against the idea, although he could see that it was a difficult issue to handle without his motives being misunderstood. Most black people in Britain are members of the working class and the Labour Party is their natural political home. Improving race relations has long been a central plank in Labour policies. Yet comparatively few blacks involve themselves actively with the party. Anything that might improve that position would be helpful but Kinnock was not at all convinced that black sections would have that effect. The only faintly comparable Labour institution is the women's section and he was not persuaded that was a good thing: certainly it had not succeeded in getting serious numbers of women into Parliament. He thought black sections would prove an additional divisive force in a party he was trying to unite. Like the Labour Party Young Socialists, now dominated by the Militant tendency, they could turn into a Frankenstein's monster, striking out against the body that created them.

He used no such lurid imagery when, in June 1984, he wrote an open letter setting out his position. He said he was in favour of the party doing more to combat racialism and prejudice; in favour of recruiting more black members and more black MPs. However,

73

I believe that the argument for constitutional change is sometimes put forward as a substitute for the demanding but more enduring and successful tasks of fundamental change in attitude and practice . . . It would create significant problems of racial definition which could lead only too easily to endless unproductive acrimony. Second, I am very deeply opposed to any constitutional change which, whatever its good intentions, would by its very nature inevitably have to be racially segregationist. That would be a terrible departure from the values of a democratic socialist party.

Anyone who opposes black aspirations, for whatever reasons, risks being dubbed a racist. The Vauxhall party produced a booklet to sell at the 1984 party conference, critical of Kinnock's position:

The Labour Party itself perpetuates racism. It is an institution rooted in a racist society and its own routine practices, customs and forms of organization exclude black people from the structures of power as effectively as if they were barred from membership . . . The history of the Labour movement is placed firmly within the framework of British imperialism.

At the conference, the proposal to establish black sections was heavily defeated by the unions' block vote, but the campaigners vowed to raise it again the following year. A meeting of six constituency black sections in Lambeth Town Hall in April 1985 provoked a main front-page headline in the *Daily Mail*: KINNOCK FACES RACE REBELLION. The story below it maintained that the black sections campaign was 'the biggest internal problem since Neil Kinnock became leader 18 months ago.' The *Mail* plainly believed it had struck a seam rich in potential for embarrassing the Labour leadership. Two weeks later it ran another front page story suggesting that the black campaigners were planning their own alternative party conference that autumn. BLACK REBELS HIJACK LABOUR was the front-page headline this time.

Kinnock did not share the *Mail*'s apocalyptic view of the scale of the problem. In terms of sheer numbers the black activists were insignificant and could not hope to command a majority at the party conference. Their campaign was an embarrassment he could well do without, but it came quite low in the scale of issues likely to provoke a crisis in the party. He responded to the intensified campaign by becoming more outspoken on the issue. He told the *Manchester Evening News* at the end of April that the party constitution did not allow for the establishment of separate sections based on race or skin colour and would not do so. The party did need to be more conscious about the needs of black people and any constituency party could set up a group to discuss and act on that issue, so long as it was open to people of all races. And the following month he told journalists at Westminster:

> I am adamantly against black sections. The overwhelming majority are against them ... I would be against any development which constitutionally gave separate status on the basis of colour of skin or ethnic origins. I would not give a damn if the whole Labour Party was against me on this. That is not the case – but it is a matter of basic values.

By now 16 parties had established black sections and many were heading for a showdown with Walworth Road over the reselection of their Parliamentary candidates. They wanted to allow black section GC delegates to vote in the reselection. Head office said that would be unconstitutional: any candidate chosen with the participation of black section members would not be recognized. When Lewisham East chose Russell Profitt, a black councillor, as their candidate, it did not become official until they went through the selection process again, some months later, without black sections delegates participating.

The NEC had set up a working party, chaired by the left-wing MP Jo Richardson, to look into the position of blacks in the party. Kinnock submitted a plan to it that would effectively have led to the establishment of a black section not restricted to blacks – an affiliated organization with the object of combating racism, but with membership open to people of any ethnic origin. The majority on the working party rejected this and in May 1985, to Kinnock's great annoyance, they recommended that the call for black sections should be heeded. A minority report suggested the establishment of a black rights campaign along the lines of Kinnock's proposal. The black campaigners denounced this as a 'Labour bantustan'.

The organization committee of the NEC rejected the majority report by 12 votes to 4. The disappointed campaigners put this down to the malign influence of Kinnock. One of them, Linda Bellos of Lambeth, told a press conference that he had closed his mind to the legitimate aspirations of black people. 'We are asking for very little,' she asserted, 'a small constitutional change that recognizes that Britain is a multi-racial society.'

Two of the activists, Sharon Atkin and Diane Abbott, went to see Kinnock on the initiative of Patricia Hewitt, who had written in favour of black sections before she became Kinnock's press officer. The black sections leadership insist that it was not a formal meeting and that Kinnock has never agreed to see them officially. Official or not, it was an unhappy confrontation. 'We find ourselves at an impasse,' Atkin said afterwards. 'Neil Kinnock is a very intransigent person who finds himself unable to accept black people in black sections in any shape or form. I reluctantly said to him: "We will have to go to conference and have a battle." It was a waste of my time and his.'

Although Hewitt told the press later that Kinnock had not regarded the meeting as a waste of time, he responded with equal vigour at a lobby briefing the following week. He said he found the black sections campaign 'repellent and segregationist'. He reported that Atkin and Abbott had denied that and avowed that membership was open to anyone considering themselves black. 'Can I consider myself black?' he had asked them. 'Patently not,' was the reply, 'because you're so obviously white.'

In June two black candidates were selected in winnable seats without black sections participating – Paul Boateng, a GLC councillor, in Brent South, and Keith Vaz, a solicitor, in Leicester East, where the sitting Conservative member, Peter Bruinvels, had a majority of only 993. Vaz had been a member of the NEC working party that recommended the establishment of black sections. Kinnock and his supporters maintained that the two selections weakened the argument for black sections, because they showed that blacks could advance in the party without them.

The following month the NEC, against powerfully expressed opposition from Tony Benn and Eric Heffer, confirmed by 15 votes to 7 the decision of the organization committee not to establish black sections. They decided instead to recommend that the party conference set up a Black and Asian Advisory Committee. That was approved by the conference, where black sections were again rejected by a large majority.

The committee was ineffective. In May 1986 a conference to launch it was called at the House of Commons, but was halted after repeated interruptions by black sections campaigners, who branded Jo Richardson, chair of the committee, as a racist. Richardson said she would resign from the post at the next party conference and several other members also quit. At the party conference that year the proposal to establish a black section was again defeated, marginally less heavily than before. The leaders of the movement plan to raise it year after year and to work on the trade unions until some of the large block votes switch to their side. The TGWU, with its considerable black membership, would be the most glittering prize. But it is a long-term strategy: it would take years to approach a conference majority.

Meanwhile, Kinnock hoped that the expected success of perhaps half a dozen black candidates at the next general election would take the steam out of the issue. But he was reckoning without the cussedness (or independence of spirit, depending whose side you are on) of the constituency parties. In December 1986 the GC at Streatham, a South London seat with a Conservative majority of 5,500, insisted for the third time that year on involving its black section in selecting its candidate, who was therefore not recognized by the NEC. It was an absurd situation because, even with black sections delegates voting, the GC had rejected Paul Sharma, an organizer of the black sections campaign, in favour of Anna Tapsell, a social worker, by a comprehensive 27 votes to 4. So the issue was not the substantive one of who should be the candidate, but the purely symbolic one of who should be allowed to vote: gesture politics gone crazy.

*   *   *

Kinnock was the first leader of the Labour Party since the Second World War to be chosen for the position with no experience as a government minister. While his freshness was part of his initial appeal, it could also be exploited by his opponents as evidence that he did not have the necessary background in statesmanship to be entrusted with his country's most senior elected office. In the series of interviews he submitted to after the election, one of the questions he was most often asked was how he felt his inexperience would affect his performance if he were elected Prime Minister. 'They ask me,' he told an interviewer, 'Mr Kinnock, how can you hope to be Prime Minister when you've never been so much as a corporal in the army of government?'

A traditional way for politicians to impress people with their urbanity and seriousness of purpose is travel overseas. It was a weakness of Kinnock's predecessor, Michael Foot, that he rarely left Britain and had never been to the United States. Kinnock, by contrast, rather enjoyed travelling abroad to meetings of bodies such as the Socialist International. Yet as a mere Opposition front-bencher he could not expect to command much publicity for those forays. As leader, when he went abroad from now on he would be accompanied by a coterie of journalists. Overseas travel was therefore valuable publicity, as well as providing beneficial experience in its own right.

His first trip was routine, a day in Brussels in November 1983, to speak at a meeting of the Socialist International, where he criticized the placement of American cruise missiles in Britain and nuclear weapons in Germany. He struck further afield just after the Christmas holiday, when he took Glenys and their two children to Athens at the invitation of Andreas Papandreou, the Greek Prime Minister.

The most publicized issue between Greece and Britain was the Greeks' call for the return of the Elgin marbles, on display at the British Museum since being taken from the Parthenon by Lord Elgin more than a century earlier. Melina Mercouri, the former film star who was now the Greek Minister of Culture, had been to Britain in the spring of 1983, campaigning for the return of the marbles to what she considered their rightful home.

Kinnock thought she had a strong case. His socialist opposition to imperialism embraced what had come to be known as cultural imperialism, the enforced removal of works of art from their place of origin. To a newly-elected leader, almost everything seems simple and possible. Before he left London he outlined what appeared an eminently reasonable solution: the marbles should be returned to the Parthenon but under a time-sharing agreement by which they would spend a few months every year in London. How, he wondered, would the British feel if part of the crown jewels were in another country? 'The Greek people must have access to the marbles ... They are as Greek as Wembley Stadium is British.'

The trouble with such patently even-handed compromises is that they seldom satisfy any party (except presumably, in this case, the owners of shipping lines carrying bulky freight between Britain and Greece). When he dined with Mercouri at a *taverna* on the second night of his visit, she insisted that the marbles must go back unconditionally. At a press conference following their formal meeting next day, Kinnock was asked whether a Labour Government would return the marbles. He said yes, but was not prepared to abandon his timeshare scheme entirely. He recommended a system of rotation of art treasures to make them accessible to the largest number of his people. And he had found a simile to replace Wembley Stadium: 'The Parthenon without the marbles is like a smile with a tooth missing.'

Had the visit not occurred so early in his leadership he would have been more circumspect. He quickly learned how easy it is to commit your future government to any amount of apparently attractive legislation – but that one of the skills of the job is to avoid commitments, especially on such peripheral issues. Nobody has ever won a British election by wooing the Greek vote.

For symbolic reasons if for no other, the United States had to be the target of his first major foreign foray. The alliance with America was the most important single element in British foreign policy and would remain so under a Labour government. Kinnock wanted no truck with the almost automatic anti-Americanism of the far left. Yet he knew that his party's defence policy, which included ridding Britain of US nuclear bases, could be seen as a threat to the NATO alliance. He would not counteract that impression in a single visit, but as an initial gesture it might help.

He arrived in Washington on 8 February 1984. Several routine meetings with officials were scheduled before he got to the senior people – Caspar Weinberger, the Defence Secretary, George Shultz,

Secretary of State, and finally 45 minutes with President Reagan, who seemed 'a pleasant enough chap'. While his most substantive talks were about the defence policy, most publicity was given to his discussion with Shultz about US actions in Central America. Kinnock said the Americans were engaged in 'government by death squad' in El Salvador. Shultz responded by telling reporters that the Labour leader's views were 'misinformed and possibly misguided'. Kinnock capped that by confiding that Shultz 'got out of his pram' during the meeting – an expression he then had to explain to the baffled newsmen. 'That is a colloquialism that signifies a departure from normal, calm, diplomatic expression.' The phrase intrigued the London press, ensuring him of front-page coverage, inspiring learned discussion about the origin of the term and, most important, diverting attention, at least temporarily, from his differences with the Americans over defence.

After Washington, Moscow. On Wednesday 21 November 1984 Neil and Glenys, with the foreign affairs spokesman Denis Healey, set off for the chilly Russian capital. After his gung-ho performance in America, he had been advised to adopt a more restrained demeanour this time and in particular not to be too fulsomely polite to his Russian hosts: historically, there is no more potent charge that can be laid against a Labour leader than that he is too friendly to the Reds. That was one reason why he took with him a list of Soviet citizens denied permission to emigrate, with the intention of raising the matter with the leaders he met.

He was also sensitive to the presentational side of the trip. He decided not to sport the fur hat that is traditional for Western visitors on these occasions: he thought it made him appear faintly ridiculous. Better to risk a frozen forehead. He also declined to fraternize with the journalists who accompanied him on the flight over. They were in economy class at the back; he in first class at the front – and there, respectively, they stayed.

The press had already given him a send-off that showed how carefully he would have to conduct himself and how little of their goodwill he could expect. Four tabloids – the *Express, Mail, Star* and *Sun* – had included the words TRIP OF SHAME in their headlines or reports of the visit. They were quoting David Owen, leader of the Social Democratic Party, who said Kinnock would be carrying a message to Moscow of which millions of Labour voters felt ashamed. Owen said that Labour's unilateralist policy was closer to that demanded by Russia than that of any other socialist party in Western Europe. Kinnock retorted that nobody knew what the defence policy of the SDP/Liberal Alliance was.

The flight landed 20 minutes late in freezing fog. Confronted with a reception committee of elderly party officials in overcoats, Healey, anxious to parade his great experience of these visits, said jovially: 'Same old Mafia, I see.' It is not recorded how the interpreters conveyed this quip to Boris Ponomarev, head of the international department of the Communist Party, and the other gentlemen in question. The visitors were told that President Chernenko was ill (he was in fact only a few months from death) but would see them the following Monday.

Next day Neil and Glenys had separate engagements, both marked by a degree of unpleasantness. Neil told Georgi Arbatov, the Kremlin's chief adviser on foreign relations, that although Labour had a non-nuclear defence policy he disagreed with Soviet proposals on nuclear-free zones, especially since the Baltic area was not to be included. Glenys met members of the Soviet Peace Committee who criticized CND because of its opposition to the deployment of Soviet nuclear missiles in Europe. She defended that position. 'I made it very clear that if there were Soviet ss20s on Greenham Common my objections would have been as strong as to the Americans,' she said afterwards. 'They seem to have extremely acrimonious feelings which are in some part reciprocated by Western peace groups.'

The British coal dispute dominated Neil's meeting with Soviet trade union leaders the following day. He refuted suggestions made in the Soviet press that the miners were on the point of starvation and denied some of the more extreme allegations of misbehaviour by police towards the pickets. And he implied that he believed the strike was already lost: 'My view is that the Labour movement lives to fight and win on other occasions.' To say that a defeat for the miners would mean a defeat for the whole trade union movement was 'a cataclysmic interpretation – I do not agree with it.' Later he commented to the British press corps about reports from London that left-wing MPs were planning to disrupt Parliament to get a hearing for the miners' case, and about a speech in which Eric Heffer criticized him for not supporting the miners with sufficient fervour. 'Don't start moaning behind my back,' he warned the MPs.

He began to get impatient at the meetings that had been arranged for him in Russia. While Glenys was assigned the unlikely role of talking to journalists on *Pravda*'s agony column, Neil had a long session with some economists who explained how the world recession was not affecting the Soviet Union. Not by nature a patient listener, he broke two pencils under the table in frustration and told journalists afterwards: 'I didn't come all this way to listen to propaganda.'

His temper became more frayed during their weekend in Leningrad. The programme was made up chiefly of visits to museums, including shrines to Lenin. He found the atmosphere of reverence overbearing. 'That's how to create a church,' he said gruffly while being taken round

Lenin's apartment; and as he left he murmured to a photographer: 'Next time the manger in Bethlehem.' At another point he raised his eyebrows meaningfully to Patricia Hewitt, who told reporters: 'He disapproves of Lenin worship absolutely.' He and Glenys pulled out of a visit to yet another museum pleading weariness, and went shopping instead. They also became tired of the ballet – three successive nights of it. He did manage one joke, though. Told that Lenin wrote 200 pages of a book in 16 days, he remarked: 'Even more than Roy Hattersley.'

Back in Moscow, his meeting with Chernenko lasted the best part of two hours. Kinnock proved that whatever his other qualities he was no medical expert: he declared that the President looked fit, though short of breath. The Russians revived an offer they had made before, that if a Labour Government was to go ahead with its non-nuclear policy they would scrap some of their own missiles and aim others away from Britain. There was nothing in writing ('We were not in the business of making treaties,' Kinnock pointed out) and press commentators were sceptical of the value of the offer, claiming that missiles could be re-aimed at a few minutes' notice. At Question Time in the Commons, Thatcher called the offer 'absolutely worthless' and similar to one made in 1978.

Glenys was meanwhile visiting a school, and was embarrassed when the children chanted 'Thatcher' as she arrived. Throughout the trip, Neil's lack of a hat was a subject of comment. On a visit to a war cemetery in Leningrad, an official took the hat from his own head and tried to press it on the visitor. 'It's all psychological,' Kinnock explained. 'You people snuggle down under your hats and just think it's cold.'

During this trip the Kinnocks first became aware of the distinctive style the press was developing for reporting their overseas excursions. Because they are not members of a government they naturally cannot expect the same easy access to senior politicians and officials as a Prime Minister warrants; nor do they command equal resources in terms of organization. The result is that arrangements sometimes go wrong and appointments are altered at the last minute. To the accompanying reporters each postponed meeting is a snub and every blip in the schedule evidence of administrative chaos. Kinnock's shoot-from-the-hip style of repartee makes it easy to charge him with gaffes and indiscretions. The reports start to read like a Marx Brothers screenplay.

Indignities suffered by the reporters themselves are added to the mix. In Moscow they were put out because their cars were not allowed to follow the official motorcade in the special fast lane reserved for visiting dignitaries. Their train to Leningrad arrived later than the Kinnocks' and they were accommodated in a hotel several miles from the city centre. It all makes for readable copy, especially in Conservative newspapers, but from Kinnock's viewpoint it buries the real purpose of the visit.

It had therefore been a frustrating journey in several respects but it did produce one positive result. An Intourist guide who married an Englishman in January 1984 had been refused an exit visa to join her husband. Hers was one of the names on the list Kinnock took with him. After he arrived back in London, it was announced that she would get her visa.

In January 1985 Kinnock went on a four-day trip to Nicaragua as a guest of the Sandinista Government, attending – along with President Fidel Castro of Cuba – the swearing-in ceremony for the newly elected National Assembly. Changing planes in Mexico City he attacked as 'fundamentally mistaken' the United States policy of support for the right-wing Contra rebels trying to overthrow the Sandinistas. He asked to visit the zone where fighting was taking place, offering to carry a gun if necessary; but transport could not be arranged. He did look at some of the slum areas, where money that was being spent on fighting the Contras could usefully have been diverted, and described as 'pathetic' the British aid effort of £60,000 a year. As soon as he returned to London he introduced the second half of a theatrical fund-raising Night for Nicaragua, featuring such as Ian McKellen, Victoria Wood, Peggy Ashcroft and Harold Pinter.

He and Glenys began the 1985 summer recess with a visit to East Africa, beginning in Ethiopia, where a two-year famine had caused countless deaths from starvation. A conference of the Organization for African Unity was nearing its end in Addis Ababa when they arrived, and he managed to schedule conversations with several of the continent's leaders, sometimes chasing them to the airport departure lounge. Then he flew over the famine areas with the Royal Air Force, in a plane dropping emergency food supplies to the hungry.

Here the Kinnocks were the victims of a blatant piece of mis-reporting which they cite to this day when grumbling about their treatment by the press. A number of papers asserted that Glenys refused to accompany Neil on the flight because, as a pacifist, she would not travel in a 'war machine'. This was untrue. She was not scheduled to go and she is decidedly not a pacifist. To be opposed to nuclear weapons, she insists, is not the same as refusing to countenance war in any circumstances. The denial was sparsely reported, as was the rest of the trip, to Kenya and Tanzania. A coup in Uganda meant that reporters travelling with the Kinnocks were diverted to covering that more sensational story.

Two months later Kinnock and Denis Healey went to Paris to meet French socialists. It happened that President Alfonsin of Argentina, who had taken over from the military junta after the Falklands war, was also there on a state visit. The two Labour leaders took the chance of arranging a meeting with him. Afterwards Kinnock, praising him for reintroducing democracy to Argentina in adverse circumstances, said he was a man Britain could do business with.

The Conservative tabloids, led by the *Mail* and the *Sun*, raised a storm. Thatcher, taking her cue from them, pointed out that Argentina had so far refused to end its formal state of war with Britain. The Paris talks would upset the Falkland islanders and pull the rug from beneath Britain when the issue of sovereignty over the islands was raised at the United Nations. Kinnock pointed out that they had not discussed sovereignty, only practical measures for improving relations between Argentina and Britain.

It is a slow process, but, despite the manner in which they are reported, the cumulative effect of such visits is to build an image of an international figure, concerned with radical causes and gaining experience of the world of diplomacy. An additional bonus is that he can free himself momentarily from domestic pressures. Even Nicaragua and East Africa seemed restful compared with some of the troubles building up for Kinnock and Labour at home.

4   *The Beast of Bournemouth*

Almost unanimously, the press were predicting a rough time for Kinnock at the 1985 party conference, due to begin in Bournemouth on Sunday 29 September. Earlier in the month he had suffered two important defeats at the Blackpool TUC. Not that they had caught him by surprise: the portents had been so unfavourable that he was glad he had decided at the start of his leadership only to address the TUC every other year – and this was a year he would miss. Congress had passed resolutions calling on him to commit a future Labour Government to retrospective action that he opposed – giving amnesty to all miners convicted of offences during the strike and repaying the NUM's fines for contempt of court; and reimbursing Labour local councillors who had incurred personal surcharges for defying the Government's policy on rates. It was expected that these resolutions would be duplicated at Bournemouth, and that the conference would be dominated by the Militant tendency and their supporters on the far left.

The opinion polls reflected that assumption. The worst was a Gallup poll in *The Daily Telegraph* of 19 September. It showed the Alliance in the lead with 35% of the vote, the Conservatives and Labour both at 29%. It meant that, two years after Kinnock assumed the leadership, the party was back in a position scarcely stronger than when he took over.

The press were wrong. Not for the first time, and certainly not the last, they had underestimated Kinnock. After possibly the most triumphant conference a leader has ever enjoyed in personal terms, Labour's rating rose to nearly 40%, and seldom slipped by more than a point or two through the following year. He achieved the transformation by rounding on his enemies and turning against them the very issues they assumed would damage him. Two years after becoming leader, he was at last visibly and indisputably in command.

*   *   *

In his early gallop to Westminster, serving in local government was a step Kinnock had missed. Many Labour MPs have used their local town halls as stages in their political careers: indeed without the promise of advancement there would be few volunteers to sit on councils. It is unpaid work and involves many hours of meetings and community service, especially in large cities. Those who do offer themselves, therefore, tend to have their eyes on higher things. And in the Labour

84

Party they are often drawn from the ranks of those same activists who have come to dominate constituency Labour parties by virtue of their willingness to put in the hours.

It is all very different from the traditional image of Labour councillors earlier in the century. They were gruff, comfortable worthies who always seemed to be wearing their Sunday best: striped suits with bulging waistcoats and fob watches. (Not many were women.) Like today, they were the same people who dominated the local party, perhaps trade union officials or small tradesmen. And if there was sometimes a whiff of Tammany Hall – the nod and the wink, the greased palm, the contract going to an old friend – they would at least get things done. The rubbish was cleared, the drains unblocked, the council flats built.

How unlike the big-city Labour councillors we have today come to know, if not universally to love. They are often under 30, engaged in social work or teaching, wearing flak jackets, jeans, training shoes and lapel buttons proclaiming their position on issues of controversy. They are skilled in that special kind of oratory that involves rapid gesticulation and an angry, fever-pitched and mostly indiscriminate devotion to radical causes. There were not many of that new breed in South Wales when Kinnock was starting out in politics. He has never truly liked or trusted them.

In the early 1980s the country's best-known figure in local government was Ken Livingstone, a former borough councillor of Lambeth in South London and, since 1981, leader of the Greater London Council. His term of office began as it was to continue, in controversy. Labour fought the election under the leadership of Andrew McIntosh, a veteran on the right of the party. At their first caucus meeting, the Labour group elected Livingstone to replace him – an incident since exploited by the party's opponents to sustain their argument that, although Labour might adopt a moderate posture when facing the electorate, it shows its true extremist colours as soon as it has achieved power.

Livingstone is smooth, smart, chirpy and exceptionally good on television. He has never been a close ally of Kinnock, although since becoming a Parliamentary candidate he has been careful never to criticize him outright. During their first months in office, Livingstone and his supporters on the GLC became symbols of a new target for the Conservative press: the 'Loony Left'. The Labour Party in London had come during the 1970s to embrace a coalition of special-interest groups representing ethnic minorities, single parents, the disabled, the homeless, social security claimants, homosexuals and others. Livingstone's GLC, along with several Labour-controlled London borough councils, came under attack for voting grants of money – small enough sums, to be sure – to bodies catering to those interests. It became a standing joke that a sure way of gaining a council grant was to put forward a project for a crèche for the children of black lesbian single parents. Livingstone also aroused hostility by inviting to London representatives of Sinn Fein, the Irish political party that supports the IRA.

Kinnock and the mainstream party had sympathy for many of those causes (though not Sinn Fein), but could see that to place – or to seem to place – their interests above all others could alienate the majority, who by definition were not members of those groups. Against the odds, though, Livingstone became a popular figure in London. On television he was able to argue for his policies with measured reason and even with a sense of humour, both rare attributes on the Labour left. He became especially popular when his council unprecedentedly reduced the fares on the London buses and underground – although the Law Lords forced them to put them up again when a resident of one of the outer boroughs, sparsely served by London Transport, successfully claimed that his rates were being used to subsidize public transport in the city centre.

If some of the GLC's excesses irritated Kinnock, they infuriated the Conservatives, who devised a root-and-branch solution. They included in their 1983 manifesto a plan to abolish the GLC and six other metropolitan county councils. The proposal was not based totally on vindictiveness. The two-tier city administrations, established by the local government reforms of the early 1960s, had never worked well. Too many of the umbrella authorities' responsibilities overlapped with those of the borough councils. But the Government's proposals, published in October 1983, seemed still more unwieldy. Although some of the GLC's functions would revert to the boroughs, many others, such as the administration of the fire service, would have to be performed by newly-established committees of appointed officials, some 20 in all. The plan seemed likely to render control of those services less efficient as well as less democratic.

After some revisions by the House of Lords, the Bill was passed and the GLC duly abolished on 31 March 1986. The council elections due in 1985 were cancelled. Livingstone made a final gesture of defiance when he and three of his colleagues resigned and forced by-elections. Kinnock swallowed his antipathy towards Livingstone and joined in the campaign. At a press conference on 11 June 1984 he cited a poll showing that 64% of Londoners wanted the GLC to continue, against 17% who did not. The abolition plan 'offends deeply against democratic values', he said. The four councillors won their by-elections, but the councils were not reprieved.

That was only one prong of the Government's assault on local government. The second would cause Kinnock greater difficulties with his party. The Conservatives, as the party representing property owners, have traditionally been against high rates, maintaining that local councils are profligate in spending the revenue derived from them. For the most part, though, the central government at Westminster has in the past avoided interference in the way councils spend their money, preferring to let local democracy take its course. Thatcher and her colleagues, bent on reducing all types of government spending, thought it time to change all that. In 1981, two years into the first Thatcher administration, Michael Heseltine, Secretary of State for the Environment, announced measures to try to control local council spending. His technique would be to use the leverage provided by the Government's control of the rate support grant, an important supplement to the revenue raised by local authorities as rates.

Heseltine ruled that councils exceeding spending targets set by the Government would have their support grant cut or receive no grant at all, depending on the scale of their offence. He guessed that some of the higher-spending councils, especially in London, would choose to maintain their spending level and make up the grant shortfall by raising rates still further. He warned them that, were this to happen, he would be forced to introduce legislation limiting the sum they could raise on the rates.

Labour councils reacted angrily. They avowed that they would not cut jobs and services, sorely needed by their poorest residents, for the sake of conforming with centrally-imposed restraints. In December 1981, the London Labour Party called a meeting to discuss how to combat the threat. Delegates resolved that councils should refuse to set a rate at all rather than levy a sum that would force them to make cuts. The most outspoken delegate was Ted Knight, leader of Lambeth Council and a veteran of the far left within the party and outside it. In 1954 he was expelled because of his connection with the Trotskyist paper *Socialist Outlook*, but was later readmitted. Knight wanted to pursue the rates dispute to what he saw as its logical conclusion – the defeat of the Government. It was 'a crisis of such dimensions that either you persuade the Government to retreat or force the very existence of that Government on to the agenda.'

There was no such act of mass defiance. Instead, many councils did what Heseltine had warned them against – increased rates to make up for the loss of their grants. An exception was Liverpool, which was to prove an exception to many rules in the months ahead. There the City Council, under the influence of the Militant tendency, did not make a rate for 1984 but was sustaining services and therefore running into heavy debt, threatening to default on its loans. Kinnock visited Liverpool on 4 June that year and gave the council moral support, blaming the crisis on the Liberal/Conservative coalition which formerly ran the city and which, he maintained, had starved local services of funds. He urged the Government to find money to bail Liverpool out.

Unusually, the Government – not quite ready for full-scale confrontation with local councils – complied with his suggestion. Patrick Jenkin, who had become Secretary of State for the Environment after the 1983 election, patched up a financial settlement to keep the city going for a year. The showdown with Liverpool and the other defiant councils would wait until 1985.

True to their threat, the Government announced soon after the 1983 election that they planned to introduce a bill setting a legal limit on the rates to be collected by between 12 and 20 selected councils that had persistently spent above the guidelines. The 'ratecapping' legislation, as it was called, was passed the following year and scheduled to go into effect in the spring of 1985.

In July 1984 Labour council leaders from across the country met at Sheffield, whose Council leader, David Blunkett, is the only municipal figure on the NEC. They decided on a policy of 'non-compliance' with ratecapping although they were not unanimous about the form the defiance would take. Some wanted to adopt deficit budgeting – setting a rate within the Government guidelines but avoiding cuts in services by budgeting to spend more than they would receive. Hard-liners, led by Ted Knight, advocated following the Liverpool example and refusing to set a rate at all. This is against the law and renders councillors liable to personal fines (called surcharges) that go towards compensating the council for revenue lost due to the rates not being set on time. A further punishment is disqualification from office. The Government might then have to appoint commissioners to set rates and run the authorities in place of those disqualified.

Knight persuaded a majority of the council leaders to support his strategy. He believed that Jenkin, faced with an act of mass defiance, would capitulate. The municipal leaders agreed that they would stand shoulder to shoulder, not allowing Jenkin to pick them off individually. John McDonnell, deputy leader of the GLC, called on members of his council to resign if they felt unable to go through with the policy and the risk of personal bankruptcy it entailed. Knight made the same call to Lambeth councillors, some of whom took the hint and quit.

But the line did not hold. One reason was a speech Kinnock made to a meeting of Labour councillors in Birmingham in February 1985. The 'dented shield' speech has gone down in the annals of the hard left as one of his worst acts of treachery. Kinnock urged town hall socialists not to make gestures by resigning, breaking the law and risking loss of office:

> Better a dented shield than no shield at all. Better a Labour council doing its best to help than Government placemen extending the full force of Government policy ... We don't want to weaken the broad coalition by wrangles over legality or public dramas or exciting

excursions. Our basic concern is – and must remain – jobs, services and democracy.

The speech received a mixed reception. Ted Knight said Kinnock had shown himself out of touch with rank and file; and he vowed: 'There will be no dented shields in Lambeth.' John Austin-Walker, leader of Greenwich Council, said: 'We are not prepared to cling to office to make Tory cuts.' Even David Blunkett, who often supported Kinnock in the NEC, thought his intervention had weakened the possibility of effective defiance. But more moderate leaders supported him. Dick Knowles, leader of Birmingham City Council, stated: 'Defiance of the law is not to the advantage of the working class. You have to be pretty rich to defy the law.'

A few days later Patrick Jenkin met the council leaders but did not back down. Kinnock authorized John Cunningham, shadow spokesman on the environment, to attend the meeting and urge moderation. In the Shadow Cabinet Cunningham had consistently stressed that the rule of law was more important to socialists than almost anyone else, since it was they who wanted to improve society by statute. For Labour Councillors to flout laws as an act of policy had a bearing on whether the electorate perceived Labour as being fit to hold office. And now a crucial convert to the Kinnock/Cunningham strategy showed his colours. Ken Livingstone, who expected to be nominated shortly as Parliamentary candidate for the safe Labour seat of Brent East, advised councillors to stay in office to defend their electors against the Conservative cuts.

The GLC had to set its rate in March, a few weeks before the borough councils. On 10 March Livingstone provoked the anger of his deputy McDonnell by voting with the majority of his Labour group to set a rate 2½p in the pound below the maximum allowed under the rate-capping legislation. That set an important example for the other threatened councils. At first they voted to delay setting a rate rather than refusing outright. Then, one by one, they decided that they had no alternative but to set a legal rate. The revolt fizzled out.

Livingstone and Knight had until then been joint editors of the hard left journal *Labour Herald*. On 12 April it carried a three-page editorial headlined CHALLENGE KINNOCK'S ROAD. It accused Kinnock of seeing opposition to the Conservatives in purely Parliamentary terms, ignoring the possibility that direct action could bring down the Government. Kinnock had turned his back on the miners and other trade unionists who advocated direct action, the editorial said. He had mounted an offensive against those resisting the drift of the party to the right. The article called for the creation of a coalition of left-wing trade unionists, left-wing MPs and party activists to combat the rightwards trend. It was signed by Knight and McDonnell, Livingstone's deputy leader, but, significantly, not by Livingstone, who resigned from the paper soon afterwards.

Kinnock had learned a lesson from the miners' dispute, where he held back for months from voicing his criticism of Scargill's leadership to avoid accusations of damaging the cause of striking workers. Such solidarity, he now saw, could have harmed the men he was trying to support, by encouraging the leadership to persist with a policy he knew to be mistaken. In any case, no matter how many gestures of support he made, it was never enough for the extremists: each would be followed by a demand for a still greater degree of commitment. This time, on ratecapping, he was not to be deflected from speaking his mind. In an interview with the *Manchester Evening News* on 26 April he said:

> My advice to Labour councillors throughout has been to stay in office in order to shield the people as best they can . . . I understand the dreadful pressures of local councillors who can see the problems of their locality and want to deal with them. The only way to change that situation is to get the power to alter the regime of central government and ensure they do get those resources. Excluding yourself from office . . . is no answer.

By June 1985, only Knight's Lambeth and Militant's Liverpool were holding out. Now the members of those authorities sought from the Labour leadership a commitment to pay back the surcharges when Labour achieved power. They argued that there was a tradition of socialists breaking the law in defence of righteous causes. Kinnock and Cunningham quarrelled with the logic of the argument and were strongly against any such commitment. Cunningham pointed out that people who broke the law on conscientious grounds did so knowing the consequences and being willing to accept them. They did not ask for others to bail them out. In June Stephen Bubb, Lambeth's chief whip, wrote to Kinnock on the subject. Kinnock replied:

> I do not accept . . . that chaos in local government brings benefits either to the people of the borough or the Labour Party. In fact I believe the reverse to be the case. The NEC supports the right of councils to set budgets to meet the needs of communities but insists Labour councillors stay in office to protect local services.

Lambeth eventually set a rate after two Labour councillors broke ranks with the party group, but it was not in time to avoid the surcharges and disqualification – and then further costs as the councillors unsuccessfully appealed to the law (to institutions they vilified as capitalist courts and Tory judges) to quash their penalties. Now the campaign for reimbursement was intensified. Knight used his influence with town hall unions to get it placed on the agenda of the TUC in Blackpool in September, where delegates approved the motion calling on a future Labour Government to commit itself to paying the money back. Later in the month Knight composed a front-page editorial for *Labour Herald*, urging the party conference to pass a similar motion, and demanding that Kinnock should take heed of it when they did.

*   *   *

Rebel councillors were not the only people insisting that Kinnock throw government money at them even before he had been given the keys to the safe. Arthur Scargill and the NUM were urging him with growing vehemence to commit his future government to repaying the fines incurred by the union for contempt of court during the strike. Since the strike, Scargill and his supporters on the far left had adopted as an article of faith the argument that the miners had not been defeated, that the very struggle had been a triumph of revolutionary politics, and that regardless of its outcome it had changed the course of British history. The action was now to be continued in a campaign for Labour commitments to repay the fines, to reinstate miners who were dismissed during the strike and to grant total amnesty to men jailed for violent offences on and off the picket lines.

The campaign reached its height towards the end of June 1985 and Kinnock blamed it for the the narrow defeat of the Labour candidate at the Brecon and Radnor by-election on 4 July. Tony Benn fired the first salvo. He announced the draft of a Private Members' Bill calling for free pardons for miners convicted of violence. Kinnock, talking to reporters while campaigning in the by-election, commented: 'It can't be taken seriously by anyone. I cannot even imagine that it was drafted with any serious purpose.'

The press gave Benn's plan considerable coverage, but in the rogues' gallery of scare figures on the left, Scargill was now a more potent figure. So the miners' leader's speech a few days later at an NUM conference in Sheffield received wider publicity still. Scargill repeated the call for amnesty, adding to it a demand for Labour to dismiss all Coal Board managers and a warning to his men to get ready for more industrial action. The by-election was now only two days away and Kinnock foresaw that the speech could harm the chances of the Labour victory predicted by the polls in what had been a safe Conservative seat. He made a swift counter-attack in a bid to limit the damage, issuing a statement while he was at the conference of the Electricians' Union at Blackpool. He supported the reinstatement of sacked miners *except* those convicted of violence. As for a new strike, Kinnock said coalfield families knew, after they had suffered so much, that while defiance in defeat was a fine instinct, common sense to prevent further defeat was vital:

> I listen to them. They speak from bitter experience. They will never forget the strike or its lessons – indeed they live daily with the reality and its results and the extra power now held by the board. They know that the only security in their industry will come from a Labour government elected through the ballot box. That is how we are going to do it. That is the only way we would want to do it. All other courses are fantasy.

But the harm had been done. At the by-election the Liberal overturned a Conservative majority of over 18,000 and beat the Labour candidate by a tantalizing 559 votes. This was tangible proof of the damage done to Labour's electoral prospects by the posturing of the left. Kinnock was determined now that it had to be assaulted head-on.

His first chance to put this new robust policy into effect came at the end of the following week, when he shared a platform with Scargill and Benn at the Durham Miners' Gala. Without mentioning either man by name, he weighed into their speeches of the previous weeks. In a clear comment on Scargill's assertion that the strike had changed the course of history, he declared:

> We do not want glorious historic defeats – there have been too many of those. I will settle for plain, ordinary, everyday victories . . . What we need to do is to ensure that every word, every action, every statement, everything that we do to educate, agitate and organize is geared completely to victory . . . In everything we say and do we work in the clear knowledge that we address an audience which is hesitant, an audience that is in need of convincing . . . It is making sure that our real ideas and our real policies are not covered up in a great blanket of distractions and delusions which our enemies will be glad to exaggerate and thicken until it smothers us in defeat.

He knew that, however powerfully he spoke, he would not deflect Scargill and his allies from pressing their claims for amnesty and reimbursement. The point of speaking out was to give the clearest possible public indication of his position in the hope of isolating the extreme left. The first test of whether he had succeeded came at the TUC in September. It was bound to be a contentious Congress in any event, for there were powerful calls from many trade unionists to expel the right-wing Engineers' and Electricians' Unions, which had defied TUC policy by accepting Government money for their ballots on political funds. Scargill was determined to introduce further controversy by proposing his motion on amnesty and reimbursement. He was given an enthusiastic standing ovation which belied the closeness of the vote – his motion was passed by only 64,000 of the nine million card votes cast. He would have lost if Clive Jenkins had been able to persuade his ASTMS executive to vote against the motion.

Kinnock maintained his truculent opposition to the reimbursement pledge, commenting:

> Arthur Scargill is president of the National Union of Mineworkers. I am leader of the Labour Party. It is on my view of the manifesto that we will fight the next election ... Many people have suffered financial losses as a result of Mrs Thatcher's policies. I am thinking in particular of pensioners who have lost literally thousands of pounds. No one is suggesting we should reimburse them.

Bolstered by his success at Blackpool, albeit a narrow one, Scargill was determined to get a similar proposition approved by the party conference in Bournemouth. Kinnock was equally determined that he should not. He had been given the news of the TUC vote while he was travelling to Blackpool. A BBC crew had boarded the train at Preston and told him. At that moment he decided that he would make two speeches at the party conference at the end of the month, one specifically against reimbursing the miners.

The Sunday papers of 29 September, when the conference was to open, were full of foreboding. They agreed nearly unanimously that there was no chance that Bournemouth would be anything but a disaster for the Labour leader, capping his second dreadful year in succession. But Kinnock remained in a fighting mood. *The Sunday Times* that day published an unusually outspoken interview with him. The reporter, Patrick Bishop, described a day spent with him in his constituency, when Kinnock had time to speak frankly about the troubles that were said to be closing in on him. He thought they were being exaggerated, by virtue of what he called the 'High Noon' school of journalism, where 'the lawman, usually in the mould of Son of Paleface, is locked in a series of showdowns with the desperadoes and outlaws that inhabit the wild and rocky places of the Labour movement' . . .

> You see it's always the same question . . . Why is your party in bloody chaos? . . . Why aren't you arranging the assassination of Arthur Scargill? There was a respite until the TUC conference when I was back on the ropes again. They don't want to know what you say or do about South Africa or unemployment.

On recompensing councillors and miners:

We've had these gestures before and they've been passed [at conference]. We had an undertaking in 1982 that we'd introduce retrospective compensation for councillors who took on the Government. It was all written down in black and white and when it came to the manifesto there wasn't a word about it. Without any arrogance it was one of the conditions of doing this job that the interpretation has to be mine . . . If anybody thinks they can do a better job they can get on with it. That's why my word has got to count. As for the miners they'll get the emotional response that the miners always get. There are damned good reasons for being emotional about the miners but you can't run a party or a country on the basis of emotion. As long as they don't expect that to be holy writ . . . A leader of the Opposition is going around offering indemnities, amnesties, God knows what. It's a fairy tale. It's gesture politics.

When he arrived in Bournemouth on Saturday 28 September he was equally boisterous and gave the first hint of the tactics he was planning to employ against the outlaws and desperadoes. Modern practice is for the leader to give his speech on the Tuesday afternoon of the conference. Kinnock never has it in final form until the early hours of that morning, after a final brainstorming session following the Monday evening round of trade union receptions. But the outline had been worked out in his office over the previous weeks by such as Charles Clarke and John Reid, a Scot for whom he has a high regard and who occupied a pivotal place in his private office until adopted as a Parliamentary candidate in Scotland that year.

Kinnock knew enough of what he was planning to say to be able to tell reporters his intention of standing firm against all the extreme demands. His resolve was strengthened by a BBC opinion poll which found that four out of five Labour voters thought Scargill was harming the party. According to the *Sunday Express* Kinnock was going to tell the extremists: 'Grow up or get out.' The *Mail on Sunday* called it a 'kamikaze mission'. He would be saying no to the miners, no to the rebel councillors, no to black sections. Some papers added, almost an afterthought, a fourth group destined to get the thumbs-down from the leadership – the Militant tendency, and in particular its followers who ran Liverpool City Council.

*   *   *

The Militant tendency is the popular name for the Revolutionary Socialist League (RSL), one of the numerous British Trotskyist groupings. It gets the name from its weekly newspaper *Militant*, sold at strategic street corners across the country. The Labour Party has never embraced Trotsky's belief that capitalism is doomed to collapse and universal revolution the only way to achieve social justice and power for the working class. Those groups on the British left that do share this opinion have always been fragmented by differences over fine details and, in particular, over tactics.

Because men and women of the far left hold their views with such conviction, they are seldom willing to sink even minor disagreements for the sake of forging alliances. So certain are they that each one of their principles is incontestably correct that to weaken on any of them is unthinkable. That is why there are so many small parties with confusingly similar names, their members all claiming to be the true heirs of Trotsky. None of the groups is powerful enough to exert any real political influence on its own. By contrast, the strength of the mainstream Labour Party lies in its being a coalition of many philosophies and nuances from the socialist middle ground, generally embraced and expressed with moderation, sinking doctrinal differences for the sake of unity and bent on achieving power democratically.

Trotsky advocated that his supporters, because they were so few, should seek to exert political influence by a tactic of 'entryism' – gaining admission into a country's main socialist party and slowly capturing its institutions, while making no compromises on the purity of the faith. The Labour Party believes there can be no common ground between people wedded to democracy and those who advocate revolution. Consequently it has from time to time throughout its history been forced to expel from its ranks those who do not accept its views on strategy, even though such expulsions grate with the party's traditional libertarianism.

In his book *The March of Militant*, Michael Crick traces the birth of the RSL in Britain to 1955, when it was set up by a small group including Ted Grant, then a member of the Labour Party. (He is still on Militant's executive committee and was one of those expelled by the Labour NEC in 1983.) The new party became the British affiliate of the Trotskyist Fourth International. In 1964 it replaced its newspaper *Socialist Fight* with a new monthly paper called *Militant*, edited by a young man from Liverpool, Peter Taaffe.

Taaffe remains nominally editor today, although his more important role is as the organizational chief of the tendency. The policies advocated by the paper have also survived largely unchanged. Its central economic demand is for full nationalization, under workers' control, of the '200 monopolies' that it identifies as dominating the British economy. It advocates a huge increase in public spending and increased 'democratization' of Labour Party practices, including NEC control of the manifesto. Although the initial aim is to gain control of the party through manipulation of its existing democratic procedures, *Militant*'s central philosophy is that the necessary radical changes in society can only finally come about through revolution.

The paper's main influence initially was exerted on the party's youth wing. Labour has always had trouble with its young members, who, impatient with the slow process of democracy and its inherent possibility of defeat, try to steer the party towards extremism. Several times the NEC have disbanded the youth section for that reason. They did so in 1955 but tried to reconstitute it five years later as the Young Socialists. Within two years that group too had run out of control and was severed from the party, being taken over by a Trotskyist faction led by Gerry Healy, later to form the Workers' Revolutionary Party.

In 1965 Labour again tried to establish a loyal youth movement and set up the Labour Party Young Socialists (LPYS). This was to prove fertile ground for Militant supporters to gain strength within the party. They used the traditional tactics of the left wing: by regular attendance at branch and committee meetings they were able to win majorities over less committed members who did not turn up as often. By 1970 Militant supporters were in firm control of the LPYS national committee, and the newspaper itself came out weekly instead of monthly. Its estimated weekly sale today is around 20,000 copies. When in 1972 the Labour Party decided to grant the LPYS a seat on the NEC, the effect was virtually to guarantee Militant representation on the party's supreme executive body. (Today the LPYS seat is held by Linda Douglas, a Militant sympathizer and the first black NEC member.)

It is against the rules of the Labour Party for political factions to be formed within it. The Militants were able to skirt this restriction by asserting that theirs was not an organized party with formal membership but a group of people who supported the line of a particular newspaper and helped distribute it. Since they operate an efficient security system, disproving that assertion was the party's most difficult task when the decision was eventually taken to move against Militant in the 1980s.

A few senior Labour figures became concerned about the entryist tactics of a number of Trotskyist groups, especially Militant, in the early 1970s. Reg Underhill, the National Agent, produced a report on them but, by a slim majority of four, the NEC decided to take no action on it. In 1976 the tendency strengthened its presence in party headquarters when Andy Bevan, one of its most articulate adherents, was appointed youth officer. Four years later Underhill, by then in the House of Lords, updated his report and, although party officials were still reluctant to take action, the press made much of it. A 'red scare' was precisely what Labour did not need a year after having been ousted from office. Combined with the defection of leading right-wingers to the new Social Democratic Party, it gave the impression of a party slithering rapidly away from the middle ground, with its new leader Michael Foot powerless to halt the process.

Three Militants had been selected as candidates in the 1979 election and all had been defeated, but now a handful were chosen in winnable seats. In 1981 Foot was prevailed upon to endorse a further inquiry. Ron Hayward, the General Secretary, and David Hughes, the National Agent, were mandated by the NEC to look specifically at whether Militant was a separate political party and thus in breach of Labour's constitution, and if so whether its leaders should be expelled. They quickly decided that, despite the claim of its supporters that it was simply a group supporting a newspaper, the tendency was indeed a distinct party. They recommended that Labour should establish a register of groups permitted to operate inside the party and that Militant should not be included on it because of the undemocratic nature of its aims.

Expelling members has always been an emotional and contentious issue in the Labour Party. It likes to think of itself as a broad church – as it is. The ugly phrase 'witch hunt' is used to argue against excluding people for sincerely held views, raising the spectre of the McCarthy hearings in Washington in the 1950s. It is a misleading comparison. McCarthy invited people to denounce acquaintances as Communists and used the charge to bar them from respectable society and from fields of endeavour where their political views were irrelevant to their performance. Labour is a political party with defined aims and strategies. It is legitimate for such a party to bar from membership people whose aims and strategies are in conflict with its own. Even the broadest church cannot embrace members whose faith contradicts its essential theology. As Foot said at the 1982 Blackpool conference: 'There is a sharp distinction between witch hunts and real offences against the constitution'.

Militant's leaders were determined to fight hard against the moves to expel them, even (unsuccessfully) seeking a High Court injunction. Partly for this reason, the matter progressed painfully slowly. Although Militant was not included in the list of approved organizations within the party, the NEC decided that before expelling anyone they had to establish his or her membership of the tendency beyond any doubt. It should not have been too difficult in the case of the ruling group; but it was, because the Militants deny that they constitute an organization in the formal sense. After exhausting the possibilities of delaying tactics, the five members of the newspaper's editorial board – Ted Grant, Peter Taaffe, Keith Dickinson, Clare Doyle and Lynn Walsh – were finally expelled in February 1983.

The barred leaders did not include any of the Militant supporters who were running for Parliament under the Labour banner. In the general election that June, Dave Nellist in Coventry South-east and Terry Fields in Liverpool Broadgreen were elected as Militant's first two MPs. Pat Wall, whose connection with Militant went back to its very beginnings, lost by 1,600 in Bradford North, where the deselected former MP, the Labour right-winger Ben Ford, won 4,000 votes standing as an independent. Wall had been the subject of controversy a year earlier, when he made a well publicized speech forecasting civil war and bloodshed in the struggle for a socialist society.

A few weeks before the general election, Militant gained its most important success in local government when Labour in Liverpool won an overall majority on the city council after ten years of rule by minority administrations. In the early 70s the Liberals had been in control, led by Trevor Jones, a pioneer of what came to be called 'community politics'. The Liverpool Labour Party had been ripe for the attentions of the far left. Until the 1960s it had been dominated by the formidable Jack and Bessie Braddock, who would have no truck with extremism. Their right-wing machine survived after they had departed the scene, but with decreasing influence. The demoralized and disorganized party could find no effective resistance to the Militant activists who offered energy and commitment – two qualities the local party had lacked for years.

The city itself was declining rapidly, too. Like much of the north-west, it had been severely hit by the collapse of British industry and merchant shipping. Unemployment grew in the 70s and 80s and its housing conditions were among the worst in the country. In 1981 there were nights of rioting in the Toxteth district, wreaking further destruction on an already devastated area.

By the time Labour won its overall majority on the council in 1983, Militant was sufficiently influential in the local party to control the ruling Labour group, even though only a minority of the group were fully committed Militant supporters. John Hamilton, a long-time councillor and not a Militant member, was re-elected leader but he was simply a figurehead. The real influence was exercised by Militant, especially by Tony Mulhearn, a former member of the tendency's central committee, and Derek Hatton, the charismatic young community worker elected deputy leader. His powerful public personality meant that it was Hatton who normally spoke for the Council, not the more reticent Hamilton.

And there was a lot of speaking to do, for the Militant-dominated authority, devoted to maintaining council jobs and improving services, immediately entered a battle with the Government over the city's budget, launching its assault in 1984, a year earlier than most other councils because it was the year before the full ratecapping legislation went into effect. After winning some concessions from Patrick Jenkin in 1984 they proposed a still more extravagant budget for 1985.

Kinnock's visit to Liverpool in June 1984 had depressed him, not just because of the city's physical condition but because of the grip Militant plainly exerted on the local Labour Party. Often in divided parties there are strong figures who oppose the dominant group: if given discreet encouragement and assistance from the central party or the leadership, they can sometimes wrest control. In a few cases since the NEC established the register in 1981, constituency parties, scenting danger, had managed to head off Militant by expelling its supporters before they gained the ascendancy. But there was little sign of a mainstream group in Liverpool large or determined enough to make any such attempt.

Some of the Council's actions worried the two senior churchmen in Liverpool, the Anglican Bishop David Sheppard and the Catholic Bishop Derek Worlock. They visited Kinnock at Westminster and told him of their worries about the city's financial crisis and the effect it was having on desperately needed public services. They added that they had received complaints from leading blacks and Asians about Sampson Bond, a black Militant from London appointed principal race relations adviser by the council in October 1984. Ethnic leaders were reluctant to deal with him and there were allegations of threats against black and Asian shopkeepers.

Charles Clarke visited Liverpool in February 1985 to liaise with people who might form the nucleus of an anti-Militant faction. He had not told the Militants he was going but they found out. Mulhearn telephoned him the day before he was due to set out. 'What are you coming to Liverpool for?' he asked challengingly. Clarke said Kinnock had received complaints about intimidation of blacks, discrimination in council hiring and many other matters and had asked him to look into them.

'You can't come to Liverpool without talking to the City Council,' Mulhearn declared. 'Are you prepared to meet us?'

'Of course,' Clarke replied.

Militant's operating methods combine elements of the sinister and the farcical. Soon after Hatton became deputy leader he formed a team of beefy guards, called the Static Security Force, to accompany him to official functions and perform other appropriate duties. Now, when Clarke agreed to meet him, Mulhearn told him that for the sake of security and to avoid attention from the press, he should leave the London train at Runcorn, a suburb 14 miles south-east of the city centre. Mulhearn and Hatton were there to meet him.

'What are you doing here?' they asked as he stepped on to the platform. 'This is our territory.' Clarke explained again and they drove him to the Municipal Buildings. Little was achieved in the way of mutual understanding. Clarke then undertook his programme of meetings with the black caucus, women's groups, housing co-operatives and trade unionists. His object was to prepare the groundwork for squeezing Militant from power. It would, he knew, be a long-term enterprise. It was a question of patiently building an alternative civic leadership. The following June, Kinnock spent a day in Liverpool under the auspices of Merseyside County Council, not the City Council. He met some of the same people Clarke had visited, and had another talk with the two bishops.

A potential ally was John Hamilton, the council leader. He held office by courtesy of Militant and was keen to hang on to it, so he would not defy the deputy leader and his allies publicly. In private, though, he held many conversations with Kinnock and Clarke and told them he would like to find a way to escape the influence of his extremist colleagues. Kinnock did not regard him as a potential leader of an alternative Labour group – he did not have the political strength to serve in that role – but he was an extremely useful source of information. They spoke by phone, Hamilton calling from his home because he feared others might listen in to his line at City Hall. A former teacher, Hamilton had known Clarke since they were both on the executive of the Socialist Education Association.

In September Clarke went with Kinnock to the TUC at Blackpool. (Although Kinnock was not making a speech he spent a day in private meetings with union leaders.) Hamilton was there too and told Clarke that the following day he and the Militant leaders of Liverpool Council would be holding a press conference to announce that, because they would have no money to pay their 31,000 employees after the end of the year, the workers were going to be made redundant. Dismissal notices would have to be issued to them before the end of the month to comply with the law stipulating three months' notice of redundancies.

With Militant it is hard to separate gestures from reality but it is doubtful that the Council did actually intend to dismiss its work force. The notices were almost certainly issued only as another weapon in the campaign to drive home the gravity of the situation and persuade the Government to bail the city out as it had done a year earlier. Yet Hatton is on record as saying that it is a legitimate tactic to achieve power by first provoking chaos – and the dismissal of the 31,000 would certainly have had that effect.

Whatever the motive for the decision, it was to prove the most serious tactical error that Hatton and his colleagues made. The trade unions were bound to react angrily – which is why, in a transparent manoeuvre, the council leaders did not make the announcement until after the TUC's vote on reimbursing surcharged councillors had safely gone their way.

On the train back to London from Blackpool, Clarke told Kinnock about his conversation with Hamilton. Kinnock's reaction was a mixture of disgust and relief – disgust at the cynical manipulation of people's livelihoods to make a political point, and relief that the decision on what to do about Militant had effectively been taken from his hands. He now saw no alternative to an all-out assault on the tendency in Liverpool.

'They're playing politics with people's jobs,' he observed to Charles Clarke on the train – giving birth to a key phrase in his Bournemouth speech. The Council were treating their work force with as much contempt as any private employer. Kinnock had decided earlier that he would use the conference speech to criticize Militant, but what was to have been a generalized attack was at that point transformed to an all-out assault on the specific tactics adopted by Liverpool Council. Kinnock knew then that, however long it took, he would have to go through with the expulsion of the Liverpool Militant leaders from the party.

*   *   *

To comply with the law the Council had to ensure beyond doubt that the redundancy notices actually reached each employee affected, so a fleet of taxis was hired to take the envelopes round to the victims' homes in the last few days of the month – the week before the Bournemouth conference. That was another tactical error. Some in the Labour movement see taxis as a symbol of privilege and extravagance. If the city was really bankrupt, how could it afford such luxuries? The irony did not escape Kinnock and John Reid as they worked on Kinnock's speech over the pre-conference weekend and well past midnight on Monday 30 September.

The leader's speech is often the least interesting thing that happens at a Labour Party conference. Unlike nearly all the other speakers during the five days, he is not contributing to a debate on a specific issue or seeking to affect the outcome of a particular vote, so the speech will normally have little immediately measurable result. No vote is taken after it. The only yardstick of approval is the length and enthusiasm of the standing ovation afterwards – a rough and ready guide. Only if the speech were received in total silence would any significant comment have been made on the leader's performance and standing in the party: the rest is relative. Nor is the speech a chance to announce new policies. Policy has to be approved by the conference and the NEC, so to launch any individual initiative in that forum would be provocative, at the very least. He is not even speaking to ensure his survival as leader or to influence the composition of the new NEC, for elections to party offices

101

are held on the Monday and the results announced before he speaks the following day.

The speech, then, is often little more than a lengthy statement of convictions that the leader has expressed many times before. It will contain references to the main political preoccupations of the day and to foreign matters. It will not need to be delivered in an especially argumentative fashion because few people there will require persuading to his views. Nearly everything he says will reflect their opinions, too. If skilfully written, the speech will be paced to start with a joke or two and then to inspire bursts of applause at well-spaced intervals, either by powerfully eloquent attacks on the opposing parties or by reference to some international issue on which the party's view is near-unanimous – South Africa, say, or Central America.

The speech is televised live nationally and long extracts are generally repeated on the TV news programmes later. But despite this valuable chance of getting himself and his message across to the electors, it is rare for a leader to enhance his reputation substantially by virtue of his conference speech. He can certainly do himself harm. A poor speech will naturally raise doubts about his competence but even a good one can be turned against him by people sighing: 'Yes, yes, we know he's a wonderful orator, but does that necessarily mean he'll be a good Prime Minister?'

Yet as far as the leader is concerned the speech is his most important of the year and must be prepared the most meticulously. It is compiled from the drafts of his advisers on specialist areas. Having read those, he decides which points he wants to highlight. The actual process of cobbling it together resembles one of those scenes in old Hollywood musicals about popular song writers, where the one at the piano experiments with a melody and the lyricist, pacing the room, comes up with the perfect words.

Kinnock is a natural pacer. He strides up and down his office experimenting with phrases to illustrate his points. His advisers will chime in with suggested improvements. When a passage is agreed one of his assistants will dash up to the word processor and run it off. Kinnock will try it out again from the text and maybe adjust it some more. It is a time-consuming process. A full draft will be ready by the week before the conference but there will be changes right up to the time of delivery, culminating in a final burst of creative frenzy in the hotel suite when most other delegates are in bed.

Kinnock keeps closer personal control of the speech in all stages of its construction than do many other politicians, who leave the bulk of the work to speech-writers. He shares the Welsh love of oratory: some of the most memorable phrases in his speeches have sprung from his own imagination. In any case, he does not keep strictly to the advance text.

He will often lead himself up a tributary, when something he says sparks a thought that he wants to pursue. Like most good political speakers he thrives on heckling from the audience and is among the best at delivering withering and often witty rebukes to those who interrupt. This is not so much evidence of a cruel streak as of a relish in roisterous political debate.

He accepts that on occasion his native garrulousness tempts him into speaking too long. As the conference speech is a set piece it is legitimate to spin it out for an hour, but to go on much longer is to tax the patience of the audience both in the hall and, to an even greater extent, at home watching on television. As Kinnock neared the end of an hour there was a hint of restlessness among the delegates seated in the raked auditorium of the brand-new conference centre on the cliffs just west of Bournemouth's town centre. That was the point at which he eventually broached the theme of extremism and impossibilism, beginning with a vivid portrayal of how impossible promises came to be made and what happened to people foolish enough to believe them:

> You start with far-fetched resolutions. They are then pickled into a rigid dogma, a code, and you go through the years sticking to that, out-dated, misplaced, irrelevant to the real needs, and you end in the grotesque chaos . . .

– now he was raising his voice until he was nearly shouting, and excited murmurs were already rippling through the hall –

> . . . the grotesque chaos of a Labour council – a *Labour* council – hiring taxis [he almost spat the word] to scuttle around a city handing out redundancy notices to its own workers.

There was uproar. The TV cameras zoomed in on the audience to locate Hatton shouting 'Lies' above the hubbub. Suddenly they switched back to the platform, just in time to see Eric Heffer, staring blankly ahead of him, climb from the stage, walk to the back of the auditorium and out through the doors. Nobody could remember any similar walkout by an NEC member during the leader's speech and the noise grew louder as left-wingers applauded Heffer and booed Kinnock, while loyalists raised counter-cheers for the leader. Kinnock stood at the rostrum, a little flushed, waiting for the turmoil to subside, his mind fixed on the next sentence in his speech. It could not have been more appropriate. It was the remark that had come to him and Clarke on the train back from the TUC at Blackpool. After a few moments, when the stir raised by Heffer's walkout had quietened sufficiently for him to make himself heard, he delivered it, emphasizing each word with deliberation:

You can't play politics with people's jobs.

The cheers this time were initiated by his own supporters. There was more booing from his opponents. He again waited for calm to return, and pressed home his point, deviating a bit from the script:

The voice of the people – not the people in here but the people with real needs – is louder than all the boos that can be assembled. The people will not, cannot abide posturing. They cannot respect the gesture generals or the tendency tacticians. It seems to me that some of them are latter-day public schoolboys. [That is one of the most potent insults in the socialist lexicon.] It seems to them that it does not matter whether the game is won or lost but how you play the game. These games players end up isolated and try to blame others – the workers, our leadership, the trade unions, the people of the city for not showing revolutionary consciousness; or somebody else.

He paid tribute to those councils that had fought for people's jobs and services using less extreme methods than those adopted by Liverpool but to greater effect. They had been forced to make hellish choices and use their best creative talents to defend their employees and those they were elected to defend. They realized that 'life is too real to mistake conference resolutions for accomplished facts or to mistake individual enthusiasm for a mass movement'. He was referring in particular to Sheffield, the council led by his new NEC ally David Blunkett. Only 24 hours later, Kinnock would have faint pangs of regret about that tribute.

Meanwhile, what had happened to Heffer? He had been, in his own words, 'shaken to my foundations' by Kinnock's assault on Militant and Liverpool, where his constituency is located. He was close to tears as he walked out of the auditorium and went to the terrace of the conference centre, where for a while he stared out to sea in silence. A group of reporters had followed him out but he would not speak to them. 'Why don't you go and listen to the rest of Neil's speech?' he asked them bitterly. A conference official gave him a cup of tea and he dropped it. He needed his wife. 'Where's Doris?' he asked plaintively.

He composed himself and went back into the hall, where Kinnock had finished speaking. His re-entry was cheered loudly by many delegates. John Hamilton, leader of the Liverpool City Council, shook him by the hand. He found Doris and left the hall, telling reporters that he could not sit there and listen to 'good working class people' being attacked in that manner.

'Gaitskell gave leadership of a similar kind and he upset the party,' he declared, adding that he had not been aware of the effect his walkout would have. He had been surprised to be chased around the conference centre by reporters. 'Perhaps I'm slightly naïve about these matters. After all, Neil fought the leadership on a left-wing ticket. I have been a moderate in comparison with some of the things Neil has said in the past . . . I think it will upset a lot of people.' However sincere his motive for the walkout, it did not help Heffer's political career: a year later he lost his place on the NEC.

Hatton gave an impromptu press conference immediately after Kinnock's speech. 'The line he was taking against Liverpool Council was an absolute disgrace and a travesty of justice and there were many untruths in it . . . Rantings and ravings will not alter our policies . . . It needs a bit of tact and understanding – real statesmanship.' Robert Parry, Labour MP for Liverpool Riverside, went further: 'Kinnock showed today that he is the biggest traitor since Ramsay MacDonald. He is the man who kicked Liverpool in the teeth when it was down on the ground.'

Kinnock's senior colleagues from the right of the party took an opposing view. Although they had welcomed Kinnock's rational approach in his two years as leader they had been unable to forget that he sprang from the left – to that extent Heffer was justified in observing how the assumption of the leadership had smoothed the sharp edge of his radicalism. This was what the right had been waiting for. Said Denis Healey: 'I think Neil's speech was of historic importance. He has shifted the centre of gravity not just of the Labour Party but of the Labour movement as a whole, decisively. We shall look back on this day as the moment when Labour won the next election.' Roy Hattersley agreed. It was, he affirmed, the best speech he had heard in his 27 years in the party. 'It was historic because it will change the country's perception of the Labour Party. We look like a party determined to win. We look like a party which is interested in the views of real people rather than people from caucuses.' He quoted Neville Cardus: 'Good batsmen influence the course of the game, great batsmen change the course of the game. Today's speech changed the course of the game.'

Indeed, the entire right wing of the party leadership was jubilant, not to say rampant. As he left the conference centre John Cunningham, shadow spokesman for the environment, was surrounded by Militant supporters who accused him and Kinnock of failing to maintain the unity of the working class. Emboldened by Kinnock's speech Cunningham tore into them: 'Don't give me all that claptrap. I'm from the working class. Your activities and behaviour demonstrate that you have no place in the party.' And support from Kinnock came from more surprising but none the less welcome sources. The actress Glenda

Jackson, born across the Mersey from Liverpool in Birkenhead, sent him a message: 'At last, at last – thank you, thank you, thank you.' In the bars of the Bournemouth hotels that night, right-wingers were in an assertive mood. For the first time since James Callaghan stepped down as leader, they felt they were back in charge. Yet at the same time the soft left, the Tribune Group and their supporters, were also pleased with the speech. Kinnock's real achievement was to have isolated the hard left from the rest of the party.

Most of the press agreed that the speech had sealed the leader's command over his party and had weakened the left wing. KINNOCK THE DESTROYER was the *Mirror*'s exultant front-page headline. In an editorial it praised Kinnock's 'conviction, compassion and courage'. The *Star* had BOY OH BOYO. The *Daily Mail* commented: 'Only when there is blood on the stage – the blood of his own party – can we be sure that a Labour leader means business.' But the other view was expressed by two papers at the opposite end of the British political spectrum. The Communist *Morning Star* wrote: 'Kamikaze Kinnock yesterday crash-landed on his own front-line troops, helping to sink Labour's election hopes.' While the *Sun* believed that the speech destroyed his hopes of becoming Prime Minister. The booing from left-wingers showed how badly he had misjudged his own party:

> People who saw it on TV know now that there is not one Labour Party but two or maybe three, each one more extreme than the other – and they won't vote for any of them.

Sensational though it was, the speech was not the sum total of Kinnock's anti-Militant strategy at the conference. The following day, one of the motions to be discussed in the local government debate was one proposed by Hatton's Liverpool party, seeking to commit Labour wholeheartedly to the council's illegal policy and to full reimbursement of penalties imposed on councillors. Because of the union leaders' anger at the Council's treatment of its employees it was certain that the motion would be defeated overwhelmingly. Kinnock could use the scale of that vote to legitimize the moves to expel Hatton and his colleagues that he was planning after the conference. The debate on the Liverpool motion went as expected until the time came for David Blunkett to sum up: he had been the obvious choice as the spokesman to explain the NEC's opposition to the motion.

Despite the flattering references Kinnock had made to Sheffield Council in his speech, Blunkett had not shared in the general jubilation. He regarded himself as a man of the left and found something distasteful in the overnight resurgence of the right. He had spent much of the previous evening discussing the situation with his political friends and wondering what he could do to heal the rift that he believed the speech had created. He was annoyed that Kinnock had given him no advance warning of what he planned to say – as the only municipal leader on the NEC, he felt he had a right to know. He did not therefore feel obliged to tell Kinnock or Charles Clarke about the plan he had devised after an almost sleepless night, although he did give a hint of it to Derek Hatton. He sought out the Liverpool deputy leader on Wednesday morning and told him: 'You're going to have to think about whether you're willing to withdraw that resolution when you've heard what I'm going to say, because I'm going to spell out a proposal. I want you to listen.'

Blunkett did not think there was much point in going through the ritual of voting down the Liverpool resolution for what would have been the third year running. Better, surely, to use the occasion to attempt something constructive in relation to the city and its finances. So at the very end of his speech he made this offer to Hatton: would he agree to withdraw his motion in return for a commitment by the NEC to set up an inquiry into Liverpool's cash crisis, perhaps pointing to a solution?

The television cameramen had by now learned where Hatton sat in the hall and they switched to him instantly, showing him in urgent consultation with Tony Mulhearn. Blunkett had deliberately not given Hatton any more than an inkling of his offer earlier, to prevent him working out his position in advance with his colleagues. He thought there was a better chance of his saying yes if caught off balance.

Blunkett is blind so he did not know about the consultations between Hatton and Mulhearn. It was frustrating. He could hear from the hubbub that something was going on but he could not tell what. So he cried out: 'Will you do it, Derek, will you?' No answer. 'Will you?' again, then: 'Are you coming Derek, are you coming?' Behind him Eric Heffer tugged his arm and whispered: 'He's walking up to the rostrum now.'

Hatton shook Blunkett by the hand, leaned towards the microphone and shouted. 'In order that unity can happen and we can go out and make sure this Government is defeated – yes.'

Delegates were carried away on a tide of emotion. The melodrama could scarcely have been more perfect had it been scripted – the blind man peering uselessly into the audience, listening for signs that his risky grandstand play was going to work. The prodigal son seeming to come home and repent – although a little cool consideration would have shown that Hatton had sacrificed nothing except the chance of another empty gesture, leading his troops to an heroic defeat at the hands of the union block vote. All the same, at the time it looked as though peace might be breaking out. There was cheering and weeping. Kinnock, not at all happy at the turn of events, was canny enough not to show his true feelings in the face of such a response from delegates. He walked to Blunkett, put an arm round his shoulder and whispered: 'You skate on thin ice. Well done.'

Afterwards they had a less cordial talk. Kinnock's advisers, Charles Clarke and John Reid especially, were angry that the process started in Kinnock's speech the previous day had not been allowed to reach its logical conclusion in a massive anti-Hatton vote. But when Blunkett assured Kinnock that he was not trying to undermine him and that he thought the proposed inquiry might strengthen the leadership's hand, peace was re-established. Blunkett was given a coveted invitation to the afternoon drinks party Kinnock holds at the end of the conference for his particular friends. The Sheffield leader was too important an ally on the NEC to sacrifice for a single misdemeanour.

Hatton was not invited to the drinks party but he and Kinnock did exchange a few words at one of the many other social functions during conference week. The Liverpudlian began to lecture the leader about revolutionary politics, expressing his surprise that Kinnock could not see the advantage of backing a general strike to support the miners or the beleaguered local authorities, or both. Such a strike, Hatton asserted, could put Kinnock on the road to Downing Street.

'I certainly want to get there,' Kinnock replied, 'but frankly I think I would stand a better chance by riding on the back of an elephant and jumping over Buckingham Palace.'

*   *   *

A measure of Kinnock's propaganda triumph over Militant was that the debate on reimbursing the miners, which commentators had assumed would be the most bitterly contested of the week, came as something of an anti-climax. Part of the battle had been won for the leadership on the Saturday before the conference, when the NEC, meeting to decide their attitude on the main resolutions, decided by a single vote, 15 to 14, to oppose Scargill's motion. Michael Meacher, formerly of the hard left but increasingly a Kinnock loyalist, had voted with the leader after a lot of pressure from Kinnock and a long struggle within himself to decide what was right. By deserting the left he provoked predictable wrath from his former allies. 'What you did,' Tony Benn told him, 'will be on your conscience for the rest of your life.'

It is rare for a party leader to make more than one speech during the conference but Kinnock had decided some weeks earlier, on the train to Blackpool, that he wanted to follow up his Durham speech and his reaction to the TUC vote by unmistakably dissociating himself from Scargill's tactics in this most public forum. The events of the previous days had primed the atmosphere for him. There was even some booing for the miners' leader when he introduced the debate – something that few would have been bold enough to indulge in before Kinnock's anti-Militant speech. Eric Hammond, the electricians' leader, also raised applause – although mixed with hostility from the left – when he likened the miners to 'lions led by donkeys'. Ron Todd, leader of the TGWU, responded: 'I'm an animal lover. I prefer donkeys to jackals.'

Kinnock was given a rousing reception when he stood up to accuse Scargill of responsibility for splitting his union, for the loss of thousands of jobs in coal mining and for tactical blunders – errors that had combined to hand power over the demoralized miners to the NCB. Many were leaving the industry because they were frightened to death of being called out on strike again and undergoing another period of extreme hardship.

They're utterly demoralized. Young men are accepting redundancy to pay off debts run up during the strike. It's pathetic. It's terrible . . . We would be dishonest in this party to give an undertaking of retrospective payments to anybody. The cavalry will not ride in to pick up the tab.

When a Scargill sympathizer yelled from the hall, asking what Kinnock had done to help the miners during the dispute, he shouted back: 'Well, I wasn't telling them lies. That's what I was not doing.' He referred specifically to Scargill's repeated claim during the strike that coal stocks were on the point of exhaustion, when they never were.

After his second rousing ovation in the week, he sat in his place on the platform to await the result of the card vote. It was better than he had dared to hope a few days earlier. The motion to reimburse the miners had been passed, sure enough, but by only 630,000 votes – by 3.54m to 2.91m. This was less than the two-thirds majority needed to put reimbursement into the party's official programme from which manifesto pledges are selected.

In interviews at the end of the conference Kinnock pressed home his advantage. He told Paul Potts of the *News of the World*:

I decided I would seek the opportunity to address the whole movement about the choices and issues before the Labour Party . . . Even though it's said I've got a hot temperament I don't think you can lead the party or a country with sudden passion. You've got to be very deliberate . . . The response has been truly overwhelming but no-one should kid themselves – there's still a long slog ahead.

He added that people's feelings for Labour had been dammed up by the charges that the party was not fit to govern and that he was not assertive enough as leader. 'Now the dam has burst.'

That new-found confidence was quickly supported by evidence. Labour Party headquarters at Walworth Road reported a surge of new inquiries about membership. And *The Observer* on 6 October published the first Harris poll taken after the Militant speech. Labour had roared into a seven point lead with 39% of preferences, against 32% for the Conservatives and 27% for the Alliance. For the first time, Kinnock had overtaken David Owen and David Steel as the man thought most likely to make a good Prime Minister.

But he was right to be circumspect. While a speech can alter perceptions, changing reality is a longer and altogether less glamorous process. There was, as he said, a long slog ahead.

5   Seeing Red

Blunkett cannot really have thought that his foray into peace-making was going to effect a miraculous cure of the Liverpool crisis, that Hatton and his colleagues would be so stirred by the scenes at Bournemouth that they would collectively renounce the philosophy they had been preaching all their political lives. His initiative had been based on a false premise: that the Militant councillors were actively searching for a fiscal solution to Liverpool's budget crisis, whereas their actions had made it clear that what they sought was a political victory, a visible routing of the enemy. Failing that, an heroic defeat – such as the miners had suffered – was greatly preferable to a pragmatic compromise.

Hatton and his colleagues made this plain to a team of trade union leaders who visited the city soon after the conference. John Edmonds, the new General Secretary of the General, Municipal and Boilermakers Trade Union (GMBATU) was one of them. Although some of his members were among those handed redundancy notices (and others were in Hatton's Static Security Force) he went with an open mind. Certainly he was as opposed to the Government's squeeze on municipal budgets as anyone in the Labour movement. But, as he told colleagues on his return, it was not long before the true nature of the dispute became apparent. At their first meeting, Hatton told him: 'We refuse to abandon the weapon of chaos.' The union leaders recognized that using chaos as a weapon meant using their members – the chief victims of that chaos – as battle fodder. That was Kinnock's view too.

All the same, the Blunkett initiative went ahead. Kinnock visited Liverpool a fortnight after the conference. It is hard to imagine how relations between him and the Militant leadership could sink any lower after the Bournemouth showdown, but by the time he left Liverpool that seemingly impossible state had been achieved. Kinnock was jeered by Militant supporters as he arrived at the municipal offices. After his meeting with Council leaders, he went on a scheduled visit to a housing co-operative. Hatton and Mulhearn did not accompany him but took advantage of his absence to hold a press conference, giving their version of what had transpired between them. Mulhearn asserted that the Labour leader had undergone 'a miraculous transformation' in the two weeks since his conference speech and was now giving his full backing to Liverpool's struggle for extra resources.

Returning from the housing co-op, Kinnock indignantly denied

Mulhearn's claim. 'You have been given a misleading impression of what actually happened,' he assured reporters. He said he had reiterated that councils must stay within the law to win the battle for jobs and services. 'I repeated for the umpteenth time that they must not fantasize about what would happen if I were to make insistences and demands on governments.' No amount of Parliamentary support for Liverpool's illegal actions would persuade the Government to find the extra resources needed.

> If very active insistence by me and demands that proper provision should be made *could* have that effect, then naturally I should spend every day of every week making precisely these demands. But that was not the reality confronting us.

If Mulhearn could read a miraculous transformation into that declaration, said Kinnock, he was truly 'a seer of visions'. And to cap a fruitless day, the Liverpool leaders rejected Kinnock's plan to appoint mediators to look into complaints from minority groups against Sam Bond, the Council's principal race relations adviser.

The investigation into the city's finances, the key element in the Blunkett compromise, was undertaken by the treasurers of four local authorities, headed by Maurice Stonefrost, the former director-general of the GLC. They went to Liverpool to look at the books and by the end of October were ready with their recommendations on overcoming the estimated deficit of £80m. The most important were increases in rates and rents and the introduction of some 'creative accounting', by which the cost of housing repairs would be transferred from the revenue account to the capital account.

Kinnock's response was to issue a statement urging councillors to accept the report. In doing so he implied further criticism of their conduct.

> The sums of money which exist or can be secured have not been invented by the inquiry. They were there all the time for those who wanted to look ... Playing politics with people's jobs must stop and political dogma give way to realism.

Hatton answered by accusing Kinnock of playing into the hands of the Conservatives in attacking the people of Liverpool. Jack Cunningham went on television to boost the Kinnock line and two Liverpool MPs, Eric Heffer and Eddie Loyden, issued a long statement in support of the councillors. Their statement concluded:

> We therefore trust that the atmosphere of charged statements and

continued press arguments will cease and that the councillors, together with all those concerned, will be left in peace to decide what happens next.

There was precious little chance of that. Predictably, the Council decided to reject the Stonefrost report because it involved increasing rents and rates. The Militant councillors were not interested in raising more revenue from their electors: they wanted from the Government what they felt was rightly theirs and they would continue to demand it. A few weeks later they announced their own solution – a £30m loan from a consortium of Swiss banks to tide them over the crisis. John Cunningham warned them not to expect a future Labour Government to help them pay off the debt.

That was, in effect, the end of the Blunkett initiative. The rejection of the Stonefrost report left the way clear for Kinnock to initiate the inquiry into the Liverpool District Labour Party that he had been wanting to launch since the conference. The NEC were due to meet in the last week in November. To get them in the mood for action Kinnock made yet another uncompromising anti-Militant speech, this time to the Fabian Society on 12 November 1985. He attacked the tendency as too dishonest to acknowledge its membership, too cowardly to act as a separate party outside Labour and too contemptuous of the people it called comrades to tell them the truth. Its adherents were parasites on the Labour movement, breaching the party's trust and exploiting its libertarian instincts:

> They use impossibilism as a calculated means of setting artificial demands so that they can accuse the party leadership and union leaders of timidity or betrayal when those demands are not recognized. The Labour Party, with its traditions of openness and tolerance, is not readily equipped to deal with such perversity.

The NEC met on 27 November. David Blunkett proposed a motion calling on Larry Whitty to institute an inquiry into the Liverpool party. Then Tom Sawyer of the National Union of Public Employees (NUPE) proposed an amendment, seconded by Neil Kinnock, that the inquiry team should be drawn from the NEC itself and the district party suspended until it was completed. The motion as amended was carried by 21 votes to 5, the five being the left hard core – Eric Heffer, Tony Benn, Margaret Beckett, Dennis Skinner and Frances Curran. The soft left voted solidly with Kinnock and the right: something that would not have happened a year earlier.

Benn spoke against the idea of centralized control being exerted on party branches and Heffer said people should stop attacking each other and unite to fight the Conservatives. Roy Hattersley replied that there had been actual and political corruption in Liverpool. In a television interview Kinnock called Militant 'a maggot in the body of the Labour Party' and he explained his strategy: 'I want them out of the Labour Party. The inquiry is not a soft option, it is a tough option. We shall act toughly.' Militant was on its way out and social democracy on the way in. The future for Militant was, in his view, 'very bleak and very short term'.

Dennis Skinner did not wholly agree. He warned his NEC colleagues that the weeding-out process might last longer than Kinnock hoped: and he was right. The original January deadline was extended to the end of February, as the team interviewed more than 100 witnesses in their search for evidence of irregularities in the running of the Liverpool party. Larry Whitty said they were prepared to take 'as long as necessary to ensure that natural justice prevails'.

The hearings were in secret but that did not prevent the press from speculating about them – indeed it gave them scope for the manufacture of some highly-coloured tales. Reports said that some sessions would take place in a 'safe house' in Liverpool where witnesses would be protected from possible Militant vengeance: in fact most were held in the Engineering Union's office near the city centre. Two of the inquiry team flew to Aberdeen to take evidence from Irene Buxton, formerly a close friend of Hatton's who had split with him and the Militant tendency at about the same time. The *Sunday Mirror* revealed the existence of a dossier on intimidation and corruption: a council worker had been beaten up after speaking out against Militant; others had received threatening telephone calls.

Mulhearn said such allegations of corruption and intimidation were 'a monstrous slander'. Yet an interview in *New Society*, published in the week the NEC agreed to the inquiry, suggested that, at least as far as intimidation was concerned, there was substance to the charges. The man interviewed was John Hamilton, who had plucked up the courage to place his head momentarily above the parapet. He told the magazine:

I am the leader but I don't have power. Militant are trying to box me off from the media. They say I'm out when I'm in. The press aren't helping by not recognizing me as leader, giving Militant an enormous public image ... How much is Militant and how much is gangsterism? You can't get a job here unless you belong to Militant. It's not for no reason that Hatton has minders.

The inquiry, combined with Kinnock's sustained invective, had one desirable effect even before it was complete: it emboldened local parties to weed Militant supporters from their own ranks. A handful of parties

(*Above*) The Dream Ticket: At the 1983 party conference at Brighton, Neil Kinnock and Roy Hattersley acknowledge delegates' cheers after their election as leader and deputy leader. On Kinnock's immediate left, Eric Heffer already seems to view the prospect with foreboding.
(Stefano Cagnoni/Report)

(*Left*) Three years on at Blackpool in September 1986, Neil, now firmly established as leader, hugs Glenys after his acclaimed conference speech. Behind them is the party's new rose emblem, launched two days earlier.
(Andrew Wiard/Report)

(*Above*) With the coal dispute in its dying weeks, Neil Kinnock finally responds to pressure from miners' supporters to visit a picket line. Early on a cold January morning in 1985, he stands outside the mine at Celynen South, near Newbridge in his South Wales constituency, while a picket shouts at a strike breaker. (*Stephens of Cardiff*)

(*Opposite*) At the Durham Miners' Gala in July 1984, with the strike four months old, Kinnock and Arthur Scargill manage a public show of solidarity, despite growing differences between them over the conduct of the dispute. (*Stefano Cagnoni/Report*)

FOREIGN FORAYS

(*Above*) In November 1984, Kinnock places a wreath on the tomb of the unknown soldier in Moscow, while foreign affairs spokesman Denis Healey looks on.   (*O. Porokhovnikov/TASS*)

(*Below*) In Ethiopia in August 1985, he watches relief aid for famine victims being loaded on to RAF planes.   (*Andrew Wiard/Report*)

FRIEND AND FOE

(*Above*) Kinnock's patron and predecessor as leader, Michael Foot.   (*Jon Blau/Camera Press*)

(*Below*) Eric Heffer, consistent hard left opponent of the leadership, who walked off the platform at the 1985 party conference at Bournemouth in protest at Kinnock's attack on the Militant tendency.
(*The Photo Source*)

THE MILITANT EXPULSIONS

(*Above*) Tony Mulhearn (*left*) and Derek Hatton shout to their supporters and the press as they wait to appear before the National Executive Committee at the party's Walworth Road headquarters in May 1986. (*The Press Association*)

(*Below*) Larry Whitty, general secretary of the party, runs the gauntlet of hostile Militant followers as he arrives at Walworth Road for the hearings. (*The Press Association*)

(*Above*) The Chesterfield by-election. In February 1984, Kinnock campaigns for the return to Parliament of his ideological opponent, Tony Benn, watched by another stalwart of the hard left, Dennis Skinner.
(*Daily Telegraph*)

(*Below*) On the march for jobs, marking the 50th anniversary of the original 1936 march from Jarrow.
(*The Press Association*)

(*Above*) Glenys outside Molesworth Common cruise missile base with Joan Ruddock (*left*), former chair of the Campaign for Nuclear Disarmament.   (*Andrew Wiard/Report*)

(*Below*) Neil and Glenys Kinnock in 1987 with their children Rachel (15) and Stephen (17).
(*David Gamble*)

began disciplinary proceedings and expelled a few Militants – not enough to weaken the tendency significantly but at least an indication that opinion in the party was moving. The trend worried such as Heffer, who wrote in his book *Labour's Future*:

> The truth of the matter is that the right of the party have got the bit between their teeth and, whether it is liked or not, the left will be witch-hunted in ever widening circles.

The publicity given to his anti-Militant moves helped Kinnock's long-term personal strategy. The image was being presented of a leader and a party on a genuine mission of reform. It plainly worried the Conservatives. In a Commons debate on the inner cities in mid-December their chairman, Norman Tebbit, devoted a large part of his speech to an assault on Militant and on the Labour Party, which he found guilty by association. Kinnock tried to intervene. When Tebbit refused to give way, the Labour leader made taunting and mock threatening gestures with the collar of his jacket. As Labour MPs shouted their protests, Tebbit said he could eat Kinnock for breakfast and added: 'I don't know where he's been but he seems a little carried away with himself.'

Kinnock later denied the imputation that he had been drinking, explaining that he had been to a decorous family dinner party in a restaurant to celebrate his daughter Rachel's 14th birthday. In fact he was exceedingly angry at Tebbit for trying to score party political points during what should have been a serious debate about one of the country's most intractable problems. The feud continued next day when the two men met by chance in the Commons lobby. Tebbit accused Kinnock of being frightened to go on television with him, adding he was not impressed by the Labour leader's macho gestures. When Kinnock asked him how old he was, he replied: 'I'm not too old to take you on, sonny boy'. Kinnock retorted that he wished Tebbit was younger, but meanwhile he should grow up. The papers suggested that both men might be under strain.

It was an unseemly incident, whoever was to blame. Since his election as leader Kinnock had consciously acted with more restraint than was once his custom: he used to retail with some relish the story of his dust-up in the lavatory at a party conference after he declined to vote for Tony Benn for the deputy leadership. His quick temper has occasionally led him half-seriously to threaten violence to people who shout insults as he leaves or enters buildings. It is part of the aggressive streak that can be admired in an ambitious young man in South Wales, swaggering noisily with his friends in the pubs of Tredegar; but it looks undignified in a political leader.

(Kinnock can usually keep the instinct under control, although he did blow his top embarrassingly in December 1986, when he roughed up two young men, one of whom had foolishly banged him on the head with a rolled-up newspaper while he was with Glenys at an Indian restaurant near their home in Ealing. Kinnock followed the men outside and sought an apology, but did not get one. According to the *Sun*, the man maintained that Kinnock head-butted him and broke his glasses. Kinnock denied it – but whatever the exact details his friends thought he was wrong to have let himself be provoked, even if his mail bag suggested that most people thought he had acted admirably.)

Apart from its implications on the way Kinnock conducts himself, the Tebbit incident was significant politically. It indicated that the Conservatives believed left-wing extremism to be a theme they could exploit at the next election. Two days later the Conservative Central Office published a pamphlet seeking to explain that the extremists were not an aberration but an ineradicable component of the Labour Party. Bernie Grant, Derek Hatton and Ken Livingstone were named as the demons in chief. 'Skilful camouflage and a ready smile have been employed to conceal the half-hidden face of today's Labour Party,' said the pamphlet. 'The success of a leader of the Labour Party is measured by the number of his own supporters he can attack.'

That was as unfair as any overtly party political diatribe, but there was a kernel of truth in the last sentence; one that was being noted by commentators not entirely unsympathetic to Labour. The *Guardian* columnist Hugo Young had observed that nearly all the highlights of Kinnock's first two years as leader had been to do with tackling the problems of his party. Only occasionally did they concern the wider political debate. Kinnock's office responded by sending Young a shaft of speeches about broader topics.

But as if to prove Young's point, the NEC was the setting for another very public row on 18 December 1985. The issue was the fate of Paul Green, a Sheffield City Councillor and Militant supporter, whose expulsion was recommended by the local party but opposed by David Blunkett, the leader of the Sheffield Council as well as a member of the NEC. When Blunkett spoke against the expulsion, Tony Benn rounded on him, saying he should have thought of the consequences before allying himself with Kinnock and the right over the anti-Militant moves in Liverpool. Benn added: 'The party starts here with the expulsion of this man and ends up joining the SDP.'

Kinnock snapped that to talk of drifting towards the SDP was a 'mischievous hallucination' on Benn's part. He went on to denounce the view that Militant supporters were no more sinister as a group than readers of *Tribune* or the soft left Labour Co-ordinating Committee

(LCC). That claim was 'part of their organized falsehood – revolutionary truth as the Trotskyists call it, damned lies as the rest of us call it.'

Because of Blunkett's opposition to expelling Green, Kinnock was deserted for this one vote by four soft left members of the NEC – Michael Meacher, Audrey Wise, Eddie Haigh and Tom Sawyer. The expulsion was approved by a single vote, 14 to 13.

*   *   *

The NEC team's majority report on the Liverpool party was eventually published at the end of February, 1986. Its main charges were that the District Labour Party exercised too much control over the City Council, and that there was an atmosphere of intimidation at its meetings. It suggested that the GC had been packed with Militant sympathizers by the ruse of affiliating more trade union delegates than was justified by union membership in the wards in question. And it named 16 people who should be charged with breaking the party rules by virtue of their association with Militant – charges which, if proved, were certain to end in expulsion. A minority report signed by Audrey Wise and Margaret Beckett recommended no expulsions. The majority report was accepted by 19 votes to 10 after an all-day meeting of the NEC.

The Militant leaders did their best to delay the process. They won a High Court ruling that the eight members of the inquiry team could not sit on the NEC while their report was being acted upon and the cases against the Militants were being heard. As the first hearings began against the accused (down to 12 after four cases had been dropped for lack of evidence), seven left-wing members of the NEC walked out. With the eight people on the inquiry also absent, there was no longer a quorum. The hearings had to be adjourned.

At a press conference at Walworth Road, both Kinnock and Blunkett denounced the walkout. Kinnock called it 'a deliberate and planned wrecking tactic' that exposed the weakness of the left's position. He announced that he would put forward an immediate proposal to amend NEC standing orders to alter the quorum to 50% plus one of those entitled to attend meetings. That would mean that the eight not entitled to attend the disciplinary hearings would not be included when calculating the 50% plus one figure. In simpler and more practical terms it meant that a walkout of seven members would not leave the Committee inquorate.

Militant leaders were exploiting every possible ounce of publicity from the expulsion threats. In May they organized a meeting in Newbridge, in Kinnock's own constituency, where Hatton denounced the local hero. Busloads of supporters came from as far away as Liverpool, but were afforded some of their own treatment when Kinnock loyalists paraded outside the meeting with placards. There are scarcely any Militants in Islwyn itself, although there is a group in Cardiff.

It was 21 May before the NEC was able to get itself organized sufficiently to conduct the first of the expulsion hearings. A crowd of Militant supporters had gathered in the soft early summer rain around the entrance to the party headquarters in Walworth Road. Carrying banners urging an end to witch-hunts, they sang the Internationale, cheered their threatened comrades and booed all but the left-wingers on the NEC. Five cases were due to be heard that day, beginning with Tony Mulhearn, president of the Liverpool District Labour Party. Even though he must have known that these were his last days in the party, Mulhearn had mustered an impressive armoury of delaying tactics. Procedural points were raised repeatedly, each one having to be considered solemnly by the NEC. Kinnock knew that if the committee deviated even by a fraction from correct and fair procedures, Militant would not hesitate to go to court to have the expulsions reversed.

It was a ludicrous pantomime, tying up 20 of the senior figures in the British Labour movement for hours on end, when they certainly had less tedious things to do: less tedious but, in Kinnock's view, not more important things. Under the constitution, the full NEC was the final arbiter on expulsions and there was no escaping the responsibility. When the constitution had been drawn up nobody anticipated that any party member would go to such lengths to exploit it. There was now a good case for changing the rules and handing such matters to a disciplinary sub-committee – which was duly done at the 1986 party conference. But as things stood in May, only the NEC could act. Kinnock was convinced that, until it did, he could never be sure that some random act of political vandalism from Liverpool would not scupper his carefully planned electoral strategy. And unless they saw it through to the bitter end now, who knew what further scope for delay the Militants might find in the ensuing weeks?

It took longer even than Kinnock had foreseen at his most pessimistic. The hearing began at 10 am with a discussion about whether the defendants should be allowed legal representation. That occupied the whole morning. After lunch Mulhearn sought a further adjournment but was refused; so the hearing proper could finally begin. The other defendants, meanwhile, were ushered to Larry Whitty's office, on the first floor of the building at the front, to await their turn. The office was chosen because it was large and comfortable – and Whitty, engaged all day at the NEC hearings, would not be needing it. Whoever decided to let the accused wait there, however, had failed to take into account that its windows were directly above the steps outside the building where the Militant supporters were gathered. This did not escape Hatton. He lifted the sash window, poked his head out and joked cheerily with his

118

supporters and members of the press. It was an irresistible picture for the television news bulletins and provided Hatton with more media coverage.

Peter Mandelson, in charge of Labour publicity since the previous autumn, was exasperated by the lack of foresight in the decision to use a front-facing office as a waiting room. It was the sort of self-inflicted propaganda wound that he had been hired to prevent. He spoke sharply to those responsible and had some rooms cleared at the back of the building on the fourth floor – near where the hearings were taking place – for the defendants to wait in.

Hatton had further publicity plans. He had booked a room in the old town hall across the road for an afternoon press conference, where he railed at the injustice of the 'kangaroo court'. By 9.45 in the evening, when the MPs on the NEC had to be taken to the House of Commons for a vote, the first case, Mulhearn's, had still not been resolved. Now it was Mulhearn's turn to hog the cameras. At the foot of the steps by the front entrance, he said he assumed the verdict would go against him, because the right-wing majority on the NEC were bowing to 'the wishes of the Fleet Street barons in expelling good socialists from the Labour Party'. Kinnock, on his way back from the vote, looked weary but adopted a determinedly chirpy manner. No matter how long it took, he declared, they would stick with it. 'I never say I'm going to do something without doing it.'

It was past 1 am before the NEC finally voted to expel the Liverpool party president. The other four cases were held over until the following day but the best-known target was allowed to escape temporarily from the net. Derek Hatton had originally been scheduled to be dealt with fourth, but he told the NEC that he needed to be back in Liverpool for an important meeting on the 22nd. So they switched him to second, promising to deal with him directly after Mulhearn, even if it meant staying in session all night. As the evening drew on, Hatton decided not to test either his stamina or that of the party leadership. He took the last train home from Euston, complaining: 'I've been hanging around all day.' Before he left, he warned the NEC not to hear his case in his absence, threatening further court action if they did. Kinnock and his colleagues did not want to risk that; so Hatton won a reprieve for a few more weeks.

After Mulhearn, the expulsion process quickened only slightly. The following day just two more cases were brought to their conclusion in 12 hours. To achieve that, Kinnock and Hattersley both had to miss Prime Minister's Question Time and ask Denis Healey to stand in for them. Kinnock was forced to cancel a speech at a Savoy Hotel dinner where he was to have presented the National Press Awards. Gerald Kaufman, the shadow Home Secretary, was his last-minute replacement; but Neil and

Glenys Kinnock did get there by 11, in time to join in the dancing at the end. Always an energetic dancer, that night he jived with special abandon. After two days of mind-numbing wrangles with stolid fanatics, it was a welcome chance to burn off some of the accumulated frustration.

The cases against Hatton and the remainder of the accused were scheduled to be heard on 12 June, but this time Hatton chose not to turn up at all, claiming more urgent council business. The High Court refused an injunction to prevent the hearing going ahead without him. When he heard of his expulsion he was defiant, insisting that he would continue to operate as deputy Council leader and to attend party meetings, as long as his local party recognized him as a member.

Two more expulsions were confirmed that day. Kinnock was playing a leading role at the hearings, effectively that of prosecutor-in-chief. He made sure that he was carefully briefed on each case and had a complete dossier of charges against each individual in front of him. Indeed it was his single-minded determination to see things through that cost him a defeat. One of the cases that followed Hatton's involved Carol Darby, accused of being a full-time organizer for Militant in Liverpool. Some of the soft left members of the NEC thought the charges against her were unconvincing. David Blunkett moved that they should be dropped; but Kinnock refused to give way gracefully and insisted on going to a vote. Darby's case was dismissed by 11 votes to 9.

The following day Terry Harrison, vice-president of the Liverpool District Labour Party, was expelled. An eighth expulsion was completed in July and two other cases were dropped. By the time of the 1986 party conference at Blackpool only one case was outstanding. Felicity Dowling, secretary of the district party, managed to delay her expulsion until after the conference, which she attended as a delegate. Hatton, Mulhearn and the others had appealed to the conference to reverse the decisions of the NEC. Monday morning, 29 September, was set aside for the debate, from which the press and visitors were excluded. The expelled Militants were at Blackpool but decided to walk out without offering any defence, in protest against being allowed only five minutes each to argue their cases. There had never been any chance of the appeals succeeding, because the major union block votes were certain to be cast against the Militants. A more important decision taken by the conference was to approve the plan to set up a National Constitutional Committee to take over the disciplinary role of the NEC. No more wearying nights at Walworth Road for Kinnock and the other hard-pressed Executive members.

It took many more months to make the expulsions effective. The district and ward Labour parties at first refused to recognize them. Hatton continued to act as chairman of the Broadgreen constituency party. Other parties used devices such as 'informal meetings' to allow expelled people to continue to attend. In August Joyce Gould, the director of organization at Walworth Road, was refused a hearing at a meeting of the Labour group of councillors. The NEC's organization committee wrote to members of the group, ordering them to reconstitute it, removing the expelled members from office. The following month Larry Whitty went to Liverpool to expedite the process but only 14 Labour councillors – including the leader John Hamilton – attended the meeting he convened. The majority, 34 of them, went to a rival affair attended by Hatton and Mulhearn. In October Whitty called another meeting of the group, but felt obliged to suspend it when Hatton and Mulhearn turned up. Then the majority of Labour councillors refused to sign a commitment to abide by the party rules for Labour groups on councils.

When the group was eventually reconstituted in November, the Militant majority took their revenge on John Hamilton for siding with Kinnock and Whitty: he was removed from the council leadership and replaced by Tony Byrne, the most prominent Militant supporter in the city to have escaped expulsion. Hatton was originally retained as his deputy but resigned when it became plain that Kinnock would seek to expel Byrne for countenancing such a flagrant breach of the rules. But the move against Byrne went ahead anyway. On 17 December the NEC voted to refer his case to the new National Constitutional Committee, due to come into being in January 1987. Kinnock made it plain that the Militant councillors' treatment of the long-serving Hamilton was an important reason for acting against Byrne. He said:

> Let us not forget what was done to John Hamilton. That has not been forgotten or forgiven in Liverpool. It is demoralizing for people in Liverpool to see that John Hamilton has been kicked out because there is a little clique who for one reason or another want to keep Derek Hatton in the public eye.

So Byrne seemed likely to go the way of Hatton, Mulhearn and the rest some time in 1987. The party nationally has the ultimate sanction over membership and over groups that operate in its name. If the constituency parties in Liverpool wish to remain in existence they will have in the end to obey party rules and exclude the expelled Militants from their meetings. If they refuse, the branches can be suspended and recreated by people willing to toe the line. In the case of Broadgreen – Hatton's branch – the threat is especially potent because it is the seat of Terry Field, one of Militant's only two MPs. If non-Militants took over a reformed constituency party, Field would not be reselected next time. It was a slow process, but by the end of 1986, fifteen months after the

Bournemouth speech, Militant were clearly being forced to loosen their grip on party institutions. And because Kinnock had turned the battle against the tendency into a personal crusade, Labour's opponents could not accuse him of being soft on the hard left.

*   *   *

One effect of Mulhearn's expulsion ought to have been to damp down a potentially inflammable dispute in Knowsley North, a safe Labour seat on the north-eastern fringe of Liverpool. The sitting MP, with a firm majority of 17,191 in 1983, was Robert Kilroy-Silk, a good-looking right-winger and a junior spokesman on home affairs until he quit that office in October 1985. He stepped down from the front bench because he was engaged in a fight to retain his candidacy against opposition from Militant sympathizers in the local party, who wanted to nominate Mulhearn in his place. (There is a formidable Militant presence in Knowsley, where Derek Hatton used to hold a part-time job with the Council before he found, earlier in 1986, that he could not spare the time from Liverpool politics.)

In his book *Hard Labour*, Kilroy-Silk describes how Militant packed the local party's General Committee with trade union nominees whose credentials were dubious and who would certainly vote for Mulhearn in a contest for the candidacy. With their votes Mulhearn – had he remained a party member – would have defeated Kilroy-Silk. But in November 1985, when Mulhearn was still eligible to stand, the NEC suspended the reselection process so as to look into Kilroy-Silk's complaints about the suspect delegates. Mulhearn's expulsion, along with the NEC investigation, made it likely that Kilroy-Silk would have been reselected before the end of 1986.

That, at least, was the confident prediction of Kinnock and his advisers. They would certainly do all they could to prevent the election of a third Militant MP, especially one with such a tough reputation as Mulhearn. But their confidence in their ability to save the seat for Kilroy-Silk was never to be tested. At the end of July, 1986, the MP suddenly announced that he was going to quit Parliament forthwith. He explained that his year-long battle with Militant had sapped his spirit:

> I cannot continue for three years being constantly undermined, abused, shouted at and vilified by my own party and remain an enthusiast for politics . . . I never thought this day would come, but the extremists have destroyed my wish to carry on . . . They are ruthless conspiratorial revolutionaries who represent something very different from the Labour Party I joined and will continue to belong to.

In any case he had just been offered a glamorous job hosting an afternoon talk show on BBC Television. The book about his struggle with Militant was already written and had been sold to *The Times* for a five-part serialization. His media career was off to a splendid start.

The immediate prospect looked less rosy for Kinnock. He felt badly let down by Kilroy-Silk, who had given him no advance warning of his intention to quit and force Labour into fighting a by-election where the choice of candidate was bound to be tricky. The party *had* given the threatened MP support against the extremists. That was why Kinnock described Kilroy-Silk's allegations as 'rubbish', provoking a pained response from the budding TV star: 'I'm very sad that Neil should put party on this occasion before truth.' The sale of the book to *The Times* was salt in Kinnock's wound, because Labour had been boycotting Rupert Murdoch's publications since they moved to Wapping at the beginning of 1986. They were being produced by new technology without the services of the print unions, who picketed the plant constantly until the dispute was called off in January 1987.

Although Mulhearn was out of the reckoning for the candidacy, the Knowsley North party was unlikely to select anyone acceptable to the leadership, especially since the locals felt as much betrayed by Kilroy-Silk as Kinnock did. As the selection process began, a front-runner appeared on the horizon from Strasbourg. He was Leslie Huckfield, Member of the European Parliament for Merseyside East, a politician with a reputation as a maverick. A former junior minister in the Department of Trade and Industry, Huckfield had moved steadily to the left and in 1982 he was one of 10 MPs who formed a group called Labour Liaison '82, with the intention of getting Kinnock and Joan Lestor voted off the NEC, as retribution for their failure to support Benn in the election for deputy leader. Kinnock survived but Lestor was not re-elected – and nor, ironically, was Huckfield.

He quickly lost his Parliamentary seat, too, in the 1983 general election, despite switching from Nuneaton to Wigan, which he hoped would be easier to win. When chosen for the European Parliament the following year, he promised the parties selecting him that he would not seek a seat at Westminster while serving in Strasbourg. However, he now claimed that the parties had released him from that commitment. Although it is hard for any politician to make news at Strasbourg, Huckfield had done his best by using a megaphone to harangue his surprised European colleagues.

Huckfield does not belong to the Militant organization but he did once speak at a rally organized by the tendency. He was not the kind of candidate that Kinnock, even if he could ignore their history of personal animosity, wanted to carry Labour's colours in a part of the country where he was already engaged in a struggle for the party's soul, and with a general election perhaps no more than six months away. Moreover Kilroy-Silk's former agent, Peter Fisher, warned that he would run as an independent if a left-wing candidate such as Huckfield were chosen.

At their September meeting, the NEC halted the selection procedure after complaints from members in the Euro-constituency that Huckfield was going back on his word. They alleged that the meeting at which he was freed from his 1984 promise had not been properly called. The NEC has the authority to prevent serving Euro-MPs from contesting Westminster seats, but simply to use that power would not have been enough, for the local party would probably have replaced Huckfield with someone just as unacceptable. The NEC also has the power to impose a candidate in case of necessity, although it is seldom used, since the party prides itself on the autonomy enjoyed by its branches.

At their October meeting the NEC effectively imposed a candidate by advising the party to choose George Howarth, a member of the right-wing Amalgamated Engineering Union (AEU) and a former deputy leader of Knowsley Council – scarcely a charismatic figure but loyal to the national leadership. The NEC added that if the party would not endorse Howarth he would be imposed anyway. The constituency party took High Court action to try to block the NEC move. When the court ruled against them, local party leaders said they would not take part in the by-election campaign.

Kinnock dispatched Jack Straw, junior shadow spokesman on the environment and one of his most trusted lieutenants, to organize the Knowsley North campaign without the aid of the constituency party. Straw took with him a team of people from Westminster, one a young American woman unfamiliar with the ways of the north. Buying a snack in a chip shop, she wrongly identified the bowl of mushy peas on display as an avocado dish. 'I'll have some of that guacamole,' she declared with confidence – providing Militant supporters with an anecdote for their speeches, and ammunition for their claim that Howarth's campaign was being run by outsiders unfamiliar with local concerns.

Knowsley is a bleak place of windswept and poorly maintained council estates, standing amid charmless man-made landscapes of undulating grass dotted with scrawny trees, surrounded by motorways. Many lower windows of the tower blocks are boarded up, the boards defaced with graffiti. A large industrial area, built to provide economic backbone to this post-war suburb, is notable for the number of empty factory units. There are a handful of half-hearted shopping centres. Public transport is minimal. The few substantial public buildings are council offices or leisure facilities. Were it not for the public split in the party it should have been the ideal place for Labour to fight a by-election after seven years of Conservative rule, for it illustrates two of the chief criticisms of Government policy – high unemployment and a lack of resources devoted to maintaining housing and public services.

After Prime Minister's Questions in the Commons on Thursday 6 November 1986, Kinnock flew to Liverpool Airport and drove to the Knowsley Civic Centre in Kirkby; a low, spacious building dating from the 1970s, alongside an extensive car park. Outside, he was greeted by some 50 protestors, mostly members of the local Labour Party who were not working in the campaign and who had been refused admission to the hall to hear Kinnock speak. Entrance was by ticket and tickets had only been allotted to campaign workers. 'No imposed candidate,' shouted the demonstrators. 'Let's have democracy here.'

Jack Straw and his campaign team had done well to fill the hall with some 400 party loyalists, although they had been obliged to bring some in buses from outlying districts. ('Anybody here from Knowsley?' was another quip from the demonstrators outside.) It was a subdued audience – older, on average, than the normal attendance at party functions. As Kinnock spoke, on a modified version of the platform that had been used at the Blackpool party conference, they listened attentively but without extravagant enthusiasm – except once, soon after the beginning of the speech, when a man near the front, who had slipped in despite the security precautions, shouted: 'Imposed candidate.' As he was bundled out Kinnock snapped: 'You may be able to control things by shouting people down where you come from, but you've got the wrong bloke here.' As it often does, the spontaneous putdown of the heckler drew the most eager applause of the evening.

At the end of the speech he sprang a surprise. George Howarth had been absent from the campaign trail all week with a painful twisted back. Now he was produced with a flourish, the sick man made whole. The candidate made a short speech, then joined in singing 'The Red Flag'. While most of those on the platform knew the words, not many in the hall did. They were more fluent with 'Here we go, here we go, here we go...'

Kinnock ran the gauntlet of more abuse from the angry Militants as he left and drove to the Derby Lodge at Huyton, the smartest hotel in the area, where he and his team from London were staying. He drank at the bar with Straw and some of the key campaign workers. This is the part of campaigning he likes best: the speech over, he has only to be his normal cheery self, buying his round, pressing the flesh, telling jokes, maybe a few seemingly indiscreet stories about his colleagues or his opponents. He had booked a table in the hotel restaurant for dinner at 9.30: it had slipped to 10.30 before he and his party sat down to eat, and it was past midnight by the time they got to bed.

He enjoys much of the formal business of campaigning, too; although he never really looks forward to the compulsory press conference. That was his first engagement the following day, at 8.30 am, again in the Civic Centre. He had some harsh words for the members of the local party who had demonstrated the night before. He resented their having taken the national party to court, involving expenditure of funds needed to fight elections. He thought it likely that, after the by-election, the NEC would take action against the Knowsley North party. Questioning turned to the national political scene, to opinion polls showing the Conservatives regaining the lead. 'Our polls in the seats we have to win to gain a majority show that we're in the lead there.' What if there were a hung Parliament? 'Those who think there will be one are confusing arithmetic with politics.'

Then two TV interviews. So far, it had been the kind of morning that makes life seem one long interview: the eternal search for the right answer freshly phrased; the constant lookout for the banana skin that the interviewer is trying to slip under your feet. After that, he was ready to go on the campaign trail proper, where life as an extended interview gives way to life as a series of photo opportunities. First to the industrial estate, to visit a firm of printers owned by two Labour supporters who started it with their redundancy payments when a big local printing works closed down. They were printing the by-election literature and, partly so that they would not have far to deliver it, they had allowed the large shed at the back of their works to be used as a campaign head-quarters. A score of volunteers were seated at a central table, stuffing envelopes. Kinnock was photographed with them, with the two proprietors, holding up a poster, looking intelligently at a computer terminal. What happens to all those pictures? He seldom sees any of them.

He enjoys exchanging badinage with party workers and has a special way with women of a certain age. They confide in him, he in them, and he twinkles reassuringly. They discussed the candidate's problems with his back. 'I expect everyone here has had back problems,' he observed sweepingly. The talk moved on to possible treatments and he disclosed how, at the Derby Lodge the night before, he had had his first disappointing encounter with a jacuzzi: 'You know when you're bathing the kids and make the water swirl around – well that's all it is. Nothing happens.' The women clucked with sly pleasure. They might have guessed as much.

If the cameras were busy at the print works they were frantic at his next and last port of call, the Westvale primary school, where he crouched repeatedly for picture sessions with groups of lovable small children. He bounced them on his knee and narrowly avoided stepping on one: 'I can see the headlines – Kinnock steps on children sensation.' The headmaster illustrated the deprived nature of the area with some statistics: out of 205 pupils who eat school dinners, 180 come from families poor enough to get them free. Over a generous buffet lunch, Kinnock moved between groups of parents and discussed the future of education – which used, after all, to be his special subject. There was just time to chat with the school cleaners, and sign an autograph for the local police constable, before he was driven away to the airport.

Labour's achievement at Knowsley North was to overcome the embarrassments of having to impose a candidate and alienate the local party, then of the absence of the candidate for several days in mid-campaigning, and to turn it into a fairly normal by-election in a safe Labour seat. The Liberals tried to exploit the Militant issue but found it counter-productive, because the Labour camp were able to assert that they had actually done something to halt the spread of the tendency's influence, rather than merely denounce it. There were the usual allegations of dirty tricks; and a bizarre incident involving dead rats apparently being thrown over someone's garden fence.

Despite early fears that the Liberals might prove a threat, the swing to them was held to 14%, not nearly enough to weaken Labour's grip on the seat. Howarth won with 17,403 votes, a majority of 6,724 over the Liberal, Rosemary Cooper. The Conservative, Roger Brown, polled only 1,960 votes, a quarter of his party's tally in 1983. It would have been an overstatement to call it a triumph for anyone, but Labour had avoided disaster by making the best use of their organizational skills and employing the big stick against the troublesome local party. In sanctioning such decisive action, Kinnock was sounding a warning to other potentially rebellious local parties. The message of Knowsley North was that all the indignant posturing in the world cannot alter the fact that, in the end, the leader and Walworth Road are in charge.

*　　*　　*

Militant's other main source of strength within the party, the Labour Party Young Socialists, was just as hard to deal with as the quagmire of Merseyside. In April 1985 the Youth Trade Union Rights Campaign (YTURC), an offshoot of the LPYS, organized a half-day strike of students to protest against unemployment among young people and the iniquities of the Youth Training Scheme. Kinnock denounced the strike. 'The kids are being exploited by a bunch of dafties,' he said. The following month the NEC decided to launch an inquiry into YTURC and to bar its officers from working at the Walworth Road headquarters.

Kinnock did not want to disband the youth movement – a tactic that had been tried too often in the past and had never proved an effective long-term solution. To wield the big stick against an organization of enthusiastic young people can provoke sympathy and support for them even among people who do not share their extreme views. But there were things the party could do to weaken Militant's grip on the LPYS. Like the moves against the Liverpool Militants, they would require great patience. Victory would go to whoever had the greatest staying power – and Kinnock was confident that it would be him.

The squeeze on LPYS began at Walworth Road itself, where it was decided to merge the post of youth officer, held for ten years by the Militant supporter Andy Bevan, with that of student officer. The 1986 Blackpool conference agreed in principle that the upper age limit for LPYS should be cut from 26 to 21: that would bar about half the membership of 10,000, including many of the most active Militants. The same resolution – passed by an overwhelming 6,051,000 votes to 256,000 – called for a new annual youth conference attended by members of several party bodies, not just the LPYS. And there are plans to have the youth representative on the NEC elected on a wider franchise, so that the seat will not automatically go to a Militant supporter.

Kinnock is convinced that it must be a paramount aim of Labour to attract young people and that not enough has been done in that area in the past. The radical nature of the party ought to make it more attractive to the young than its rivals, but many youngsters are put off by the intense ferocity of the arguments deployed by those trying to recruit them and the commitment to the hard political grind that seems to be demanded of them. So there has been a conscious effort to soften the appeal, and Kinnock has taken a strong hand in it personally. In November 1985 he hosted a reception on the terrace of the House of Commons to launch Red Wedge, a group of established pop singers prepared to commit themselves to Labour. They included Billy Bragg, Paul Weller from the group Style Council, Attila the Stockbroker, Spandau Ballet, Strawberry Switchblade – all big names in popular music. 'We want to reach out to young people as a way of saying: "Come and look at us and find out",' said Kinnock, adding: 'Red Wedge is not the style of my latest haircut.' Earlier that year, as part of the same strategy, he had agreed to be seen in a pop video of Tracy Ullman singing 'My Guy', after meeting her on a television programme aimed at young people.

'He's got great charisma,' said Ullman, when asked why she had invited him. 'It wasn't any political reason or anything. He's just a nice bloke – very natural.' Some doubted the wisdom of such non-political exposure but on balance Kinnock thought it had helped both his and the party's image. 'Anyway,' he said, 'Rachel [his daughter] had a whale of a time.'

*   *   *

There was a final setback for Militant at the very end of 1986. The tendency has never succeeded in establishing a powerful presence in the trade union movement. So its followers were delighted and surprised when, in June, John Macreadie, an avowed Militant, was elected general secretary of the Civil and Public Services Association, the largest civil service union, by the narrowest of margins – 20,424 votes to 20,303. But the union executive was still dominated by right-wingers, who began receiving complaints that some branches had not been given the opportunity to vote. An inquiry by the Electoral Reform Society upheld the complaints and the ballot was retaken. This time the turnout was 65.5%, compared with only 39.9% on the first ballot; and the result was a resounding victory for the right-wing candidate, John Ellis, by 42,228 votes to 31,791. After the result was declared Ellis called on the Labour Party to take action against the LPYS, who had been campaigning enthusiastically for Macreadie.

So, 15 months after the Bournemouth speech, Militant had suffered some serious blows, most of them inflicted by the Labour leadership. Kinnock's extensively publicized achievement in curbing the extremists was reflected through most of 1986 by his and his party's standing in the opinion polls. Despite Kinnock's reservations about 'High Noon' politics, such gladiatorial enterprises are invariably good for the ratings.

*   *   *

The trade unions have to be handled much more subtly. Scare-mongering newspapers conjure up a lurid prospect of a government in hock to the unions and at the beck and call of their extremist leaders. They remind voters of previous Labour administrations, especially those led by Harold Wilson, when the TUC barons appeared to wield more real power than the Cabinet. They scorn what they portray as the old method of settling industrial disputes: union leaders trooping to Downing Street where, over beer and sandwiches, a pliant Prime Minister would give in to their every whim. The resulting pay deals, the story goes on, were the reason for the galloping inflation of the 1970s.

In recent years Arthur Scargill has been the favourite union bogey-man for the media. Despite Kinnock's blatant hostility towards him, the miners' leader is said to be the man who will really hold power if Labour is elected. The record shows that the opposite more often applies: Labour governments in the past have lost office because of their *failure* to create harmonious relations with the unions – which provide most of the party's income. The 1970 defeat was brought about partly by the opposition of organized labour to the abortive attempt by Harold Wilson's Government to introduce legal restraints into industrial relations, as set out in the notorious document *In Place of Strife*. Under this plan, pay increases would have been set by the Government and the freedom to strike restricted.

Wilson's later bid to replace this with a 'social contract' with the unions, based on solemn and binding understandings over pay levels but with no legal sanctions, was equally unsuccessful. The Thatcher victory in 1979 followed the 'winter of discontent', the series of industrial disputes that undermined the Callaghan administration. Since then the unions have seen their power reduced by Conservative legislation.

Relationships of mutual dependence are never easy to handle. The Labour Party could not exist without union financial support. Equally, without the party the unions could not make their voices heard at the highest levels of government. Yet unions tend to be unpopular with everyone except their own members. They make news only when taking or threatening industrial action, to the inconvenience of the populace at large. Because of Labour's close identity with the unions, major national strikes nearly always decrease support for the party (the coal dispute of 1974 being a notable exception). That was one of the considerations – although not the most important one – in Kinnock's decision to distance himself from the striking miners. At the same time, if a Labour leader persistently falls out with the unions he had better watch his back, since their block votes at conference and their strong presence on the NEC give them the power to decide policy and even, as a last resort, to initiate a change in the leadership.

The unions and the party get on better when Labour is out of office. Then, they sink their differences and work towards the aim of winning the next election. When it is won, the new government are never able to do as much for their chief patrons as either side would like. Disappointment and anger rear their heads. The first months of a Labour government see the unions determined to make life easy for the administration they helped elect; but the honeymoon seldom lasts long.

Kinnock inherited the leadership at a time that, though inauspicious for the party as a whole, placed him in the strongest possible position *vis-à-vis* the unions. The second successive election had been lost, this one by a shaming margin. The Conservative Government had declared open war on organized labour by banning union membership at GCHQ in Cheltenham, by introducing laws limiting the right to picket and call a strike, and by trying to end the unions' financial links with the Labour Party. The unions were demoralized. The new leader represented the only hope of a Labour victory. If the unions withheld support from him, they would be consigning themselves to a long exile – a permanent exile, if the Conservatives had their way – in the political wilderness. So he was not in their pockets. They needed him rather more than he needed them.

The TUC/Labour Party Liaison Committee meets nearly every month. It is a large and in some respects an unwieldy body of thirty members – eleven from the NEC, ten from the TUC and nine from the PLP, including Kinnock and Hattersley. It has served as the forge in which Labour's policy towards the unions has been hammered out since Kinnock became leader. For nearly two years the committee worked on a document that would amount to a definitive statement of how the unions and the next Labour government would relate to each other. It was called *A New Partnership, A New Britain* and it was to be presented to the TUC Congress in Blackpool in September 1985, as part of the Jobs and Industry Campaign that had been launched several months earlier to give focus to Labour's plans to cut unemployment and regenerate Britain's declining industrial base.

Kinnock introduced the document at a press conference on Tuesday, 6 August. The final wording was agreed by the Liaison Committee in June and went to the NEC for approval the same month. At the NEC there were complaints from the left that it begged the question of the position of law in industrial relations and pay bargaining. Benn, Heffer and their allies wanted a clause inserted to the effect that statutory wage restraint was no solution and would not be imposed by Labour. The initiative was quickly squashed by Larry Whitty, who said the wording had been formally approved by the TUC and could not be altered at this stage. Benn complained that as it stood the plan was 'violently anti-socialist'.

This view was not shared by the Conservatives, who began their assault on the document on the weekend before Kinnock was to launch it. Their campaign started with a speech by Peter Walker, the Secretary of State for Energy. He said the new agreement amounted to the most left-wing programme ever put before the British electorate and would leave a Labour government at the mercy of the unions. 'If you want Arthur Scargill to run the nation you have only to vote Labour at the next election,' he maintained. The *Daily Mail* led the paper with a report of Walker's speech headlined HOW SCARGILL COULD RULE FROM NUMBER TEN. David Owen, leader of the SDP, said it would mean 'total subservience by the PLP to their trade union bosses'. John Gummer, chairman of the Conservative Party, said the parts of the document devoted to creating new jobs would add 24% to income tax and mean doubling VAT to 30%.

When the document was finally published three days later it was, in the words of John Lloyd in the *Financial Times*, less lurid than its advance publicity. The section that had attracted all the attention was called 'Working Together'. It contained a promise to repeal the Conservative trade union legislation and replace it with new measures that would stress partnership between unions and management:

A key feature will be to provide workers with positive rights to information, consultation and representation in company decisions. The aim will be . . . to widen the collective bargaining agenda beyond wages to crucial investment decisions. We see new rights for workers as a catalyst for the extension of democratic involvement and accountability not just within the enterprise but also beyond it in sector and national planning.

The business plans of public and private enterprises, as well as regional plans, would be negotiated with the government and the unions. Details were given of the proposal for a National Investment Bank, aimed at regenerating industry and discouraging investment overseas.

Our partnership with trade union members must go beyond the place of work. It will mean working together to determine the nation's economic and social priorities.

Responding to the criticism at the launching press conference, Kinnock was forced on to the defensive. He insisted that co-operation with the unions did not mean they would dominate the next Labour government. There was no question of the work force being able to dictate management policy. Union representatives would have no power to summon managers and call them to account. There would be 'no blank cheque' for the unions.

With that phrase he was echoing Ron Todd, general secretary of the TGWU, who had used it in a television interview the previous June. Todd was not initially one of Kinnock's closest allies among the leaders of the large unions. They had got off to a bad start in April, when allegations came to the surface of irregularities in the ballot by which Todd had been elected general secretary as the left-wing candidate, defeating the right-winger George Wright. The BBC's *Newsnight* carried out an investigation and concluded that not all TGWU branches had been given the opportunity to vote.

Kinnock wrote to Moss Evans, the retiring general secretary, expressing his concern about the allegations and asking to be kept informed of the union's investigations into them. At one of his regular meetings with lobby correspondents he went further and recommended that the election should be re-run. But later he stated in a radio interview that this was not the only way to resolve the dispute. In the event Todd agreed to a re-run and won it comfortably.

On 30 June Todd was asked about *A New Partnership, A New Britain* in a television interview. He used the occasion to warn Kinnock that one union, at least, was not going to agree automatically to anything the leadership wanted:

I want the return of a Labour Government and if things start to cause us dissent what we should do is to think of the last six years of Mrs

Thatcher. If that does not bring us back to our senses then nothing will, but it is not an open cheque. I do not say as general secretary that I want Neil Kinnock as leader and Roy Hattersley as deputy leader and will sign an open cheque on anything that they want. There will be wide ranging discussions.

The Liaison Committee's document was duly discussed and approved at the 1985 TUC Congress. But in the event it was a half-hearted debate, for the union leaders had more pressing internal problems on their mind, threatening the unity of their movement. As part of the 1980 Employment Act, the Government had offered money to the unions to finance the balloting of members by post on whether they wanted to continue their political levies and on other internal matters. Because the TUC disapproved of the legislation, Congress had passed a resolution that this money should not be claimed from the Government. But the leaders of the AUEW decided that it would be unfair on their members to ask the union to foot the £1.2m cost of the ballot when it could be paid with outside money. When AUEW leaders consulted members on whether to accept, the vote was overwhelmingly in favour; so accept it they did. The electricians' union, the EETPU, also decided to apply for £200,000 from the Government, but by the time of the TUC Congress they had not actually received it. At Blackpool, most of the fire was directed at the engineers.

Norman Willis, general secretary of the TUC, had written to Gavin Laird, the tough Scottish general secretary of the AUEW, giving him an ultimatum: unless he undertook to comply with TUC policy, his union would be 'disciplined' – which meant expulsion from Congress. The EETPU would eventually have gone as well. It was not a coincidence that these were the two unions leading the way in signing single-union, no-strike deals with managements – a form of industrial relations previously anathema to the Labour movement. If expelled, the two unions would have set up a rival body to the TUC, trying to attract some of their more moderate colleagues. Laird replied to Willis's threat with a three-page letter conceding only that he would ballot his members again to see if they confirmed their previous decision. This time he would allow the TUC view to be expressed on the ballot paper and in the campaign.

Left-wingers saw Laird's letter as confirmation of the engineers' defiance and wanted the renegade union expelled. Legalistically, there was an unanswerable case for doing that, for TUC policy had been deliberately defied. The Conservatives were delighted with this unexpected bonus from their employment legislation. They may not have succeeded in getting any unions to drop their political levies, but to split the trade union movement would be an even more glorious achievement. Kinnock went to Blackpool to see if he could avert such a setback. When he got there he found Laird, Willis and two senior union leaders – Ron Todd and David Basnett, general secretary of GMBATU – in a crisis meeting. He stressed to them the importance of finding a compromise. In the end it was Todd who devised a face-saving formula. He said that Laird's letter, with its offer to hold a new ballot, could be interpreted as an acceptance of TUC authority. It was agreed to defer any decision until after the new ballot. That, too, resulted in a big majority for taking the money. The move for expulsions was quietly dropped. By the end of 1986, fifteen unions affiliated to the TUC had applied for Government money to fund postal ballots of their members.

The Government's employment legislation included a second requirement for ballots. The approval of all union members by secret ballot had to be sought before strikes were called. This law had been denounced by many on the left but the 1985 Labour/TUC document made no reference to a policy on it. This remained one of the trickiest points still to be agreed before the general election. And there was another contentious issue that the document only hinted at: the desirability of a legal national minimum wage. It called for an end to low pay, adding only: 'We are considering the whole scope of statutory support and whether it can be developed in a more comprehensive way.' Both these difficult questions were left until the 1986 Congress at Brighton.

*   *   *

It is doubtful whether any Labour leader could get away with advocating pre-strike ballots if they did not already exist. The right of union leaders to call on their members to stop working, and to have the decision ratified by a show of hands at a hastily-convened workplace meeting, is seen as the most effective weapon they have in the battle for higher pay and better conditions against recalcitrant employers. Anything that hampers the use of that weapon must make the unions' position weaker. That, at any event, is the conventional view; but Kinnock does not share it. The strongest and most consistent thread running through his political philosophy is that legitimacy can only be conferred through the ballot box. That was why he defied his advisers and tried to force through conference his one-member-one-vote plan for reselecting Parliamentary candidates. It is why he consistently denounces calls for extra-Parliamentary action in pursuit of radical causes. Given that the law on pre-strike ballots already exists, it would go against his nature and most basic beliefs to commit himself to repealing it.

He declared that position plainly at a meeting of the Labour Party/

TUC Liaison Committee on 24 March 1986, called to do some preliminary work on a document to be presented to that year's TUC congress in Brighton. A draft paper had been prepared by the trade union section at Walworth Road. It amounted to a sweeping endorsement of the divine right of trade unions to operate untrammelled by government, summed up in this central sentence:

We need to provide a right to take industrial action, irrespective of its purpose, and to protect it against all forms of legal liability.

Detailed proposals in the document included the right of strikers to claim full supplementary benefit without deductions for real or notional strike pay; and immunity of workers from dismissal for offences committed in the course of industrial action – both of them issues in the miners' dispute. Kinnock could scarcely believe that such a plan was being presented for serious consideration, since it ran so counter to his own views on industrial relations, as well as to a growing mood in the party and the union rank and file. While he believed working people should be protected against the inequities of the recent legislation, and that legal sanctions should be removed from industrial relations as far as possible, there had to be a balance between rights and responsibilities. The draft Walworth Road document provided no such balance. He told the Liaison Committee:

Nobody can imagine the Labour Party producing either in a manifesto or in legislation any such commitment to the unions in that form. It badly distorts and misrepresents the Labour Party's policy and nobody around this table can possibly go along with it.

That draft was scrapped and it took another three months for the Liaison Committee to hammer out the statement, *People at Work: New Rights, New Responsibilities*. It said:

An incoming Labour government would place strong emphasis on assisting trade unions in the development of membership involvement and participation in union decisions, including the use of balloting... In stark contrast to the Government's approach, the new framework would in no way give employers, or their customers or suppliers, any opportunity to seek injunctions and damages against a union. This new statutory framework will also entail laying down general principles for inclusion in union rule books based on a right for union members to have a secret ballot on decisions relating to strikes and for the method of election of union executives to be based on a system of secret ballots. The aim is to provide an effective right for union members.

135

It also proposed the creation of a new tribunal, with the power to enforce its decisions, to deal with any complaints of breaches of those or other provisions of the proposed legislation.

During the summer, Kinnock called in the leaders of the main trade unions individually for talks, explaining how important it was for Labour's electoral strategy that the document should be approved by the TUC. He was able to clarify for them an important point about pre-strike ballots. There would be nothing in the planned legislation to prevent an immediate walkout in the face of intolerable provocation by management, so long as a ballot were held to test opinion on whether the strike should continue. Nor would ballots be required in the case of bans on overtime. Through these concessions, Kinnock won the important support of Ron Todd, who had stated unequivocally in March that the internal affairs of trade unions should not be the subject of legislation: 'You cannot command methods of democracy from the centre or from Parliament.'

The NEC's Home Policy Committee should have been the last hurdle that had to be cleared before the document was approved for presentation to the TUC congress and party conference. The committee endorsed it by 17 votes to 8, with routine opposition coming from the left, who would have preferred something closer to the original Walworth Road draft. Kinnock told them:

> You people don't seem to talk to rank and file trade unionists, including strong Labour supporters, who want their rights as individuals improved.

Kinnock went on holiday to Corfu at the beginning of August believing that it had all been settled; but there was a final alarm before the pieces were in place. Some union leaders were still hesitant over the exact role of the courts in the formula for enforcing the proposed policy. For two days it looked as though the agreement might collapse. Charles Clarke was handling the negotiations and phoned Kinnock in Corfu to alert him to the danger. It was solved by inserting a sentence explaining that appeals from the planned new tribunal to the ordinary courts could be made only on points of law. Kinnock did not, in the event, have to fly back to make peace.

At Brighton in September, Ron Todd explained to the TUC why the TGWU and other formerly antagonistic unions were going along with Kinnock's plan. They were delivering a vote of confidence in a future Labour government. It was better to swallow hard on this agreed policy than to risk choking on the Conservatives' much less digestible measures. Norman Willis commended the policy document in more positive terms:

Balloting is here to stay – because our members favour it. And don't delude yourselves that our members, let alone the electorate, will be fobbed off with protestations about state interference in union affairs. It just won't wash.

The document was approved convincingly on a show of hands. A further satisfaction for Kinnock, on the eve of his visit to the Congress, was a setback for Arthur Scargill, inflicted by his own NUM delegation. Scargill wanted to propose an amendment to the resolution approving the joint statement. It would have declared the TUC to be opposed to state interference in union affairs – and thus would have negated the agreement on ballots. It would presumably not have achieved a majority but it was never tested, because the delegation voted not to propose it. Arthur the Terrible, who was supposed to be going to manipulate Downing Street, could not even manipulate his own colleagues.

*   *   *

The desirability of a national minimum wage has been debated earnestly on the left for years. On the face of it, the proposition seems hard for any socialist to contest. The Labour movement is devoted to helping the neediest, and a national minimum would benefit the lowest paid. But it has been opposed from both the left and right flanks of the union movement. The left object for the same reason that they are wary of strike ballots: their reluctance to involve the law in industrial relations at all. Free collective bargaining has long been a cardinal principle in the trade union movement, and anything that impinges on it is viewed with deep suspicion, especially since *In Place of Strife*. A national minimum wage is seen as an incomes policy in disguise. The objection of right-wing unions, especially those representing skilled workers, concerns differentials. This is another hallowed tenet of organized labour. Increasing the wages of the lowliest could trigger demands all the way up the scale and provoke a new wave of pay disputes.

But between those two positions, the majority of the Labour movement believed that to introduce a national minimum wage was the best way of solving the problem of low pay, particularly at a time of high unemployment when conditions in the job market favour the employer. The 1985 party conference had approved a resolution to that effect. A further document, *Low Pay: Policies and Priorities*, was drawn up by the Labour Party/TUC Liaison Committee for adoption by the 1986 Congress. It said the figure for the national minimum would be decided in the light of conditions when Labour came to power, but £80 a week was mentioned as a possibility.

At Brighton, the banner of the left-wing objectors was carried by Ron

Todd, that of the right by Eric Hammond of the EETPU. Todd, having persuaded the TGWU executive to line up behind Kinnock over strike ballots, could not do it a second time over this issue. On the eve of the conference he announced his union's rejection of the minimum wage concept, explaining:

> I have always said we want to support a Labour government and we want to work very hard to return a Labour government. But it can't be at the cost of saying: 'You have got to back everything, because otherwise you will rock the boat.' I'm afraid sometimes the boat has to be rocked.

Yet despite his and Hammond's immovable devotion to the cause of free collective bargaining, the policy document was adopted on a show of hands.

Kinnock addressed the Congress on Tuesday, 2 September, midway between the two victories for his policies. He did not mention either issue specifically. Instead, he delivered a broad attack on the Government and stated Labour's economic priorities, with the creation of new jobs coming first. He accused the Conservatives of dividing the country. Labour would operate by consensus:

> There are some, I know, who despise consensus. To them it is collaboration, supping with the Devil, corrupting even. Saloon bar revolutionaries detest consensus. But then, they never have to negotiate a deal, they never have to bargain for a settlement, they never have to achieve an agreement. They are small in influence and that is how they will remain.

It was a clear and courageous statement of his political philosophy – courageous because the word 'consensus' has seldom enjoyed a good reputation in a party where it has been the custom to speak the heady language of revolution even when adopting the politics of retreat and fudge. Kinnock was planting his standard firmly in the middle ground. And now the TUC and the Labour Party, after initial hesitation, were rallying to it.

*   *   *

Rupert Murdoch and his newspapers have played a dual role in Labour's disillusion with the press. First, their very style, especially the strident cynicism of the *Sun*, had infected their rivals, suppressing the ever fainter voice of calm reason. It is hard to recall now that when Murdoch acquired the *Sun* in 1969, the year before Kinnock was first elected to Parliament, he kept it for a time to its former political position, supporting Harold Wilson and Labour. But that did not last long and since Thatcher came to power in 1979 its support for her has scarcely wavered. As, over the years, the paper's editorial style grew shriller, hostility to Labour came to be expressed in ever more hysterical terms. *The Times* was equally vicious, even if it adopted a superficially more reasoned tone. It had been a Conservative paper before Murdoch bought it in 1981, but it has moved further to the right under his ownership. Kinnock calls it: 'The *Sun* with long words.'

In January 1986 the Murdoch papers contributed to Kinnock's deteriorating relations with Fleet Street for a reason unconnected with their style and quality. That month the Australian-born tycoon, who had recently changed his citizenship to American, moved all four of his national titles – the *Sun, The Times, News of the World* and *The Sunday Times* – to a modern production centre at Wapping, near the Tower of London. The move had been meticulously planned well in advance. Murdoch assumed he would be unable to negotiate the transfer successfully with the two print unions, SOGAT and the NGA, so he decided to do it without them. Their traditional functions had been superseded by new technology. The new machines were run by members of the electricians' union, the EETPU. The print unions established a picket outside the new plant, and outside other Murdoch buildings in London.

They were seeking their jobs back. Since Murdoch had proved that he could produce newspapers without them, they had no weapon to use against him except public opinion, an unpredictable ally. While the Wapping picket did not work as a picket (most members of the National Union of Journalists and others crossed it against union instructions), it did provide a focus for left-wing protest throughout the year, rather as the miners' strike had done in 1984. Every Saturday night there was an anti-Murdoch demonstration outside the plant, at which the strikers were reinforced by sympathizers with a variety of left-wing views. Because these demonstrations violated the new laws against picketing, SOGAT were taken to court and fined.

Murdoch offered to pay off the printers, and increased the cash offer twice in an attempt to get the picket lifted. The strikers had two ballots on the offers and rejected them. Because these long disputes seldom win votes for Labour, Kinnock would have liked them to accept, as would the union's new general secretary, Brenda Dean. But the proper democratic procedures had been followed and the strikers were adamant that they would hold out for their jobs back. That was always an unlikely prospect, but it was their decision: Dean and Kinnock had no alternative but to support them in it. As the months went by with no sign of a settlement, the mood on the picket line grew more dangerous. There were injuries and arrests.

As it happened, Kinnock had accepted an invitation to address SOGAT's 1986 conference at Scarborough in June. He receives far more invitations to union conferences than he can attend, and accepts them on the basis of an informal rota. The week before the conference, the strikers had voted by a convincing majority to reject one of Murdoch's offers. As Kinnock entered the conference hall some of the more voluble Wapping pickets crowded round him and demanded a firmer public commitment to their cause, as the miners had done two years earlier.

'What are you going to do for the printers, then?' someone shouted, while a group carrying anti-Murdoch banners chanted: 'Jobs, jobs, jobs.' Kinnock shouted back: 'Wait until you hear what I'm going to say.'

The speech gave them no cause for complaint. Kinnock said that employers, having supported the Conservative legislation demanding ballots on strikes, should now respond to the workers' feelings reflected in the ballot:

It was not this union that sought a strike. It was Mr Murdoch who wanted a strike. And he got his strike in a climate of coercion created by laws which have deliberately weakened trade unions and by a management which has deliberately broken every tradition, every convention of good industrial relations in this country. The dispute at Fortress Wapping has proved yet again that good industrial relations cannot be achieved by law but bad industrial relations can be provoked by prejudiced law.

He added that he was attracted by the examples of the United States and other countries that placed restrictions on the ownership of media organizations by foreign nationals.

Without vindictiveness but with concern about the current and potential power of press and broadcasting ownerships, I must say that it is time for us to think seriously about establishing similar citizenship conditions, not only because of the nationality-swapping history of Mr Murdoch but also because of the new reality and the increasing probability of other non-British ownerships of important media of news and opinion.

At the end of the speech he was given a standing ovation by the SOGAT delegates, who sang: 'Here we go, here we go . . .'. Afterwards Kinnock went to discuss the intractable issue with Dean and her senior colleagues in a back room. It was one of a continuing series of contacts between them – they met about once a fortnight in the early months of the dispute – but both recognized that there were not many practical ways in which the party could help the printers' cause. As he left the hall, the few hostile demonstrators outside were drowned by supporters singing 'For He's a Jolly Good Fellow'. Somebody gave him a hat inscribed: 'Wapping Official Picket'.

Almost as soon as the Wapping dispute began, SOGAT had initiated a campaign for a boycott of the four Murdoch titles. Not only were the papers themselves barred from Labour headquarters and Kinnock's office (as well as from the libraries of some Labour-controlled councils) but he and other Labour politicians would not talk to their reporters. This complicated his relations with the lobby, a self-organizing group of political journalists based at Westminster, in which all national newspapers were then represented. Apart from individual and *ad hoc* contacts with journalists, it is customary for the Leader of the Opposition to meet the lobby as a group, in their own room in the Palace of Westminster, once a week. The briefings used to be unattributable ('on lobby terms') but since he became leader Kinnock had put them on the record, as have the leaders of the two Alliance parties. (Because of the increasing use of on-the-record statements rather than unattri- butable guidance, many political journalists are questioning whether the lobby system any longer serves a useful purpose, and *The Guardian* and *The Independent* have withdrawn from it.)

After Wapping, Kinnock decided he would not answer questions from reporters who worked for the Murdoch newspapers. Since the lobby would not agree to any such restriction at briefings they organized themselves, he altered the rules. He would not go to their room but would hold his own press conference, under his own sovereignty, in the Shadow Cabinet room – a large, panelled conference room in his suite of offices in the Commons. He invited all Westminster-based journalists except those from Murdoch's papers. When the dispute ended in January 1987 he still held his own briefings but lifted the ban on the Wapping papers. The briefings are scarcely joyous occasions. Kinnock is wary, conscious that people are trying to 'stitch him up' – a phrase he has brought with him from his youth in Wales. He curbs his natural ebullience. He does not make many jokes.

*   *   *

At the end of 1986 the most serious trade union issue facing Kinnock was another consequence of the miners' strike. When the strike ended in 1985, miners who had continued working throughout, mostly centred around Nottingham, left the NUM and formed the Union of Democratic Miners (UDM). They did so after Arthur Scargill had sought to introduce new rules limiting the freedom of action of the NUM's area divisions. The

TUC, sticking to its policy on breakaway unions, would not recognize the new grouping. Nor would the Labour party allow the UDM to affiliate because its rules say it can grant affiliation only to unions recognized by the TUC. Individual members of the UDM have, however, been allowed to remain members of the party.

Leaders of the new union, especially the general secretary Roy Lynk, had been pressing for full formal recognition from the beginning. Yet, even though the Labour leadership would not have been averse to upsetting Arthur Scargill, there was nothing that could be done under the party's constitution. Kinnock and his colleagues made the occasional plea for a restoration of unity among the miners, but Scargill was not prepared to make concessions to lure the UDM back; nor did the new union's leaders see any reason to reverse their unilateral action.

Seeking a way of putting pressure on the party, the UDM leaders hit on a plan that would wound Labour where it hurt most, in the ballot box. They threatened to run candidates against the party's nominees in the East Midland seats where the new union is strongest. Most of those seats are marginal, and a split Labour vote could let the Conservatives in.

The first seat targeted by the UDM was Mansfield, where the candidate selected by the constituency party was Alan Meale, a left-winger supported by the NUM. He was a particularly provocative choice because he was secretary of the Campaign Group of hard left MPs, who had been Scargill's most consistent cheer-leaders in Parliament during the strike. The new union was also considering fighting four other seats in the area, where Labour would be vulnerable to its candidates' intervention. With the next election likely to be closely fought, the party could scarcely afford to risk four seats for the sake of what was essentially an internal squabble. Stan Orme was sent to Nottingham to mediate, but there was no obvious solution.

So as Kinnock looked ahead to 1987, almost certain to be the most fateful year of his life, he still had not pulled himself completely clear of the perilous quicksands of the Labour party's recent history. He had come a tremendous distance since 1983, but the opinion polls showed that he had still not drawn clear of the Conservatives. Few had much doubt about the chief reason for that. It was the issue that had dogged the party during the 1983 campaign and it was unlikely to be defused either by the tactic of head-on confrontation that had succeeded against Militant, or by the arm-twisting he had exerted on union leaders. The question of nuclear defence needed to be handled with even more finesse if that, too, were to be laid harmlessly to rest.

6   *The Best Form of Defence*

The defence of the realm has never been a simple issue for the Labour Party. At its purest, socialism reaches out for a Utopia where men and women throughout the world strive together in equality, mutual respect and peace. That ideal does not countenance conflict between nations. There have always been pacifists in the party, most notably George Lansbury, its leader from 1931 to 1935. But most of its adherents have recognized that in the real, impure world, good intentions are an inadequate protection against the unscrupulous and the fanatic. With Fascism the foe in the late 1930s it was easy enough for the left to unite in support of the war against Germany. Afterwards, when the socialist Soviet Union became the potential enemy, the issue was less clear-cut. For some, there was a painful conflict between ideology and patriotism.

The introduction of atomic weapons, with their horrifying potential for mass destruction, introduced an extra element into the moral and political dilemma. As the arms race between East and West grew in intensity through the 1950s, a campaign developed for Britain to withdraw to the sidelines and renounce its own nuclear weapons unilaterally, hoping by example to persuade others to do the same. Most advocates of that policy were motivated by abhorrence of weapons that could destroy millions of civilians; but some were sympathetic to the Communist Eastern bloc and reluctant to contemplate taking up arms against it.

Many on the Labour left supported unilateral nuclear disarmament for one or other of those reasons. An early split in the leadership was averted when Aneurin Bevan, the natural leader of the left, came out in support of the British nuclear deterrent at the 1957 party conference, declaring that without it British statesmen would go 'naked into the conference chamber'. That unity did not survive the 1959 election defeat. The newly-formed Campaign for Nuclear Disarmament attracted tens of thousands of people on its Easter marches to and from the weapons research establishment at Aldermaston, in Berkshire. Among the lasting images of the early sixties is that of a flamboyant Michael Foot striding under the leading CND banner alongside Canon John Collins of St Paul's Cathedral and Frank Cousins, the general secretary of the TGWU. The party conference in 1960 – against the strong urging of the leader, Hugh Gaitskell – passed a resolution making it Labour policy to give up British nuclear weapons.

The policy was reversed before Labour won power in 1964. Britain kept its independently-controlled Polaris submarines and allowed the United States to base nuclear weapons in Britain under NATO agreements. But support in the party for unilateralism remained strong. It appeared in an election manifesto for the first time in 1983, in the wordy document compiled for that calamitous campaign, led by Foot:

> Labour believes in effective defence through collective security but rejects the present emphasis on nuclear weapons. Britain and her allies should have sufficient military strength to discourage external aggression and to defend themselves should they be attacked. Labour's commitment is to establish a non-nuclear defence policy for this country. This means the rejection of any fresh nuclear bases or weapons on British soil or in British waters, and the removal of all existing nuclear bases and weapons, thus enabling us to make a direct contribution to an eventually much wider nuclear-free zone in Europe.

But there was a fudge over the timing, introduced deliberately as a sop to those on the right of the party who had serious misgivings about the policy:

> However, all this cannot be done at once, and the way we do it must be designed to assist in the task to which we are also committed – securing nuclear disarmament agreements with other countries and maintaining co-operation with our allies.

That last sentence gave scope for a wide range of interpretations of Labour's actual intentions, even among senior members of the party. Denis Healey and Roy Hattersley said it meant that implementation of the policy was contingent on concessions from the Soviet Union – turning a unilateralist policy into a multilateralist one at a stroke. But that interpretation appeared to ignore a sentence further down in the statement:

> We will, after consultation, carry through in the lifetime of the next Parliament our non-nuclear defence policy.

During the campaign the party issued a statement saying the timing of implementation depended on whether there was any move towards nuclear disarmament talks, but this made things no clearer. Then James Callaghan, Foot's predecessor as leader, made an election speech saying firmly that Britain should not give up Polaris unilaterally. The left were enraged. In a television interview Kinnock said: 'He has a personal opinion and he is entitled to offer it. He must be the best judge of the wisdom of offering it right in the middle of an election campaign.'

The internal squabbling on that issue was clearly an important reason for Labour's poor showing in the election. As soon as he became leader, Kinnock was determined to evolve an unambiguous defence policy around which the whole party could unite, even if some sections were bound to be less enthusiastic about it than others. The first of his new joint policy committees was put to work to produce the defence document passed overwhelmingly at the Blackpool conference in 1984.

It is one thing to unite the party round a policy, quite another to be able to promote it to the electorate. The most persuasive argument made by Labour supporters who oppose unilateralism is the pragmatic one. They may – in many cases do – believe that to abandon nuclear weapons is wrong and unwise. But chiefly they argue that, whatever its merits, it is impossible to sell the policy to voters taught to believe that our security depends on our possession of fearsome weapons to deter our enemies from attacking us, and that it is only the existence of these weapons that has kept the peace in Europe since 1945. To give them up would be to abandon ourselves to the evil designs of our potential enemies.

Unilateralists contest the assumptions on which those arguments are based. They believe the peace that has been maintained is increasingly precarious and the existence of nuclear weapons places the world constantly on the brink of grave peril, even obliteration. Safety can be assured only if these weapons are abandoned. Britain cannot single-handedly rid the world of all nuclear weapons but some (not Kinnock) believe that as a medium-sized power it can set a salutary example by renouncing them voluntarily, perhaps hastening the day when the major powers follow suit. Although often characterized as a moral view, it is in essence a practical one. A moral position would not distinguish between the comparative destructive power of weapons but would oppose them all. The specific argument against nuclear weapons is that they are likely to obliterate vast numbers of people indiscriminately and painfully, and have a lasting adverse effect on the environment.

Neil and Glenys Kinnock have shared the unilateralist view with a majority of Labour Party activists from their earliest days in politics. Its weakness as a political position is that its central argument is in essence an article of faith, not capable of being tested before it is put into effect. Nuclear disarmament by Britain might persuade the United States and the Soviet Union to follow suit eventually, but more probably it would not. Neil could see that to present it as a viable policy the party had to put forward realistic arguments to show that Britain could be defended more effectively without nuclear weapons than with them. Academics from university departments of disarmament studies – such as Mary Kaldor of Sussex and Malcolm Chalmers of Bradford – were summoned as expert advisers to the policy committee.

The scenario they constructed was unveiled in the 1984 document, *Defence and Security for Britain.* By giving up its increasingly expensive independent deterrent, Britain could afford to spend more on new conventional weapons systems. (The document foresaw that eventually the defence budget could be reduced as a proportion of national spending, particularly by cutting commitments outside Europe. This would free funds for improvements in welfare services. But it was held out as a long-term rather than an immediate possibility.)

It has always been more likely – or at least devoutly to be hoped – that if there were to be further conflict in Europe it would not initially involve nuclear weapons. Yet to maintain the British independent nuclear deterrent our conventional troops, so the argument ran, were being allowed to deteriorate dangerously. The process would accelerate when the old Polaris missiles were replaced by the much more expensive Trident 2. The document affirmed Labour's strong commitment to continued membership of NATO, despite left-wing opposition. It maintained that the most effective British contribution to the alliance would be to strengthen its conventional land, sea and air forces, in which the Conservatives were being forced to make fresh cuts to pay the £9 billion asking price for Trident 2.

The problem in presenting Labour's ideas is that, to argue them through, it is necessary to state truths which, although more or less self-evident, are unpalatable and may be construed as defeatist. The 1984 document stated that 'Britain's current defence policy bears little relationship to a realistic assessment of our roles and responsibilities.' The sentence was repeated in the new document approved at the 1986 conference, which added that the Conservative Government 'pursues the delusion that possession of semi-independent nuclear force would keep Britain as a great power'. Although it is apparent that Britain is no longer the major power it was until the early years of the twentieth century, it is not the kind of truth that people want to hear. The Falklands war won widespread support because it showed that Britain still could throw its weight about, albeit on a restricted stage.

That is why, of the two strands of the defence policy, expelling the American nuclear bases is more acceptable to the British public, according to the opinion polls, than abandoning the independent deterrent. This is doubtless partly because of the instinctive anti-American streak that lies buried, none too deep, beneath the surface of the British character – the 'Yanks go Home' syndrome.

Defence experts take precisely the opposite view of the priorities. They envisage few circumstances in which the British deterrent could play a decisive role in any possible conflict. The Americans, although they have agreed to go along with the policy by supplying the Trident missiles, would not object if Britain were to decide that the money could be better spent elsewhere. The unpopular US bases, on the other hand, play an important role in NATO's strategy. If they were closed to nuclear weapons, the strategy would have to be modified.

Kinnock maintains that talk of strategy in the event of nuclear war is academic, because there is no way of ensuring that the effects of nuclear weapons are confined to their targets. The 1986 explosion at the Soviet nuclear power station at Chernobyl showed how far radiation can be spread even by unleashing a fraction of the force contained in a nuclear bomb. Thus any power using a nuclear weapon in Europe would be endangering its own people as well as the enemy. But that strictly logical approach ignores the fact that deterrence is an inherently illogical theory relying on two contradictory assumptions: that nuclear weapons will never in fact be used, but that it is essential to convince potential enemies of our readiness to use them.

If the debate is about possession and not use, then why, Labour asks, is it necessary for US weapons to be stationed in Britain, when missiles based on their own soil and in their submarines are as credible a threat to the Russians? That argument is met with the charge that Labour, while seeking to abandon its full responsibilities as an alliance partner, still wants to nestle under the protection of American weapons, the so-called 'nuclear umbrella'.

Those two words have fuelled the most heated arguments in the debate over Labour's policy. Kinnock has said that he would not ask the United States to use nuclear weapons to defend Britain or British interests. Opponents of the policy say that such self-denial would expose British front-line troops in Europe to unfair risk when they were up against opponents who possessed nuclear weapons. Even those such as Denis Healey, who have been persuaded to support the main elements of the policy, are keen to retain the concept of the umbrella, although not the 'first strike' strategy – the commitment to use nuclear weapons in response to a Soviet conventional attack in Europe. But it is another academic point. Who truly believes that, if the time came for the Americans to decide whether to fire nuclear weapons, they would use any criterion other than their own strategic interest as assessed at the time, no matter where the weapon in question was based, or who was directly under threat, or what they had previously said they would do? Would they risk a bomb on Manhattan to defend London?

It is hard to make that point in so many words. For one thing, taken out of context, it could be used as an argument for keeping the British independent deterrent. For another, such scenarios, although earnestly contemplated by defence experts, are so far removed from anything actually likely to happen that they do not play an important role in public discussion of defence policy. As with other complex questions, what sways voters finally is not the detailed argument of options for action in scarcely imaginable circumstances, but the overall impression of competence in defence and commitment to it – and that can be built or destroyed with a single word. Will Labour, as its opponents maintain, leave Britain defenceless? It is a simple question that seems, on the face of it, to need a one-word answer. If, in their reply, Kinnock and the party spokesmen go into a dissertation about first strike strategy and the like, voters may assume that they are waffling because they have something to hide. That has proved a hindrance to Labour in promoting its defence policy.

*   *   *

For some time after the 1984 statement, there was not much public discussion of Labour's defence policy. The Conservatives had been surprised by the extent of the opposition to the arrival of the cruise missiles at the end of 1983 and by the persistence of the anti-cruise campaign. They had no particular reason to stress the issue, with the next election still a long way off. Demonstrations at the US bases at Greenham, Berks., and Molesworth, Cambs., continued throughout 1984. In February 1985 Glenys Kinnock joined the protestors at Molesworth, a few days after 1,750 troops and police had evicted fewer than 200 peace campers and put up a barbed wire fence round the base.

Wearing silver dove earrings, a symbol of the peace movement, Glenys explained: 'I felt I had to come to give my support. It is vital to continue to protest.' And of the eviction she said: 'It was like the dreaded night-time knock on the door. It must have been terrifying for the peace campers and I find it terrifying for everyone else in the country.' She has been photographed on a number of anti-nuclear demonstrations since.

In March 1985 Kinnock went to NATO headquarters in Brussels, where he tried to assuage fears that Labour's non-nuclear policy would weaken and divide NATO, and gave an implicit warning against NATO intervention in Britain's internal affairs. 'The cruise missiles are going back on the election of a Labour Government,' he said. 'This generates some concern in certain parts of NATO but I am sure they recognize the importance of a decision made by a sovereign government duly elected.' He stressed his commitment to continuing British membership of NATO and to strengthening conventional defence.

Later in March he was arguing against attacks from the other end of the spectrum. Tony Benn and Eric Heffer took the lead at that month's NEC meeting to have the defence policy revised to include a commitment to quit NATO, and to spend the savings from the abandoned independent deterrent on domestic needs rather than on strengthening defence. Kinnock delivered a powerful criticism of their initiative, saying it would leave Labour without a credible defence policy and be a gift for the Conservatives. He insisted that the best way to change NATO strategy was to remain a member and exert influence from within. 'We are going to stay there and we are going to make a difference,' he stated. The Benn/Heffer move was defeated by 16 votes to 9. Kinnock's most welcome supporter was Michael Meacher, who said that everything had to be subordinated to a Labour victory at the next election – the only way Britain could secure a non-nuclear policy. Kinnock nodded his approval vigorously.

He had always known that defence would be the hardest of all Labour's policies to promote. The press would be near-unanimous in opposing it and the Conservatives would label it defeatist and irresponsible. He reluctantly conceded that his Shadow Cabinet colleagues who opposed the policy – notably Peter Shore, shadow Leader of the Commons – were probably right when they said there were no votes in it. People who would be positively attracted by the policy were for the most part Labour voters already.

But Kinnock could also see that, even ignoring his own firm convictions, it would be impossible to unite the party around anything but a non-nuclear policy. The object, therefore, must be to limit the potential damage that defence might do to the party's chances at the next election by persuading the middle-ground voters, whose support was essential for victory, to vote Labour *in spite of* the party's stand on the issue. It was therefore important to dictate as far as possible the terms of the debate and its timing. Part of the problem in 1983 was that defence options had not been thoroughly argued until the Conservatives went nap on the issue a few weeks before the election. It was important, Kinnock saw, to air them fully, well in advance of the next election. Labour's private opinion polls showed that defence was not among the half dozen issues that most concerned the voters: those were such as jobs, health, education – the areas where Labour's case was strongest. This encouraged him to believe that the Conservatives would find it hard to sustain public interest in defence over an extended period.

In October 1985 he raised the issue at a weekend meeting of the Shadow Cabinet at the SOGAT conference centre at Rottingdean, Sussex, just before the Commons went back into session. He now held these meetings at least three times a year and found them invaluable for planning strategy in Parliament and in the country. It was no secret that some of his colleagues – such as Roy Hattersley, Denis Healey, John Smith, as well as Shore – were opposed to unilateral nuclear disarmament. He warned them that there could be no going back on the policy that had been agreed at the 1984 conference. Not only that, but they had to help him sell it to the electorate, a process he planned to initiate the following year. Many of his colleagues were uneasy, but the authority Kinnock had gained at the Bournemouth conference a fortnight earlier helped persuade them to swallow their reservations for the sake of unity and consistency. Their solidarity was to come under pressure towards the end of the following year, but it held up surprisingly well.

Kinnock planned to have a more detailed version of the policy presented to the 1986 conference for approval, and saw that as a good time to launch the promotional campaign. As Leader of the Opposition he receives scores of invitations to give speeches and lectures in many countries. One of them was from the Kennedy School of Government, part of Harvard University in Cambridge, Massachussetts. There were three main reasons why this seemed a suitable venue for a major defence speech. The first was that many Americans were worried about the policy and this would be a chance at least to explain it to them, even if he could not expect to achieve a miraculous conversion; the second that he was certain to be accompanied by a retinue of reporters who would ensure extensive media coverage; the third that to make the speech at an academic institution rather than on a party political occasion would underline his seriousness of purpose. He accepted the Harvard invitation for the first week in December, 1986, adding another speech to the itinerary in Georgia and later a third, at the National Press Club in Washington.

Work on the new conference statement went on through the early months of 1986. By July it was ready to be presented to the NEC. There was little substantially different from the 1984 statement, from which many key paragraphs were quoted verbatim. The new document included a stronger commitment to remaining in NATO, but coupled with an intention to persuade the allies to adopt a policy of no first use of nuclear weapons as part of 'a non-provocative conventional defence posture'. There were fuller details about the expected level of savings from abandoning Britain's independent deterrent and what the surplus could be spent on:

> Our aim is that while there will be some savings in the overall levels of military spending, there will also be some resources made available to improve Britain's conventional defences. In particular, there may be a strong case for using a significant proportion of the savings on nuclear weapons expenditure to restore the short-term economies in conventional defences which the Conservatives will need to introduce to pay for Trident.

Even if Kinnock had not planned for defence to be among the most prominent issues to be discussed at Blackpool, events in the week before the conference conspired to ensure that it would be. The Liberal

Party, meeting at Eastbourne, split damagingly on the question. Nuclear disarmers have in recent years had a strong voice in the Liberal Party, while their Alliance partners, the Social Democrats – in particular their leader, David Owen – favour a British independent deterrent. For the sake of Alliance unity the Liberal leader, David Steel, had agreed a joint policy with Owen involving the retention of nuclear weapons, possibly by co-operating with the French in what came to be called the 'Eurobomb': but this was repudiated at Eastbourne by the Liberal Assembly, causing doubts whether the Alliance could remain united.

Almost simultaneously a press report from Washington focused attention on Labour's defence policy. The producers of BBC Television's *Panorama* had decided in July 1986 to examine that policy in a programme to be broadcast on the Monday of the Blackpool Conference. A key segment in the programme would discuss the critical reaction to Labour's defence plans in the United States administration, so an interview was sought with Caspar Weinberger, the Secretary of Defence. At first Weinberger refused the invitation, not wanting to be seen to be interfering in British domestic politics. After persistent pressure from the *Panorama* producers he relented. The US administration had decided that, with opinion polls pointing to the possibility of a Labour election victory in 1987, it was important to make their view clear on Labour's policy to avoid any later misunderstanding, regardless of the diplomatic niceties. Weinberger's one concession to those niceties was to insist that it be made clear that he was not appearing on *Panorama* on his own initiative but in response to an invitation.

The gist of his contribution to the programme was leaked in Washington the week before it went on the air. He said the closure of US bases in Britain would weaken NATO and introduce a dangerous instability to the balance of power in Europe. He also warned that it might provoke an isolationist backlash in America leading to pressure to close *all* American bases in Britain, conventional as well as nuclear. He made no specific threat that the administration would bow to such pressure, although Kinnock, in his initial reaction to the reports, appeared to assume he had. Pointing out that other NATO countries – Canada, Spain, Denmark, Norway – adopted non-nuclear policies, Kinnock said:

We are committed to the defence of Britain and the democracies of Western Europe and North America. So too are the Americans. If as a consequence of our decision to become another non-nuclear NATO country the USA sought to remove all of their conventional forces, it is they who would be jeopardizing NATO.

151

The Assistant us Defence Secretary, the hawkish Richard Perle, spoke out with even less restraint in an interview on Channel 4 the same week. He said Labour's policy was 'wildly irresponsible'. Leading members of the Democratic Party, asked for comments by British reporters, added their critical voices.

Kinnock had not expected such concerted public hostility from American officials. Hitherto he had believed that although they could not be expected to welcome the policy, they would not speak out against it. On arrival in Blackpool he told reporters bitterly that critical comments from overseas officials were best made in private. 'If we ask for American missiles to leave, then leave they will,' he declared. 'Another country cannot interfere with the life of a democratically elected government.' He was still not convinced that Weinberger spoke for the whole administration and said as much in a BBC Television interview on the first day of the conference, Sunday 28 September.

Something else he said in that interview made headlines on Monday morning. He affirmed that once the American nuclear weapons were out of the country he would not expect Washington to use nuclear weapons on Britain's behalf. In other words, he would be folding up Britain's nuclear umbrella. That was not the policy as Denis Healey understood it. As soon as the shadow Foreign Secretary arrived in Blackpool on the Monday afternoon, he went to see Kinnock and urged him to find a way of modifying that remark. Healey and Kinnock do not have an intimate relationship but respect each other mutually. The leader genuinely appreciates the support he gets from Healey on the non-nuclear defence policy and values his experience in foreign affairs. He is even prepared to forgive the older man his occasional indiscretions – as when earlier in the year he told an Italian newspaper interviewer that Kinnock lacked experience. (Healey had apologized but Kinnock brushed it aside, saying it was demonstrably true: he *did* lack experience compared with Healey and other senior Labour Party figures.)

So he did not resent Healey's moderate concern in Blackpool on the nuclear umbrella question. Healey told him he ought to make it clear that he was not opposed to the use of American weapons to deter a Soviet first strike against Europe, including Britain, but he would not countenance a nuclear first strike by the Americans against Soviet conventional forces. Kinnock undertook to make the distinction clear in future interviews, but it was impossible to prevent commentators quoting the original remark against him for some time to come.

That night scores of conference delegates clustered round the large television set that had been placed in the lobby of the stately Imperial Hotel, to hear the exact words in which Weinberger denounced their party's policy. The American Defence Secretary had already assumed a villainous status at the conference and the delegates were preparing themselves to hiss his appearance. In the event, though, *Panorama* produced an alternative demon, this one from inside the party itself. Denis Healey was closely questioned by the presenter, Fred Emery, on the detailed arrangements for securing the withdrawal of American nuclear bases. Was there, he wondered, any possibility that the Americans could dissuade a Labour government from taking its intended course? Healey was doubtful:

> I don't think the Americans could persuade us, but I think that if we take the alliance seriously we have to listen to what our allies feel as a whole.

In that case, Emery pressed him, what if our NATO partners wanted us to keep the American weapons? Might that persuade Labour to change its policy?

'I would doubt it but it's not inconceivable.'

An angry murmur, soon turning to shouting, arose from the crowd round the television screen. Was Healey trying to scupper the unity on defence that had been achieved with such pain? The whole point of the policy was that US nuclear bases should go. To concede that this might not actually happen was tantamount to renouncing the policy. That evening the BBC's *Newsnight* team buttonholed delegates in the Imperial and asked for their reaction. It was overwhelmingly hostile, with the left baying for Healey's blood. 'He has misbehaved tonight and should now resign,' said Clare Short, the left-wing MP.

Kinnock was coming close to the end of his Monday evening round of parties when someone broke two pieces of news to him. First the good: it would be announced next morning that in the ballot for the NEC his enemy Eric Heffer had been defeated. Then the bad: Healey's gaffe. When he got back to the Imperial he delayed starting work on the next day's big speech and sent for Healey, who was traced having dinner at the River House at Poulton-le-Fylde – the one truly smart restaurant in the Blackpool area. He returned for the second heart-to-heart talk of the day with his leader. This time the gruff foreign affairs spokesman was the one in the dock. Healey explained that the 90-second snatch of film used in the programme was edited from an interview that had lasted very much longer. Remarks qualifying the 'not inconceivable' quote had been omitted. But he could see the damage that had been done and believed the only way out of it now was to tell the world he had not meant it. Without recrimination, Kinnock concurred.

Next morning Healey went on breakfast TV to say he now believed it *was* inconceivable for American nuclear bases to be allowed to stay in Britain under a Labour government; a view, he maintained, that had been reinforced by Weinberger's barefaced attempt to interfere in British domestic politics and bully Labour into changing the policy. Healey's tactic was to exploit latent anti-American sentiment – and it had the desired effect. On Monday night it had seemed that the gaffe might throw out of gear all the careful plans for a slick, trouble-free conference; yet by Tuesday lunch time it was already fading from Blackpool's collective consciousness.

After approving Healey's suggested tactics, Kinnock spent most of the rest of the night in his suite with his advisers, getting the speech into its final shape. By the time it was done it was 6 am. He had time to snatch less than two hours sleep. Although there was to be a long segment in the speech devoted to the defence policy, he decided to make no reference to the Healey row. He did not want to risk extending it.

Defence came at the very end of the speech. He had been in full flow for some 45 minutes and his voice was showing signs of strain. He introduced the topic with a modified quotation from the American Declaration of Independence:

I hold it to be self evident that it is the first duty of any government to ensure the security of their country. That duty does not change in any age and we will discharge that duty fully, for this is our country and we defend our country as we always have.

Patriotism was a strong theme, coupled with indignation at the actions of Weinberger and Perle. He thought they might have been put up to it by the Conservatives:

In recent days there have been some intervening voices from outside Britain. Some of their language has been lurid but it has been repudiated. It has been made clear that it has not been representative of the attitude of the administration. At least, not representative of the American administration. But representative perhaps of the present British administration ... The interventions that we have heard were not so much a product of American anxiety as a result of Tory alarm at the fact that we are defeating them.

He went on to list some of the British installations that are vital to the defence and security of the United States and which a Labour government would not close down – Fylingdales early warning station; GCHQ in Cheltenham; stations in Cyprus, Hong Kong, Scotland and Wales.

We do not propose for one instant to withdraw those facilities for we are allies and we discharge our obligations.

Undeterred by a solitary shout of 'rubbish', Kinnock went on to justify the non-nuclear policy by recounting the horrors of nuclear weapons:

> We are the first generation in history to have to deal with the existence of weapons of obliteration . . . I face it as the leader of this party who works to become the democratically elected leader of our country. I face it as an adult, as a citizen, as a father. And I tell you in no casual spirit that, like most of my fellow citizens, I would if necessary fight and give my life for my country. I would die for my country. But I could never allow my country to die for me.

That was clearly intended as the rhetorical highlight of the speech, to be shown on the evening news bulletins. The phrase provoked warm applause and when the speech was over a few minutes later he and Glenys, who had come to his side in a vivid red dress, won a standing ovation lasting some ten minutes, as well as several choruses of 'Here we go, here we go, here we go . . .' It did not have the dramatic impact of the Bournemouth speech a year earlier, but then lightning cannot be expected to strike two years running.

There was one damper on the upbeat mood inspired by the speech. The US ambassador to Britain, Charles Price, had been listening to Kinnock with grave attention from the visitors' gallery in the Winter Garden. Afterwards he was asked by reporters to comment on whether Weinberger had in fact been speaking for the administration. That evening and the next morning, every television report of Kinnock's speech had cut into it an embarrassing flash of Price stating categorically that Weinberger did indeed speak for Washington.

In a few weeks, Kinnock would be able to test the temperature in the American capital for himself. Before that, he was planning a visit to the theatre where, if things went wrong, defence theory was most likely to be put into practice.

*   *   *

Kinnock is a strong supporter of the Socialist International, the world-wide union of democratic socialist parties, and likes to attend its meetings when he can. Few things build the confidence as surely as spending a few days closeted with like-minded people, united in the common purpose of convincing the world of the efficacy of their beliefs, as they do not need to convince one another. He had been keen to go to an SI get-together in Peru during the summer of 1986, but was persuaded that the public would see the trip as extravagant and self-indulgent; so he stayed at home. The following October there was a more accessible meeting in Bonn. He decided to combine a visit there with a goodwill call on British troops in Germany and a symbolic look at the Berlin wall – a compulsory pilgrimage for aspiring leaders ever since President Kennedy went there a quarter of a century ago to declare that he was a Berliner.

Anxious to disprove any suspicion of crypto-pacifism, Kinnock put on a fine display of enthusiasm for the armed forces and their works. Flying between Hanover and Berlin, he sat for a while in the cockpit while one of his party told accompanying reporters: 'Neil would like to have been a pilot if he hadn't become a politician.' He was affable with the understandably equivocal officers he met at a military reception and next day joked vigorously with other ranks on a tour of the British garrison in Berlin, against a background of warlike sound effects from the adjoining rifle range.

Then the wall. Every politician who visits it has to mint a new phrase to describe his feelings about it. As the years have gone by, the most apposite and moving have been spoken for. Kinnock did not do badly with 'stupidity turned to concrete'. He added:

> I keep telling the Soviet leaders when I meet them that their language about development and liberation will lack any credibility until they pull down the Berlin wall . . . The wall must come down in the next 25 years . . . This is crazy, crazy.

Whether he would have a chance to contribute to this process as a world leader would depend to a considerable extent on his success in promoting his defence policy over the next few weeks, beginning with his visit to America.

*   *   *

Labour leaders seldom enjoy much affinity with the United States, where democratic socialism is regarded as a contradiction in terms. The suspicion is to some extent mutual. The United States is cast as the villain in many of the foreign policy conflicts that raise and have raised passions on the British left: South-East Asia, Central America, the Middle East. It is easy to conjure a cheer at the party conference with attacks on American policy. One of the best-received portions of Kinnock's Blackpool speech was a long and vituperative assault on US support for the right-wing Contra guerrillas in Nicaragua – more bad news for Charles Price to report back to an administration already apprehensive about the possibility of a Labour Government.

Kinnock's visit to America in 1984 had been reasonably successful in terms of press coverage and making contacts with officials. But he wanted to make at least one, possibly two more Transatlantic forays before the election to establish his credentials as someone who could get on with Americans in spite of policy differences. The Harvard invitation gave him a motive for one visit at the end of 1986.

For politicians there is never an absolutely right time to leave the country. Making forward arrangements to be absent for a week while the Commons is sitting is especially risky – but if you choose to speak at universities your options are limited, because university terms overlap with the Parliamentary session. Sod's law, or maybe the machinations of your political opponents, will ensure that there is always a pressing reason to stay at home when the date for the long-planned trip comes up. In this case the crisis that, for a fleeting moment, made Kinnock consider whether to cancel his trip, was partly of his own making.

For much of November, 1986, the press had been absorbed by a court case in Sydney, Australia, where the British Government were trying to prevent, on security grounds, the publication of a book by Peter Wright, a former member of MI5. Sir Robert Armstrong, the Cabinet Secretary, had spent a fortnight in Sydney giving evidence for the Government, but had come off the worse in exchanges with Malcolm Turnbull, the sharp young lawyer for the publishers. In one notable exchange Turnbull had persuaded Armstrong to admit that in a previous answer he had been 'economical with the truth'. A question Turnbull had raised was why the Government had not sought to prevent publication of an earlier book by the journalist Chapman Pincher, based on information from Wright and covering much of the same ground as Wright's book. Armstrong said the decision not to prosecute Pincher had been taken by the Attorney General, Sir Michael Havers.

This suggestion of a political motive for what should have been a purely legal judgment was fertile material for an Opposition conscientiously going about its innocent daily purpose of embarrassing the Government. But Kinnock's attempts to have the matter discussed substantively in the Commons had been frustrated by Thatcher, who kept her silence, claiming that the matter was *sub judice* – an interpretation not supported by the Speaker, who pointed out that Australia was an independent country whose courts had no authority in Britain, and vice versa. Kinnock saw that he could score points off the Prime Minister over her coyness in replying, and he encouraged his back-benchers to join in. At a meeting of the Parliamentary Labour Party on 19 November he rounded on Thatcher, saying:

The Prime Minister's performance resulted not from ignorance of the procedures of the Commons or of foreign courts, but from character deficiency. When she was deliberately given the

157

opportunity to repair her error, she just wasn't grown-up enough to take it.

Thatcher was quick to retaliate. On Friday 21 November she encouraged her deputy press secretary, Jim Coe, to criticize Kinnock in an unattributable briefing to lobby correspondents. A few weeks earlier *The Guardian* and *The Independent* had opted out of unattributable lobby briefings and thus felt free to report in full what happened in them, as conveyed to their lobby correspondents by friendly colleagues. According to *The Guardian*, Coe said:

The Government feels that the Opposition is playing games, with apparently the front bench and the back bench acting in concert. It is being suggested that the whole approach of the Opposition to this very important matter of security is the same as its general approach to this administration on its second term. It seems to be dealing with things other than policy, dealing with the froth of what happens rather than things that really matter. Some members of the Government have been heard to say that it is difficult to believe the Opposition is really serious about becoming the government, and that somebody looking to be a potential Prime Minister would behave in this way on a matter of national security.

Kinnock was not cowed. He responded by accusing the Prime Minister of an attempted cover-up, adding: 'They know very well there is absolutely no question of jeopardy to national security.'

The exchanges continued in this merry fashion until two days before Kinnock was due to leave for America. That was when, in Sydney, Armstrong made a remarkable correction of his earlier statement about Havers. He now asserted that it had *not* been the Attorney-General who took the decision not to prosecute the Pincher book. Kinnock pressed the question of whether the decision had been made 'for political reasons that had nothing to do with national security.'

But now it was Kinnock's turn to become an issue in his own right. A week earlier there had been a series of telephone calls between his office and Turnbull, the defence lawyer. David Leigh, the *Observer* correspondent covering the trial, phoned Patricia Hewitt. He suggested it might be useful for Kinnock to see the transcript of that day's proceedings. A transcript was sent and later Turnbull telephoned Kinnock's office to discuss it. That was when Kinnock had his single conversation with him. When news of the contact broke, Conservative backbenchers sought to make much of it, suggesting that Kinnock was acting against the country's security interests by colluding with a lawyer defending such a case against the British Government. On Friday 28

November, the day before he was due to leave for America, Kinnock wrote a six-page letter to the Speaker, explaining the nature of his contact and denying that it had any bearing on security. There had been no collusion. The charges against him were 'clearly and absolutely specious'.

Ideally, then, it was not the best of times to be flying to America to make speeches. But Kinnock saw that to cancel the trip now, apart from letting down his American hosts, could be construed as an admission that he had something to answer for. So off he flew, ignoring calls from Conservative backbenchers to return and explain himself. The skirmish could be pursued equally well across the Atlantic. On Tuesday 2 December Thatcher needed little encouragement at Question Time to call her opposite number to account, stating:

> The bi-partisan approach to security matters is totally and utterly fundamental to security in this country. The Leader of the Opposition has abandoned a fundamental defence policy pursued by his predecessors and he has now abandoned a fundamental security policy pursued by his predecessors.

Answering questions from her supporters, she appeared to agree with a suggestion that, to punish Kinnock, she should suspend the briefings on security matters occasionally given by the Prime Minister to the Leader of the Opposition. Kinnock's office responded that he had not received a briefing on the Wright case in any event. And there, in spite of sporadic attempts by Conservative backbenchers to revive it, the matter rested. What Kinnock was doing in America began to assume more significance than what he said on the phone to Australia two weeks earlier.

*   *   *

There was disconcertingly thick fog over Gatwick airport when Kinnock and his three-man entourage arrived at the nondescript VIP lounge just north of the main terminal building, shortly after 11.30 on Saturday morning, 29 November. He was travelling with Charles Clarke, John Eatwell (a Cambridge economist and his specialist adviser on America), and Andrew Fox, his young acting press officer. When they arrived they were told that because of the fog their British Caledonian flight to Atlanta would take off 40 minutes late. Almost right away, Kinnock got to work on the speech he would be delivering in Atlanta the following day. It would be a nine hour flight but he might need nearly all of that, because little work had been done on the speech so far. Lunch was served as soon as the Boeing 747 cleared the fog and cloud. Afterwards the four went up to the top deck of the first-class section, furnished with easy chairs and small tables at one end, a bar at the other.

Of the half-dozen reporters travelling on the plane only Trevor Kavanagh from the *Sun* had a first-class ticket, but he invited some of his colleagues forward. They stood and drank around the bar while Kinnock beavered away at his speech at the other end of the saloon. He did not look up. The reporters had hoped he might come and have a drink with them. In the same circumstances a couple of years earlier he would no doubt have done so; but after three years in the job he had come to the conclusion that it does not matter how a Labour leader treats the press: overwhelmingly Conservative as it is, it will invariably publish stories calculated to do him the maximum damage. He believed that the reporters on the plane – from papers such as the *Sun, Daily Mail, Times* and *Star* – were not travelling with him because they wanted to convey reasoned stories to their readers about Labour's defence policy and how it was being explained to the Americans: they had come to trip him up. They were looking for gaffes, snubs, indiscretions. Knowing that, it was impossible to relax with them over a drink. And if he could not relax, he would just as soon ask the stewardess to fetch him a can of beer at his table, so that he could sip it while working, instead of wasting time in arid, watchful sparring with men whose company he was unlikely to enjoy.

After two hours the gentlemen of the press retired, thwarted, and went back to their seats to bury themselves in the press pack, a glossy folder bearing the rose motif, that Andrew Fox had given them on takeoff. Their relations with Kinnock had thus got off to a discouraging start and were not to improve all through the ensuing week – a state of affairs reflected in the coverage given to the visit. He had in fact agreed to an airborne interview with the man from the *Star* and, as the aircraft neared Atlanta, his press officer Andrew Fox asked if he was ready to see him. Kinnock reacted irritably, venting the anger he had been holding back while seeing them all standing at the bar:

'If they want to be in on the action they don't write things like my wife is an arch-pacifist who won't go on an aeroplane because it's a war machine. He can bloody wait.' When Fox pointed out that this journalist had not been responsible for that piece of misreporting, Kinnock exploded again:

'I know it wasn't him. It's never him, never the journalist – always the bloody sub, and if it's not the sub it's the editor, and if it's not the editor it's the owner, and if it's not the owner it's a typing error. Makes you puke.' With only a half hour to go before landing, the *Star* reporter was finally granted his interview.

* * *

It was raining softly when the plane landed at Atlanta soon after dark. Through the night the rain intensified and was splashing noisily off the streets and buildings when Kinnock fulfilled his first engagement on Sunday – laying a wreath on the grave of Martin Luther King, the black civil rights leader. He attended a two-hour service at King's Ebenezer Baptist Church and after lunch went back to an adjoining meeting hall to give his speech on civil rights and South Africa. His host Andrew Young, the mayor of Atlanta and former US ambassador to the United Nations, had done a poor job of filling the hall. By the scheduled starting time fewer than 100 people were there, and several of those were press and television reporters.

There were good reasons for the low turn-out. It was still raining hard with no sign of a let-up; it was the tail end of the Thanksgiving holiday weekend; John McEnroe and Boris Becker were playing tennis at the city's indoor stadium; the American football season was reaching its climax and many were at home watching the games on TV. All the same, it was embarrassing: and Kinnock, disappointed, made Young wince with a barbed reference to the low attendance in his introductory remarks.

It was a gift for the travelling reporters, who had been augmented by British correspondents based in Washington and New York. Here was a straightforward 'Kinnock snubbed' story served to them on a plate. They added extra details. The Labour leader had not been recognized when he arrived at the airport the previous evening. Andrew Young had, according to some keen observers, closed his eyes momentarily during the speech. It was an inauspicious beginning and, despite the large audiences for Kinnock's two other speeches and the extensive exposure he received on network television, the impression that he was being ignored and humiliated lingered to permeate the coverage of the rest of the trip.

It could equally have been written that it was remarkable that he attracted any attention at all, for when he arrived the American media were obsessed with their biggest political scandal since Watergate. Earlier in November it was disclosed that the administration had been supplying arms secretly to Iran as part of a deal to try to secure the release of some American hostages in the Middle East. Moreover, it emerged that some of the money from the transaction had been funnelled illicitly to the Contra rebels in Nicaragua. Two members of the national security staff had already resigned from the White House and there were fears that President Reagan himself could be implicated.

Kinnock was forced to adapt his approach to television interviews. So engrossing was the Iran scandal that it was monopolizing television and radio current affairs programmes. So his interviews fell into a pattern. He would first be asked for his reaction to the latest Iran revelations.

161

'There's always that suspicion about politicians right around the world that there's somebody with his hand in the till,' he observed to Jane Pauley on NBC's early-morning *Today* programme. (Later, after taking judicious advice about American colloquialisms, the 'till' became the 'cookie jar'.) After mining his wisdom on that topic, the interviewers would slip in a question about Labour's defence policy and he would say his piece.

The *Today* interview was one reason for his 24-hour visit to New York, squeezed between Atlanta and Boston. He also had dinner with New York Democrats and lunch with the *New York Times* editorial board. New York's most influential newspaper gave his visit sparse coverage, but in the previous week had published a full-column interview with Kinnock by their correspondent in London. In it, Kinnock insisted that he was not anti-American, that his generation had grown up 'in the American age'. He explained:

I am more related to the United States of America than Mrs Thatcher. I feel very comfortable in America and in Italy and at home. I mean, I get along fine elsewhere, but that's in three cases air which I breathe without ever sneezing.

He had a similar pre-visit interview with the correspondent for the *Washington Post*, whose newspaper took him seriously enough to devote its main leading article to his visit on Monday 1 December. It was uncompromisingly critical:

The purpose of his visit to the United States this week is to persuade Americans that a Britain divesting itself of nuclear arms would remain a reliable ally and a serious deterrent to Soviet adventuring. He is unlikely to succeed in any part of that mission.

A similarly hostile article appeared in the weekly news magazine *Newsweek*. Noting that Kinnock's opposition to nuclear weapons was a moral position dating from when he was a teenager, the magazine concluded:

It remains for the British voters to decide – perhaps as early as next summer – whether a politician of conviction is as dangerous to them as he can be to himself.

This, then, was the ingrained attitude that Kinnock had to overcome when presenting his case to the Americans. The Harvard speech was to be the central weapon in his armoury, a closely argued text that could be referred back to later for an authoritative exposition of the policy. It had been written in the two weeks before he left London and approved by senior colleagues such as Denis Healey and Denzil Davies, the defence spokesman.

The Arco Forum at the Kennedy School of Government at Cambridge forms the central well of the airy, modern building. The upper two floors are arranged around it as balconies, rather like an Elizabethan theatre. Thus the speaker at the podium commands the attention not just of the audience on his own level but of those on the two floors above. On the evening of Tuesday 2 December all the seats were quickly taken. Students and visitors stood at the back and sides of the hall and balconies to hear the Labour leader. Outside, supporters of the Spartacist League, a Trotskyist group priding themselves on being more militant than Militant, demonstrated in the rain, shouting: 'Honour Kim Philby, hate Neil Kinnock . . . Judas Kinnock . . . Down with NATO.'

Kinnock, by contrast, was saying 'Up with NATO', while advocating radical changes in its defence strategy, especially in the 'first use' policy of using nuclear weapons to halt a conventional conflict:

> The scientific and strategic fact is that, whatever may be claimed for them in terms of balance, deterrence or security, nuclear weapons cannot be used to defend Britain. The size and location of our country means that using nuclear weapons would always either be pointless or self-destructive, or both . . . The case for an independent or semi-independent British nuclear force cannot now be sustained by any consideration of real need or by any evidence of influence or access to great position which it gives us.

He pointed out that the American commitment to sell Trident to Britain could well have gone by the board had that autumn's Reykjavik summit produced its hoped-for East–West agreement on reducing strategic ballistic missile systems. Of the 135 American bases in Britain, only three would have to be closed under the policy: the Greenham Common and Molesworth cruise missile facilities and the Poseidon submarine base at Holy Loch in Scotland. The F-111 bombers based at Upper Heyford and Lakenheath would have to be switched to a non-nuclear role – which would, Kinnock maintained, increase their effectiveness as cover for conventional troops. American ships armed with nuclear weapons would not be barred from British ports, as they had been from New Zealand when it adopted its non-nuclear policy. As for questions about loyalty to NATO, he reminded the audience that Britain commits 95% of its defence spending, that is 5% of gross domestic product, to its contribution to the alliance. That was more than any other ally and it would continue under Labour.

If that scale of British commitment is somehow considered to be evidence of an unwillingness to share alliance obligations, then words have truly lost their meaning.

The speech was greeted with loud applause from an audience which admired its cogency and sincerity, even if many among them contested its central premise. Afterwards Kinnock fielded some penetrating questions. If Britain was so committed to NATO, why not change the policy by consultation with its allies? He replied that it was a government's fundamental responsibility to choose a reliable defence policy over one it perceived as unreliable. He was asked whether it would not be more expensive to provide an adequate conventional defence force for Britain in NATO than to rely on nuclear weapons. He conceded that there would be few savings to begin with, but for the price Britain would have an effective and credible defence, instead of weapons it could never use.

After it was over, Kinnock moved to the side of the auditorium, where a crowd gathered round him. But soon rival groups were forming round two members of the School of Government faculty, both formerly senior officials in Washington. Richard Haas, in the State Department during President Reagan's first term, said Kinnock had been 'dangerously articulate' but he hoped that if Labour actually achieved power they would not go as far as he had indicated. Haas could not imagine that it would be easy to persuade a Labour Cabinet to increase expenditure on conventional forces as much as would be needed. As for whether the United States might close *all* its British bases as an act of pique, he observed: 'Britain is not the only country with a public opinion. We have a public opinion here, too. If Britain tries to redefine the bargain, people on this side of the Atlantic will resist.' Stephen Flanagan, who had worked in the Carter administration, agreed that to adopt such a policy would end the special relationship between the United States and Britain. Charles Clarke was annoyed at the attention the two men were getting, suspecting a concerted attempt to steal Kinnock's thunder.

Next day Glenys flew from London to join Neil in Washington, where they and the rest of the party stayed at the palatial British Embassy on Massachusetts Avenue. More television interviews were scheduled, plus meetings with economists, arms negotiators and senators, including Senator Edward Kennedy. The central engagement was a luncheon speech at the National Press Club, where the potential audience includes political correspondents from hundreds of newspapers around the country. Standing behind the rostrum and in front of a Christmas wreath, Kinnock delivered a shortened version of the Harvard speech to an unusually large audience for one of these lunchtime events. They applauded vigorously at the end, some comparing the speech favourably to the platitudinous observations they often hear from politicians. One of the questions afterwards was about an inter-view given to a German newspaper earlier that week by General Bernard Rogers, NATO's supreme commander in Europe. Rogers had said:

Should plans such as those in the Labour Party ever be realized, America would decide: 'Good, that does it, we will no longer expose our 350,000 soldiers to the risk of the kind of thinking which shifts responsibility for defence on to others.' The Soviet Union, with its massive strength on the ground, would laugh at us.

Kinnock responded that it was no part of the General's function to try to influence political events in NATO's constituent democracies. In any case, American troops were in Europe not just to defend Europe, but also to assist in the defence of the United States.

The final question was whether he thought too much money was spent on the British monarchy. Would a Labour government change it? He suspected a plant from one of the British reporters. Who else would know that in his early years as an MP he had been critical of the amount of money spent on royalty, and in 1977 boycotted the state opening of Parliament in protest? In his reply, therefore, he was extravagant in his praise of the royal family and the value for money they represented. He would not be caught out that simply.

He and Glenys stayed privately in the American capital over the weekend and were taken to a game of American football by Senator Gary Hart, a contender for the Democratic nomination for President. Neil was back in the Commons on Monday 8 December, to the ironic cheers of Conservatives. On balance he was satisfied with the trip. The press had done their worst to scupper it at the beginning but he had persevered and at least received a hearing from legislators and from the American public via television, radio and their newspapers. Nobody ever said it was going to be easy.

*   *   *

The almost automatic hostility of the bulk of the press is something Labour leaders have to learn to live with. That is why those few publications that do support them take on a special significance: any hint of defection from their ranks is particularly painful. While he was in America he was put out by the desertion, on the defence issue, of the *New Statesman*, a journal he had only recently reclaimed as a supporter. In an editorial in the issue of 5 December, it declared:

165

The Labour Party must change its defence policy. It has two compelling reasons for doing so: first, to make the process of making arms reductions both more stable and more likely; and second, to assist the defeat of the Conservative Government.

The *New Statesman*, as the most widely read of left-wing political journals, has always had an influence in the Labour movement out of proportion to its circulation – declining since the 1970s and now down to around 20,000 copies a week. Historically, it had generally lined up with the mainstream of the party, to the right of *Tribune*. Like the leadership, it had been opposed to unilateral nuclear disarmament until 1983 when, edited by Hugh Stephenson, it supported the new party line. Despite that, Kinnock had been unhappy with Stephenson's editorship, believing he had allowed far left supporters on his staff too much influence. At times, Kinnock felt, it read like a house journal for those noisy local politicians who were, as he saw it, harming the party's image through their unbalanced obsession with radical crusades on behalf of more or less oppressed minorities: what the popular papers delighted in characterizing as the 'Loony Left'.

When, in the middle of 1986, Stephenson announced his intention of resigning, Kinnock took an intense interest in the choice of a successor. A leading contender was Anthony Barnett, who had made himself highly unpopular with Kinnock by writing articles calling for more radical leadership. Kinnock brought to bear all the influence he could to secure instead the appointment of John Lloyd, the labour editor of the *Financial Times*. He had come to respect Lloyd's work during the miners' strike, which he believed the *FT* had reported better than any other newspaper. Lloyd had been in two minds whether to apply for the *New Statesman* job. Kinnock urged him to do so and then lobbied on his behalf with the *NS* board, whose most influential member was the former Labour MP Phillip Whitehead, likely to return to Parliament next time as the Member for his old Derbyshire seat.

Lloyd won the appointment and took over as editor in August 1986. For the first few weeks he had given the leadership stout support, which only made his stand on defence the harder to bear. The *NS* would remain on Kinnock's side on other matters but its deviation on this one pointed to the damage the defence policy could do to his electoral prospects. Party disunity surfaced again in March 1987, when James Callaghan insisted in a Commons speech that Trident should be retained and Gerald Kaufman's research assistant resigned after advocating the same policy in *The Times*. Nearly all Kinnock's actions as leader had been designed to win back the support of middle-ground voters who had defected to the Alliance, or were thinking of it. It would be cruel if those efforts were to prove fruitless because of his insistence on sticking to unilateralism. But there was now no way he could retreat, even if he had been inclined to.

*   *   *

The launch of the defence policy document, *Modern Britain in a Modern World: The Power to Defend our Country*, was timed for 10 December, two days after his return from America. Essentially it contained the policy outlined in the conference statement and the Harvard speech, fleshed out with more details of how it was intended to beef up conventional defence. It would involve making better use of manpower training reserves, installing man-made barriers to protect NATO's eastern flank (the 'explosive ditches' proposal that provoked some derision in the press) and buying more modern conventional weapons. One part of the policy that remained uncertain was the timing of the closure of American nuclear bases. He had never been specific on it. His initial position, that they would be gone within a year of a Labour government taking office, had been modified. On the American trip, Charles Clarke had spoken of a longer time scale. 'There are no circumstances that it would be more than three years, something like that, to carry things through,' he told reporters in New York.

Now the line was that nobody knew how long the technical process of removing the missiles would take. Kinnock had said that 'no stop watch' would be set in motion. At the press conference launching the new document he speculated: 'It could take a year, perhaps a little more, perhaps a little less – and that refers to the technical requirements.'

The document opened with some pointed criticism of the Conservatives' nuclear defence policy:

> The truth is that Mrs Thatcher – who relishes the title Iron Lady – is following policies which diminish Britain's defences and ... the credibility of allied defences is reduced too ... The paradox of the Tories becoming disarmers by stealth arises not because Mrs Thatcher does not want to defend Britain but because her ambitions for defence policy far exceed anything which Britain under its present economic management can afford ... Mrs Thatcher has a nuclear fixation. Her delusions of grandeur directly threaten the defence policy for Britain that *is* possible and is vitally needed.

So Kinnock was taking the fight to the enemy's camp. He was not going to be forced on to the defensive. Even if he no longer believed that unilateralism would gain many votes for Labour come the election, he did know that being shamefaced about it was a sure way of losing. After two weeks of consistent criticism of the policy in the press, it was not

167

surprising that the pre-Christmas opinion polls began to show the Conservatives in the lead.

* * *

There were two nuclear debates at the 1986 party conference. The second, on the use of nuclear power for peaceful purposes, aroused more profound passions than the first. Although defence is a matter of great contention in the country at large, in party terms it is less so because the supporters of unilateral nuclear disarmament are in such an impregnable majority.

The energy question is altogether more difficult. Like many environmental issues, it points up the division between the two chief sources of Labour support. Ideologists see the environment as a central socialist concern. The world, in their eyes, is divided between captains of industry who uncaringly pollute the air, the sea, the land and the rivers; and the mass of the people who are their impotent victims. But for trade unionists, attempts to curb industrial development for environmental reasons often involve threats to their jobs; so they resent the interference of 'do-gooders'. (An exception is the National Union of Mineworkers, whose conscientious objection to the hazards of nuclear power happily coincides with its self-interest in maintaining coal as a prime energy source.)

Yet nuclear power did not become a divisive issue in the party until the 1980s. In office, Labour had been in favour of it – indeed many of Britain's existing nuclear power stations and supporting facilities were initiated by Labour governments. But doubts about the safety of the plants had arisen as a result of incidents involving the leakage of small amounts of radioactive material and, at Three Mile Island in Pennsylvania, the narrowly averted threat of a large-scale catastrophe. The 1983 manifesto committed Labour to halting the development of the planned pressurized water reactor (PWR) at Sizewell, in Suffolk. It added that the need for a nuclear programme based on the advanced gas cooled reactor (AGR) 'will be reassessed when we come to office'. The Bournemouth party conference in 1985 was the first to approve a resolution calling for the ultimate closure of all nuclear power stations in Britain.

The explosion at the Chernobyl nuclear plant in the Soviet Union, on 26 April 1986, strengthened the case against nuclear energy. Thirty-one people were killed and many more exposed to radiation levels that would have a profound long-term effect on their health and their life expectancy. Around 50,000 people living and working within a 19-mile radius of the plant had to be evacuated. Thousands of acres of land have been rendered useless for the foreseeable future. The subsequent spread of radiation across much of northern Europe contaminated large quantities of meat and dairy products, even spreading as far as Wales. In the wake of the accident, some countries decided to mark time on nuclear power, others to move away from it back to oil, coal and gas.

The Chernobyl explosion occurred as the NEC were hammering out a long statement on energy policy to present to the 1986 Blackpool conference. The accident and its aftermath ensured that there would be tremendous interest in the topic. When the time came for constituency parties and trade unions to submit resolutions to the conference, 214 were on nuclear energy – nearly all calling for the next Labour government to renounce it.

Kinnock was influenced by this evidence of strong feeling in the party; but he was also conscious of the support for the nuclear industry among trade unions whose members worked in it – among them the engineers, the electricians and GMBATU. At the TUC conference in Brighton, a mild resolution had been passed calling only for a thorough inquiry into all aspects of nuclear power, including its safety, and a freeze on new developments until the inquiry was completed. He knew this would not be enough to satisfy the anti-nuclear majority at the party conference.

Another consideration for Kinnock was the position of John Cunningham, shadow spokesman on the environment, a former junior energy minister and a strong supporter of retaining nuclear power. Cunningham's constituency of Copeland includes the controversial nuclear reprocessing plant at Sellafield (formerly Windscale). More than 11,000 of his constituents work in the nuclear energy industry and the same number again have jobs that depend on its prosperity. He argues forcefully that a Labour government coming to office committed to cutting unemployment would be ill-advised to act precipitately to throw so many people out of work. He maintains that if Labour is serious about its plan to increase production in British industry, it would be absurd to cut the supply of energy available for new and expanded factories. Cunningham stresses that he favours the most rigorous safety standards for nuclear power stations and the closure of any that do not meet them. But he does not believe there is a future for a country that deliberately turns its back on a whole area of advanced technology. It conflicts with his vision of a modern socialist Britain.

Because he was so forthright in stating his position, Cunningham became a target for Labour supporters opposed to nuclear power. He was nicknamed 'Radiation Jack' and, being on the right of the party on other issues (he was once Parliamentary Private Secretary to James Callaghan), he became the butt of jokes of the 'fluorescent socks' nature at left-wing rallies. As the 1986 conference approached, an informal campaign got under way to persuade Kinnock to switch Cunningham from his environment portfolio to one where his views on nuclear energy would be less relevant.

Although they started their political careers on opposing wings of the party, Kinnock and Cunningham have established an excellent personal and working relationship since Kinnock became leader. Cunningham is industrious and sensible, prepared to put in long hours reading briefs, talking to interested parties and formulating policy. Along with his deputy, Jack Straw, he played an invaluable if low-profile role in the showdown with Liverpool Council – local government being one of the main responsibilities of the Environment Department. Kinnock believes that in Cunningham and Straw he has as strong a shadow team as in any other policy area. Both men have the application and realistic outlook that Kinnock requires in people who work with and for him. When suggestions began to appear in the press (notably *The Guardian*) that he ought to move Cunningham to another field of responsibility, their effect was to stiffen Kinnock's resolve to do no such thing. In a pre-conference interview on BBC Television, David Dimbleby asked him whether he intended to move Cunningham. Kinnock replied:

> Jack Cunningham is very, very good at his job and I don't think anybody can contest that. He was good from the start which is why I asked him to do it. What he's done during these three years is go from strength to strength . . . Jack Cunningham, on the basis of his own merit, his own very well developed talent which is widely recognized, is safe in that job.

Yet at the same time Kinnock knew that the party would not accept a blanket endorsement of nuclear energy, that the conference resolution would have to refer either to phasing it out entirely or to reducing the country's dependence on it. He became personally involved in drawing up an NEC statement that would embrace such commitments, yet not in a form that Cunningham would find so unacceptable as to warrant his resignation from the front bench. At the Welsh Labour Party conference on 19 May, Kinnock was reflecting Cunningham's views when he declared:

> Lists of complaints about the dangers of nuclear plants and vague suggestions that alternatives for energy and for jobs should be available somehow, somewhere, some time, do not meet the needs of a country that has nuclear power and has had it for decades . . . Airy declarations certainly cannot form a programme for a party that is serious about governing this country and doing its duty by the people.

The draft of the conference energy statement came before the NEC in

July. Cunningham was invited to attend the meeting, along with Stan Orme, the energy spokesman, and John Smith, spokesman for industry. It was, as usual, an overlong meeting and it was past 10 pm before the subject of the energy statement was reached. The three Shadow Cabinet members were solemnly ushered in to be reminded that they were there only as observers and would not be asked to contribute to the discussion.

Cunningham found it hard to contain himself as he was forced to sit and listen to Eric Heffer denounce his views and speculate on his future in the Shadow Cabinet, as though he were not in the room. He wondered ruefully what organization other than the dear old Labour party would keep three of its senior members sitting around for hours and then bind them to silence on a subject about which they certainly knew more than anybody else present.

The statement had to make clear that the party was against an excessive reliance on nuclear power: even Cunningham had been forced to recognize that. He was anxious, though, that it should contain no commitment to a precipitate closure of nuclear stations before alternative arrangements had been made for the employment of those working in the industry and for the replacement of the power they produced. The form of words finally devised was one that Cunningham could go along with, although without great enthusiasm. The NEC committed the next Labour government to

a diminished and diminishing dependence on nuclear power, in a decades-long process of ending its use – and thus the gradual phasing out of existing nuclear plants.

The qualification 'decades-long' made the policy tolerable to Cunningham. The environmental group Greenpeace had produced a plan for phasing out British nuclear power stations in four years. The NEC statement showed that it had in mind a much longer term than that.

In detail, the statement said Labour would carry out safety reviews of the old Magnox stations, built between 1956 and 1971 and using Britain's first reactor. Those found unsafe would be closed. Two AGRs under construction, at Torness in Scotland and Heysham in Lancashire, would not be proceeded with, unless they were in commission by the time Labour took office. Nor would a Labour government proceed with the proposed PWR at Sizewell, or with research into Fast Breeder Reactors, or with imports of nuclear energy from France.

One of the most difficult issues was the Thermal Oxide Reprocessing Plant (THORP) being built at Sellafield, in Cunningham's constituency, at a cost of £1,600m. The NEC statement argued in great detail that there was no need to reprocess ceramic oxide fuel and that two-thirds of the plant's projected throughput would be from overseas contracts – other

171

countries dumping their waste on Britain because of the political difficulty of handling it locally. Labour would sign no fresh contracts for such disposal. Should they scrap the plant, then? Cunningham argued against this, pointing again to the cost in terms of jobs in his constituency. Kinnock was among the chief architects of the compromise reached: to continue building the plant but not use it for reprocessing:

> Instead, we shall use the facility and the scientific and other skills concentrated there to develop the technology of waste disposal and storage.

Critics of that proposal saw no logic in planning to use an expensive scientific facility for a purpose other than the one for which it was designed. The pledge to keep THORP going in some form was certainly a satisfying victory for Cunningham, whose constituents were also gratified by two further promises in the NEC statement:

> Because of the accumulated expertise in the area, we intend to develop, at Sellafield, a 'centre of excellence' in waste management. We also propose to create a science park in West Cumbria to promote and diversify industrial development based on the knowledge and experience at Sellafield.

There was little doubt that the gradualist approach to a non-nuclear energy policy, as spelled out in the NEC statement, would gain a comfortable majority at conference. A greater problem for the leadership was an alternative energy resolution proposed by the NUM. It called on the party to make clear its opposition to nuclear power. It instructed the next Labour Government to halt the nuclear power programme (including THORP, Torness and Heysham), end the dumping of nuclear waste, phase out all existing nuclear power plants and switch investment and manpower into alternative fuels, especially coal.

The NUM resolution caused lengthy controversy at the NEC meeting at Blackpool on the Sunday the conference began. At first, Kinnock argued for the NEC to recommend rejection of the motion because it was in direct conflict with the Committee's own statement on several important points. The soft left, the all-important 'middle ground' of the NEC, were unwilling to take such a rigorous stand, on the grounds that the Scargill motion, as they had come to call it, was virtually certain to get a majority, no matter what the NEC recommended. That would present Scargill with the prestige of a victory, and maybe help restore the reputation that had been so damaged when Kinnock weighed into him in 1985. Why, it was argued, should the leadership take on the miners' leader for a second successive year, in the virtual certainty of defeat? What kind of tactics was that?

That reasoning gave Kinnock pause, but when the meeting broke for lunch no decision had been taken. During the break Tom Sawyer and David Blunkett took him aside and pointed out that it would be possible for him to accept the bulk of the NUM resolution without difficulty. There were fewer than a half dozen points at which it clashed directly with the NEC statement. In response, Kinnock hit on the unconventional notion of giving the NEC's blessing to the resolution but with reservations, and making the reservations public. Nobody could recall when that had been done before, but equally nobody could think of a reason not to do it.

The reservations had the effect of turning the motion into a version of the NEC statement. The first concerned the timing of the removal of nuclear power stations: the NEC pointed out that it could not possibly be done within the five-year life of the next Labour Government. On THORP, Torness and Heysham the NEC referred back to the position in its own statement. And they rejected the blanket call to stop dumping all nuclear waste.

When the energy debate took place on Wednesday, Scargill declined to accept those qualifications as part of his motion, but that did not prevent Eddie Haigh from reiterating them when he spoke for the NEC. Scargill insisted that closing all nuclear stations within five years was possible. He tried to dampen other union leaders' fears of job losses by saying that their members could be absorbed into other energy industries as the switch was made. He also suggested that the high levels of radiation found among sheep in north-west England could have been caused by discharges from Sellafield rather than the Chernobyl accident.

It was a noisy debate. A speaker from Cunningham's Copeland constituency opposed the miners' motion and was shouted down when he referred to Scargill as 'el supremo' who, if he gained a larger role for his union in the supply of energy, could manipulate Kinnock in Downing Street like a puppet. Eric Hammond, the electricians' leader, had a job making himself heard above the catcalls (provoked mainly by his members' strike-breaking role in the News International dispute at Wapping). He was proposing a resolution seeking to commit the party to the TUC policy of an inquiry into the nuclear industry, combined with a freeze on construction and development of facilities. That gained the support of Bill Jordan, president of the Amalgamated Engineering Union, who said the Scargill policy would cost his members 140,000 jobs. In the day's most emotional speech a Harwich delegate, Bill Johnston, said that if nuclear energy put at risk the lives of 270,000 East Anglian schoolchildren, 'I'd say it's worth a million bloody jobs'.

173

Then came the votes, and the NEC statement was carried comfortably, while Hammond's motion was defeated. The miners' resolution, without the NEC qualifications, was passed, but by fractionally less than the margin it needed to make it part of the manifesto – it won 66.3% of the votes, instead of the required 66.6%. That meant that a Kinnock government would be free to move away from nuclear power at their own deliberate pace.

Cunningham was comfortably re-elected to the Shadow Cabinet and was keen to keep the environmental portfolio. Kinnock was inclined to let him, not just because he thought him good at his job but because he did not like the idea of switching his team around merely to satisfy critics in *The Guardian*. A complicating factor was that one of the new faces elected to the shadow Cabinet was Dr David Clark, an expert on environmental issues. After a weekend of bargaining, Cunningham stayed as shadow Environment Secretary while Clark was added to his team with specific responsibility for 'green' subjects such as conservation and anti-pollution measures. That meant that Cunningham stayed in overall charge, but Clark would be the front man on questions relating to radiation hazards. It was not an ideal solution but, as Kinnock reflected, the art of leadership lies in knowing when to compromise.

7 Glenys and the Fleet Street Factor

A persistent and, on the face of it, curious theme ran through the press reporting of Kinnock's stand on non-nuclear defence: speculation about the role of his wife Glenys. It was said that the reason for his dogged refusal to budge was her commitment to unilateral nuclear disarmament as an article of faith, so firm that she would not let him countenance compromise. It was even hinted that the very future of their marriage might depend on his holding fast. So often was this published that eventually it became accepted as substantiated fact. Neil was cast as the henpecked husband, dominated by a woman portrayed – laughably to those who know her – as a ferocious harpie, a Lady Macbeth whose taunts drove him on against his better judgment, a Joan of Arc to his Dauphin.

'It's totally untrue,' Glenys told *The Sunday Telegraph* in September 1986. 'Neil and I have a very equal relationship. It's not one where either of us feels it necessary to impose wills on the other.'

Nobody who knows them doubts it. Yet repeated denials do not deter the press and political opponents from continuing to make the same assertion. The simplest explanation for the persistence of the legend is that Neil is the first leader of a major British party in living memory to be married to someone with an independent political life. Their marriage was founded on a base of politics. They met at Cardiff University in 1962 when he sought – with instant success – to recruit her to the Socialist Society: she was a fresher and he, at the beginning of his second year, was chair of the society. She came from a more political family than his. Her father, Cyril Parry, was secretary of the Anglesey Labour Party and an office-holder in his union. Kinnock's father Gordon was a loyal member of the miners' and then the blast furnace-men's unions, but had never been active in party politics.

Glenys joined the Campaign for Nuclear Disarmament at the peak of its success in 1960. She was then 16 and did not join the Labour Party until a year later. At Cardiff she and Neil soon ran the Socialist Society in tandem, he as president and she as secretary. They enjoyed a bonus year of this partnership when Neil had to stay on for a fourth year to resit his history exam before being awarded his BA in 1965, and then stayed a further year for his Diploma in Education. He became president of the Students' Union and she was chair of the local committee of the National Union of Students. That was where they had their first taste of factional fighting. Both resigned from their posts after a successful attempt by opponents to dictate who would be on the Cardiff delegation at the NUS annual conference.

Once they started going out together, neither Glenys nor Neil seriously considered marrying anyone else. Although their political views were the same, it was in other respects an attraction of opposites. North Wales is the stronghold of the Welsh language, which Glenys speaks fluently. The north Welsh are gentle, introspective, sensible, hard to draw out. 'They're so tight they make Scotsmen seem generous,' is the perception of their southern compatriots, who, by contrast, are mercurial extroverts, talkative and stimulating companions, romantic and occasionally unrealistic.

So it is with Glenys and Neil. She has none of the sharp edges or rasping tones that characterize many female politicians. Certainly the pair discuss politics: with their backgrounds it would be amazing if they did not. The best description of their relationship is that she tries to keep him in check, persuading him to pause for thought before engaging in actions dictated by his instincts that she thinks risky. Often she succeeds but sometimes not. That is why the press image of the rampant, dominant Glenys makes no sense.

After their marriage in 1967 they kept up their interest in politics. Neil was now a tutor organizer of the Workers' Educational Association in South Wales and Glenys, who had also obtained a Diploma in Education, was teaching at a grammar school at Abersychan, just north of Pontypool. They bought a small house in Pontllanfraith, near Blackwood, and together transferred to the Bedwellty Labour Party from Ebbw Vale. Within a year Neil had become the political education officer of the local party and in 1969 won the Parliamentary nomination. It was one of the safest seats in the country, so he was assured of his ticket to Westminster. Glenys was temporarily less active because she was starting their family, although she was at the selection meeting as the Young Socialist delegate. Stephen was born in 1970 – the year Neil was first elected to Parliament – and Rachel almost two years later.

The family moved to London in 1971, first to Kingston and then to Ealing, where the children go to a comprehensive school. Through most of Stephen and Rachel's childhood, Glenys worked as a teacher and continued her political activities, attending demonstrations in support of CND and the Anti-Apartheid Movement. Once or twice the whole family went on a demonstration together.

When they moved to London they bought a small terraced house in Pontllanfraith to use for constituency visits. Neil is meticulous about his monthly surgeries for constituents. Starting at 9.30 on a Saturday morning, he will sometimes stay there until mid-afternoon, without a break, so that he can see all the people who are waiting. The most common problems are to do with council housing and social security. Like other MPs Neil cannot guarantee a positive response but often a judicious letter helps speed things up. He will either draft it there and then in longhand, or dictate it to his agent, Doreen Moore, sometimes while the constituent is still there.

Glenys does not always go with him to the constituency, because the children often need her in Ealing. But she makes several visits to Islwyn during the year, to events such as the constituency party's annual dinner. She is popular with the local people. Some of them, including Doreen Moore and her husband Barry, are old friends from the days when she and Neil used to live there permanently. They both enjoy going back.

When Neil became leader of the party in 1983, he and Glenys talked about what role she could best play. Three considerations had to be balanced. She naturally wanted to help him become Prime Minister, but she was also anxious to pursue her own political and professional interests and not to function as a traditional politician's wife, the dutiful hostess occasionally let out on her own to open jumble sales.

The third and, they both agreed, the most important object was to ensure that they could enjoy as normal a family life as circumstances allowed. They were determined to protect the children from the circus of constant publicity, although as it happens both are now considering fairly public careers. Rachel has thoughts of becoming an actress, or a teacher like her mother. Stephen is doing A-levels in languages and history with an eye to a university place and then a possible career as a journalist. Another interest he shares with his father is his enthusiasm for rugby. He has played for the London Welsh junior teams since he was eight. Neil used to coach and referee in boys' rugby before the leadership started to eat into his time.

They are a close-knit family, so far as that is possible where the father has so time-consuming a job. Neil believes in conventional values, as he explained in an interview with the feminist magazine *Everywoman* in September 1986. Asked what influence the 'permissive society' had on his thinking, he replied in a way that did not endear him to the party's most radical supporters:

There's only one answer to all that. I'm a father. And no matter how much I try to convince myself towards the course of 'enlightenment' I know damn well that, put to the test, I'm what people would call a reactionary. I know it, I try and rationalize it, but it's no good. I come to the same conclusions all the time. My children stand a chance of being hurt in the foreseeable future by the indulgence of what's called permissiveness.

An important sacrifice Glenys made when Neil became leader was to stop working full-time as a teacher. Instead she took a part-time job, for half a week, teaching children reading and language development at Wykeham Junior and Infants' School in the north London Borough of Brent. During the 1985 teachers' dispute, she joined picket lines outside her school, attracting press photographers – and inevitable criticism from Conservative newspapers. She has grown used to that and does not let it deter her from continuing her political activities. She still attends the occasional CND and Anti-Apartheid demonstration.

Switching to part-time work left her with Mondays and Fridays free for political engagements. She was surprised how many invitations she received to attend functions independently of Neil. She began accepting them at about the time of the 1984 European elections and they kept coming: now she receives around 50 a week. At first she was nervous about speaking in public but she took some tips in self-confidence from the American feminist Gloria Steinem, who advised her that when experiencing the customary terror before a speech she just had to keep telling herself: 'You won't die.' As a speaker she has nothing like Neil's electricity, his ability to bring an audience cheering to their feet, but her experience as a primary school teacher means that she can put even the most detailed message over with low-key simplicity and clarity and can gauge when attention is slipping.

The invitations she accepts are those that fall within her specific areas of interest, especially education and overseas development. A typical day out was Friday 14 November 1986. With Sue Nye, the diary secretary from Neil's office in the Commons, she took the 9.10 train from St Pancras to Derby, where she was met by Margaret Beckett, the local MP, and the regional Labour Party organizer, as well as some cameras from local TV stations. It was the day after the Knowsley North by-election and reporters asked for her reaction to the result. She does not as a rule answer questions about such matters, emphasizing that she has no authority to speak on behalf of the party, but this time she did allow herself to say that it was a good result and she was keen to see a general election as soon as possible.

The main purpose of the visit was to open a new school building at Belper, not far from Derby. Three schools had been merged into a single one, catering for children between 10 and 18, on two sites. There were good photo opportunities for the local papers when, as part of her tour of the school, she visited the animals kept in a shed for the rural studies programme – rabbits, chickens, goats and pigs. As she went round the new building she discussed educational philosophy with the headmistress, Rosemary Ingham, like Glenys a strong believer in non-sexist education.

She went for a short interview with sixth-form students, who had prepared questions on that topic and others. Glenys told them how disappointed she was, when looking at the new science text book Rachel had brought home from school, to find that only two of the laboratory pictures showed girls. She talked about sexist terminology – 'tramp' having a different meaning for men and women; terms for women derived from food – honey, sweetie, tart. Someone asked if there should be a rule against wearing political badges in schools. She thought not: sometimes she wore her CND badge to school – not consciously, but if it happened to be on the coat she was wearing.

She had lunch in the pupils' dining room and then went to the school's second site for the opening ceremony. The headmistress spoke of Glenys as a role model, rather than as the wife of the leader of the Labour Party. In her reply, Glenys again emphasized the importance of giving opportunities for girls to develop their potential. Interviewed afterwards by local radio stations, she insisted on only talking about the school she was opening and educational issues. She refused to be drawn on wider political questions.

Then she drove back to Derby to look at a children's hospital, accompanied by Phillip Whitehead, prospective candidate for the area. More chances of pictures for the local papers. A final interview, with tea and scones, in the hotel by the station, before relaxing on the late afternoon train home. In essence these outings are part of the permanent campaign to keep Labour in the public eye. Neil encourages them; and because she is doing things connected with her own interests she has come to enjoy them too.

At the party conference she dutifully accompanies him on the trade union cocktail circuit and spends quite a lot of time in the guest seats on the conference platform. When he makes his big speech she is there beside him, in her scarlet outfit, to share the applause. But she also addresses fringe meetings on her own subjects. At Blackpool in 1986 she spoke on the Sunday night about the developing world at a meeting on 'Labour and Internationalism' organized by the Tribune Group. Next day she hosted a lunchtime meeting of One World, a group she chairs. Funded by a number of trade unions, One World campaigns for better trade and aid terms for developing countries and seeks to examine the connection between poverty in the Third World and the policies adopted by governments, multi-national companies and financial institutions of the industrialized rich countries.

On Tuesday, in the space between the end of the afternoon conference session and the start of the union receptions, she chaired a meeting calling for better provision of child care for under fives. By Friday she had slipped back into the role of a wife, chivvying Neil after the final party, urging him to pack his suitcase (she eventually did it for him) so they could get started on the drive home. Enough was enough.

The party had claimed its full share of them both. It was more than a week since they had seen their children.

*   *   *

The newspapers adopt a consistent tone in their coverage of Glenys, while blowing hot and cold over Neil, depending on how he is perceived to be faring politically. When the opinion polls show Labour to be losing, he is portrayed as a bumbling ideologue with a bottomless capacity for getting things wrong and taking bad advice, destined to be a loser. When the party's fortunes recover he is transformed miraculously into a cool political operator, maybe a little shallow and inexperienced but otherwise a man to be watched, a force to be reckoned with.

Glenys, on the other hand, is stuck in the Lady Macbeth role. When Neil looks like winning we are warned to beware the dangerous schemer, measuring up the Downing Street curtains with one hand, while with the other drawing up her blueprint for a non-nuclear, non-sexist Britain which she will impose on her malleable milksop of a husband. When the prospect of Downing Street recedes temporarily the papers ask, as the *Daily Mail* did on 22 December 1986: 'Who is to blame as Kinnock's popularity plummets?' No prizes for the answer, in large white lettering on a black background: 'Glenys the Menace'.

The article began as it meant to continue:

> It is doubtful if Neil Kinnock has made a major pivotal decision all his married life which has not had the approval, and frequently the lead, of his wife Glenys . . . Her influence on him, and on the shape of the Labour Party and therefore the very history of the nation, is un-relenting.

An editorial alongside the article described Glenys as 'Mrs Thatcher's secret weapon', who pushed Neil into unilateralism. And in case we still did not get the point, the accompanying illustration showed her pulling the strings of a Neil puppet bearing a CND banner.

Just after Christmas it was announced that Glenys would be suing the *Mail*, not because of the generally hostile tone of the article but for a paragraph in it that seemed to reflect on the way she performed as a teacher. The decision to sue was a difficult one, taken in close consultation with Neil and his inner circle of advisers. That they decided to go ahead indicated that they had effectively written off any hope of forging useful relations with the press and decided that they would have to contest the election without the help of Fleet Street. Because of the cordial relations Neil used to enjoy with Parliamentary journalists, it had taken him longer to reach this conclusion than the facts seemed to dictate.

180

When he first joined the Shadow Cabinet he enjoyed more genial relations with the press than most of his fellow front-benchers. He is naturally gregarious and appreciated their company more than that of his sombre political colleagues. He served for a while on the NEC's press and publicity committee. Some journalists, who were of his age and shared his and Glenys's interests, became personal friends. They would have dinner at each other's houses. Yet Kinnock would never let himself trust them too far. A lifetime of radical politics had taught him that the owners of newspapers do not, as he puts it, keep dogs and let them miaow. They are required to bark, and bark they do.

His current deep antipathy for nearly all journalists dates from the year leading up to the 1983 election. He was sickened by their merciless gibes at his friend and mentor Michael Foot. They were writing things, he felt, that they would not dare say to Foot's face. It offended his sense of fair play. He sought their company less – particularly those responsible for the articles that so angered him.

When he became leader there was a brief honeymoon period. Then he detected that the coverage was getting patronizing, turning to plain hostile as the Conservatives and their Fleet Street supporters began to see him as a potential winner. They began to taunt him for failing, as they saw it, to speak out about the miners' strike and denounce the picket line violence. During a particularly virulent phase of that campaign, he had a visitor in his room in the Commons. Dora Gaitskell, Hugh's widow, was a life peeress and over 80. She suffered from severe arthritis that made walking difficult and painful, yet she had hobbled through the long corridors from her room in the House of Lords. She went in and perched on his settee:

'I just came to tell you I think they're all snobs,' she said.

'Who?' he asked.

'All these people who write condescending and cruel things about you.'

Kinnock shrugged. 'I can't afford to let them run my life, but it's lovely of you to say so.'

Lady Gaitskell persevered: 'I travel on the buses and the people on the buses aren't snobs and they think you're a good man – so don't take any notice of the snobs.'

He asked why she had come to see him.

'That was all I wanted to say,' she replied, slowly rising from the settee. He pressed her to stay for a cup of tea, then she walked slowly back to the Lords.

He derived a little – only a little – amusement from tracing patterns in his press coverage. For a year or so after he became leader, the 'Welsh windbag' slur was dragged up whenever he spoke for a bit too long. When the writers grew tired of that there was a spate of stories hinging on the word 'embarrassed'. Describing the latest (and usually abortive) spoiling move by the far left, the commentators would assert: 'This is certainly going to embarrass Kinnock.' A man who has spent nearly all his adult life as an active politician is unlikely to embarrass easily. Glenys suggested that he should sign his letters 'Embarrassed of Ealing'.

His relationship with the press is worsening and represents a real dilemma for him. Parliamentary democracy, if it is to work properly, demands a reasonably impartial press. Overwhelming media bias towards one party distorts the process by negating the assumption that all sides have a reasonable chance to put forward their views in a favourable light, so that the voters may choose between them. Unwilling at first to admit to himself that this condition did not apply in the Britain of the mid-1980s, Kinnock decided to try to change things single-handed. He went through a period of telephoning reporters and editors after the first editions had appeared, to complain about specific items. *The Guardian* was a target for this treatment during its series of articles about civil nuclear power which persistently questioned John Cunningham's position.

The Guardian is the least hostile of the serious newspapers; but it was for that very reason that Kinnock felt so troubled about its apparently blinkered attitude on this issue and believed he might be able to do something about it. But he quickly realized that to establish himself as a kind of one-man press council, a caped crusader swooping telephonically on Fleet Street in the small hours, was unproductive, even in dealing with a reasonably responsive and potentially sympathetic newspaper. The war was being fought on too broad a front for individual acts of derring-do to alter its course. The reporting of his American visit in early December (which *The Guardian*, incidentally, covered more sympathetically than anyone else) had finally convinced him of that: the *Mail* article on Glenys merely confirmed it.

The day after it appeared, Roy Hattersley said on BBC radio:

British newspapers, by and large, are now more prejudiced than they have ever been, more irresponsible in their use of facts than they have ever been, and in some instances more dishonest than they have ever been.

He said newspapers had developed a 'strange partnership, co-ordinated and calculated' with the Conservative Party and its politicians, singling out Rupert Murdoch's *Times* for special obloquy. The following weekend *The Sunday Telegraph* responded with an article of the very kind he was complaining about. 'When will Kinnock grow up?' asked the headline, accusing the Labour leader of retreating into a bunker and adding a note of special peevishness by pointing out that he had invited only two political journalists to his Christmas party. Nowadays he invites only those he personally trusts to his parties – such as his friend Julia Langdon of the *Sunday Mirror* – because he knows that otherwise a garbled and half-invented version of some off-guard remark or incident will appear in the gossip columns. The *Mirror* papers and their owner Robert Maxwell are his most reliable friends in the media and Maxwell contributes money to party funds. It is not an ideal relationship so far as Kinnock is concerned, because Maxwell's reputation as a capitalist tycoon is in some respects no better than that of Rupert Murdoch, a demon figure for the left. But Labour is not so weighed down with media friends that it can afford to be too choosy.

Kinnock finds television less biased than the newspapers – although he was angry about the *Panorama* programme on defence policy during the 1986 conference. He is likely to concentrate his election efforts on the screen, where he thinks he has an advantage over Thatcher. He also makes a point of talking to the local media – newspapers, radio and TV – whenever he travels out of London. He thinks he gets a fairer hearing outside the hothouse atmosphere of the metropolis.

*   *   *

It is part of political lore that an Opposition Leader's performance in the House of Commons can be decisive in establishing his reputation among voters. The foundation for the belief is probably that the political commentators themselves are based in the Palace of Westminster, and that is where they most often see politicians in action. Of party leaders who have won elections in the last 30 years, Macmillan and Wilson were outstanding in Parliament, Heath and Thatcher less so. Of the two Prime Ministers who failed to win re-election in that period, Home did poorly at the dispatch box and Callaghan well. Their electoral showing thus appears to bear no direct relation to their argumentative skills – although this would no doubt change if TV cameras were allowed into the chamber.

Since Parliament is the forum in which Britain's democratic system operates, it is logical that how politicians perform in it should be among the factors voters take into account when weighing up the rival claims on their support. The headline KINNOCK LASHES THATCHER can never do the reputation of the lasher much harm, or the victim's much good. Although there is no intrinsic reason why a talent for verbal sparring should have any bearing on someone's ability to run a government, persistent failure on the floor of the house would be reflected in the tone of the entire press coverage of a leader, contributing to an overall impression of incompetence.

Kinnock's performances in the chamber are inconsistent. In his early days he won something of a reputation for his ability to speak convincingly and often passionately without notes. When he became education spokesman in 1979 he began writing his speeches in advance, a conscientious safeguard against inadvertently letting slip anything that might conflict with party policy. But his written Commons speeches have only occasionally equalled the power of his earlier ones, and sometimes they have gone on too long. He has never seemed certain of the level at which to pitch them. The Commons is a difficult audience (and sometimes a sparse one). Speaking there is far removed from delivering an inspirational message to a packed and largely sympathetic meeting, rally or conference.

A reputation for oratory is a mixed blessing. Kinnock has always been aware of the danger of being regarded as a maker of fine phrases and little else – the 'Welsh windbag' syndrome. That is why on occasion he deliberately strips his speeches of vivid imagery and pyrotechnics, giving them the arid texture of academic lectures. He is given to quoting worthy passages from his favourite political philosophers, R. H. Tawney and Aneurin Bevan, whose writings move and inspire him, and form the basis of his convictions. Yet it is impossible to spread that inspiration to others by means of a handful of maxims.

He enters spiritedly into the ritual of Prime Minister's Question Time because it is required of him, although in truth he thinks it rather pointless and does not enjoy it. This accounts for his variable effectiveness here, too. Sometimes he lets himself become too shrill, either because of his genuine concern about the topic under discussion – perhaps health, education or some aspect of welfare – or due to his frustration at Thatcher's refusal to give what he considers a straight answer. At other times he lets his questions run away with him and tries the patience of the House.

Kinnock's most ferocious clash with the Prime Minister came in February 1985. Like many Commons rows of recent years, it was over a security matter. He accused her of lying about her involvement in the decision to prosecute Clive Ponting under the Official Secrets Act. Ponting had been charged with leaking documents concerning the sinking of the Argentinian battleship, the *Belgrano*, during the Falklands War; but he was acquitted. Thatcher wrote to Kinnock denying that she had lied and demanding withdrawal of the allegation. Kinnock refused. For some days the two exchanged petulant letters. Political correspondents wrote that they could not recall when relations between a Prime Minister and a Leader of the Opposition had been so low. Kinnock switched his attack to whether Thatcher had misled the Commons over the sinking of the battleship itself – a theme that the Scottish MP Tam Dalyell had been doggedly pursuing for months. By the time the dust settled both sides claimed victory. Neutral observers judged that honours were roughly even.

Kinnock came less well out of the two scandals of 1986 which could have damaged the Government gravely. The first was in January, over the future of the Westland helicopter company. Two ministers resigned – Michael Heseltine as Defence Secretary in protest at the company accepting an American rather than a European takeover bid, and Leon Brittan as Trade and Industry Secretary after the leak of a letter, critical of Heseltine, was traced to his office.

The Government was clearly in trouble and Labour supporters were looking forward eagerly to the debate on the question on 27 January. They hoped to see Kinnock make life uncomfortable for Thatcher. He had already made one powerful speech on the débâcle. But this time, under pressure of barracking from the Tory benches as soon as he stood up, he gave one of his least effective performances as leader and she escaped further embarrassment with little difficulty. Then, at the end of 1986, during the Government's Australian court case over Peter Wright's book on MI5, Kinnock's contacts with the defence lawyer gave the Conservatives the chance to deflect the fire from the Government back to him, accusing him of lacking patriotism.

The Conservatives believe that Kinnock's advocacy of a non-nuclear defence policy makes him vulnerable over a range of questions basic to the country's survival. In an article in the *Sunday Express* at the end of 1986, Thatcher wrote: 'The path of unilateral concession, chosen by the Labour Party, is a recipe for weakness and instability.' Every time issues of defence and security came up at Question Time – and that has happened more often than usual since Thatcher became Prime Minister – she would hammer away at the theme.

As the general election approached, the Conservatives stepped up their attack on a second front where they thought they detected equal potential for embarrassing the Labour leadership. This was the political complexion and sometimes surprising activities of a few Labour-controlled local authorities – those the press had succinctly labelled the Loony Left. The theme here was that although Labour may have moderated its national image, its true face was still represented by the activities of extremists on local councils, even after the abolition of the GLC.

Bernie Grant, leader of Haringey Council in North London, was singled out for particular hatred and ridicule. In October 1985 there was a riot on the Broadwater Farm council estate at Tottenham, in which a policeman was killed. In interviews directly afterwards, Grant seemed to take the side of the rioters, although he later expressed his regret over the killing. Kinnock made a point of condemning the killing unequivocally from the beginning. At the end of 1986 he went to

Tottenham to unveil a memorial to the dead policeman. He is aware of the harm that could be done if he were to be thought anti-police, which he decidedly is not. After a violent Saturday night outside Rupert Murdoch's Wapping plant in January, 1987, Government ministers repeatedly challenged Kinnock to denounce the assaults on the police in ever stronger terms, as they had done during the miners' strike. The Conservatives believe law and order to be one of Labour's weak suits.

At the end of 1986 the north London borough of Brent became a special target for Conservatives. The council were seeking to discipline a headmistress, Maureen McGoldrick, for allegedly having told someone in the local education authority that she did not want another black teacher in her school. The much-publicized case dragged on through various council committees and the courts. The predominant view was that the headmistress was being unfairly victimized; but for some weeks the council persisted with the case. A direct request from Kinnock to let it drop was ignored for a time, and complied with only after more weeks had passed.

In November 1986 came the clearest sign that the Conservatives thought the excesses of local authorities could be exploited with profit in the run-up to the election. In the debate on the Queen's Speech the Secretary of State for the Environment, Nicholas Ridley, said:

> Town halls founded on civic dignity have become an arena for aggressive political posing, disruption, wild accusations, threats and fear .... I am told that people dare not speak out for fear of what might happen to them and their families. Perhaps they cannot really believe it is happening in England in the 1980s, in a democracy. It is more like Poland or East Germany – the knock on the door in the middle of the night . . . No amount of rose-tinted public relations can dispel the stink emanating from Labour town halls.

Ridley's hyperbolic attack was not isolated. On the same day Norman Tebbit, the Conservative Party chairman, made the same point in a speech at Ilford, Essex:

> The wreckers have moved to take over the town hall Labour parties and are poised to take over the Parliamentary Labour Party, too. They have a clear vision. They already see Neil Kinnock as just another ex-future Labour Prime Minister. Tomorrow's leaders of the Labour Party are there in these town halls today.

Although John Cunningham, the shadow environment spokesman, dismissed Ridley's exaggerated charges in the House, it soon became apparent that Labour leaders were worried about the potential for damage in his and Tebbit's remarks. A few days later Larry Whitty, the party's general secretary, wrote to Labour groups on local authorities pointing out that the results of the local elections, due on 7 May 1987, could have a strong influence on the timing of the general election. He warned the councillors:

> We must therefore take particular care over the presentation of policy initiatives as these can, too easily, be distorted and misrepresented by our opponents, eclipsing our other achievements.

Those are precisely Kinnock's sentiments, although Whitty had expressed his strictures more moderately than is his leader's custom. But the issue would not go away. After the death of Guy Barnett, the Labour MP for Greenwich, the local party obstinately chose a far left candidate for the February, 1987 by-election – Deirdre Wood, a former member of the GLC. The selection was above board and there were no grounds for a Knowsley-style intervention by Walworth Road. The press mounted a personal campaign against her, based not just on her politics but also on embarrassing aspects of her family history. She lost the seat to Rosie Barnes, the SDP candidate, by 6,611 votes. Labour's share of the poll fell to 34%, more than 4% below the 1983 figure; but the main factor in the SDP victory was a massive switch of votes from the Conservatives, who had voted to keep the far left candidate out. Kinnock's aides blamed what they called 'the London effect'. In a letter to Frank Dobson, chairman of the London group of Labour MPs, Patricia Hewitt wrote: 'The "Loony Labour Left" is taking its toll; the gays and lesbians issue is costing us dear among the pensioners.'

The previous month an issue had arisen that looked as though it might prove as productive for Labour as the 'Loony Left' was for the Conservatives. Although the parallel is not exact, the City of London bears much the same relationship to the Conservative Party as left-wing councils do to Labour – in both cases the party approves of the institution's objectives but has reservations about some of the methods used in pursuing them. In January 1987 came a spate of revelations about some dubious techniques that had been employed in one of the big City battles of the previous year, the takeover of Distillers Group, the whisky manufacturers, by the brewers Guinness. It emerged that Guinness had organized a group of friendly financiers to buy its shares to keep the price up and make its bid for Distillers worth more. Several executives resigned.

Because the Conservatives are identified with the City, such scandals, based as they are on greed and shady practices, are assumed to harm them, as strikes are said to damage Labour's electoral prospects. (That belief was not altogether confirmed by a Harris poll in *The Observer*. After the Guinness affair became headlines, the pollsters found that 81% of people said it would make no difference to their voting intention.) Labour supporters saw the row as an additional argument against selling off nationalized industries so that rapacious speculators could make profits from them. As far as Kinnock himself was concerned, the revelations confirmed his own antipathy towards the City, expressed unequivocally in *Making Our Way* – his first book, published in the autumn of 1986. The book dealt mainly with Labour's plans for Britain's economic recovery. Explaining the proposal to create a British Investment Bank, partly to support industries taken into social ownership, Kinnock blamed the financial institutions for the poor performance of British manufacturing industry. He maintained:

> The British financial sector does not play the monitoring and restructuring role that the industrial banks do in other countries ... In these circumstances the contempt expressed for 'the City' by a wide spectrum of opinion, ranging from working managers and pressurized entrepreneurs to me and my fellow socialists, is entirely justified.

Since the bulk of Kinnock's literary output has been the texts of countless speeches, it was no surprise that the book's style was rhetorical. What emerged most strongly from it was his conviction that manufacturing is not just the most economically beneficial undertaking for Britain in the 1980s and 1990s, but is also morally superior to the service industries that have taken up some of the slack as industry has declined. Despite his assertion that 'service industries are not to be despised and they are not demeaning', he does not warm to the idea of a nation of hairdressers, travel agents and gourmet chefs. In his 1984 conference speech he characterized some service industries as 'fruitless fripperies' – a philosophy inherited from his childhood in the valleys, where work with the hands was about the only respectable work there was.

The book won a mixed reception. In *The Guardian* Ian Aitken pointed out that left-wingers would not be amused to discover that 'socialism' merited only one reference in the index, and that a wrong one. He also observed that, although Kinnock could not bring himself to mention the words 'incomes policy' – the phrase that has haunted so many labour administrations – he did write about a 'revenue and rewards' policy, which sounded suspiciously like the same thing.

Mixed with the book's quite radical economic proposals were calls upon impatient Labour supporters to adopt a moderate though determined approach to the business of reform. It ended:

> I believe that it is better to get on with the job than be paralysed by the size of it. Better to work for decisive victories of socialism than to

wait for some interminable date when they can be universal. Better to light a candle, than curse the darkness.

*　　*　　*

Neil Kinnock, the apostle of consensus and realism in 1986, had moved a distance from the Neil Kinnock of less than a decade earlier – the scourge of the monarchy, enemy of privilege (he wanted to abolish the House of Lords), critic of Wilson's and Callaghan's moderate leadership and a founder member of the Campaign for Labour Party Democracy which he left in 1980. His 'conversion' is resented on the left of the party, where political virility is still judged by how rigidly you adhere to bewhiskered dogma and how passionately you insist on impossible demands. Yet he has won some fellow converts in the PLP by hammering home his point about zealotry: that in the long run the force of progress is impeded by extremism, because it is exploited by reactionary elements among the enemy and alarms potential supporters, driving them into the arms of alternative parties.

There are obvious parallels here with Harold Wilson's tactics. Wilson was a former Bevanite who – like Bevan himself – moved decisively towards the centre when the leadership beckoned. Kinnock naturally resents the comparison and it is inexact in most important respects. Once Wilson's position as leader became virtually unassailable, he did not trouble to court the good opinion of the party rank and file. Frustration at his leadership simmered below the surface, and broke through disastrously after his resignation in 1976. The resentment that he and Callaghan provoked led directly to the introduction of compulsory reselection of Parliamentary candidates and the creation of the electoral college for the leadership. The party has yet to recover fully from those years of turmoil, although under Kinnock the completion of its convalescence is in sight.

Lacking Wilson's status nationally, Kinnock has recognized the importance of keeping the party behind him in everything he has done, both to safeguard his own position and to avoid more internal contention. Even his best publicized act of bravado, the assault on Militant, has been performed with a meticulous regard for correct procedure. He is convinced that, if he is seen to be acting fairly, the great majority of Labour supporters will give him their backing. He believes this is the only way the party can be led effectively, avoiding the kind of long-term damage he inherited. Not that there is any immediately obvious alternative leader. Any of his senior colleagues would provoke such hostility from one or other faction in the party that none could function effectively. In electoral terms, too, he is a lot more attractive than any who might fancy their chance of mounting a challenge to him.

The great majority of MPs, no matter how extreme their position, would prefer to be in government than in opposition. They will therefore give Kinnock's moderate leadership a reasonably easy ride so long as it seems likely that he can deliver an election victory. As soon as the polls turn seriously against him, though, the muttering in the ranks gets louder. This was noticeable in two instances early in 1987 when, probably as a result of the nuclear defence debate, the Conservatives were ahead in most opinion polls.

The first hint of disaffection came when Norman Buchan, frontbench spokesman on the arts and a member of the Tribune Group, resigned his portfolio after Kinnock decided that, under a Labour government, some responsibility for broadcasting would remain with the Home Office rather than being transferred wholesale to a restructured arts ministry. It was a comparatively arcane point of principle, but since the shadow Home Secretary, Gerald Kaufman, is on the right of the party, left-wingers saw it as a rightist coup. They criticized Kinnock in unusually bitter tones at a PLP meeting and made their views known to journalists.

The second occasion when the left broke ranks was over a security leak of the kind that was coming to characterize the Thatcher administration. Duncan Campbell, a writer on the *New Statesman* specializing in exposing official secrets, had made a programme for the BBC which revealed details of Zircon, a supposedly secret British communications satellite said to be devoted to eavesdropping on the Russians. The BBC, having made the programme, decided not to screen it, so Campbell instead wrote the story for the *New Statesman*. The Government bungled their attempt to suppress it and Kinnock criticized them for that, giving Thatcher an uncomfortable time in the House. He said that if the revelation was truly harmful to national security there had been ample time to suppress it earlier.

This 'responsible' attitude was clearly aimed at mitigating part of the effect of his intervention in the Wright case in Australia, where Thatcher had accused him of undermining the Government's security efforts. In electoral terms Kinnock's stand on Zircon was certainly well judged, for patriotism has never been a vote loser. But it angered backbenchers on the left, who again felt freer to criticize their leader with the party performing poorly in the polls. They admired Campbell's persistence and initiative in getting the report published and would have liked the Labour leadership to mount an attack on the development of the spy satellite itself. (The whole party was able to unite a week later in condemning a further raid by the Special Branch, when they swooped on the BBC headquarters in Glasgow and took away cart-loads of films, tapes and files.)

As well as being criticized by the left, Kinnock also generates a degree of suspicion on the right, where, in addition to reservations about the defence policy, some doubt the sincerity of his conversion to the ranks of the pragmatic. It is pointed out that after the next election, whoever wins it, the centre of gravity in the PLP will have shifted leftwards. This is certainly true if you judge by looking at the known political posture of the new batch of candidates in winnable seats (and even more so in unwinnable seats, although the point is academic). Only six sitting MPs lost their nominations in the reselection process, but one unforeseen effect of the new rule was the early retirement of a number of moderate MPs who would formerly have been expected to continue for at least another term. In their sixties, they saw no real point in ending their careers with a bruising battle against constituency activists. So they stood down gracefully, invariably to be replaced by figures from the left.

Pointing to this potential shift in the balance of the PLP, the party's enemies speculate that Kinnock could fall victim to the fate of Andrew McIntosh in the GLC. He lost the leadership of the Labour Group to Ken Livingstone immediately after an election had put Labour in power at County Hall. This was what Tebbit was referring to in his Ilford speech about 'the wreckers' in November 1986.

There are three reasons why what happened to McIntosh will not happen to Kinnock. The first is that MPs who arrive at the Commons spitting fire often find themselves restrained by the disciplines of Parliament. Whether in government or opposition, the party whips are always hovering, preaching the virtues of loyalty to the leadership. And in government, the prospect of office in itself proves a powerful incentive to loyalty. Several MPs likely to receive appointments in a Kinnock administration distanced themselves from the far left as the election drew near. Michael Meacher was the most obvious example but there were others: Stuart Holland, spokesman for overseas development, quit the Campaign Group at the end of 1986.

The second structural reason why Kinnock appears safe from a far left hijack is the new college system of electing the leader. Even if he were to lose the support of the majority of MPs, they nowadays count for only 30% of the votes in a leadership election. The unions, who hold the whip hand with 40%, would almost certainly oppose any move by MPs to replace Kinnock.

There is a nice irony here. Both the new electoral college and compulsory reselection came about as a result of pressure from left-wingers. They wanted a new method of choosing the leader because the rightist bias of the Parliamentary party, which previously had the choice to itself, made it hard for anyone from the left to gain the post. Yet at the same time they were pushing for reselection, which swung the PLP to the left. A left-wing candidate for leader would stand a better chance now if the choice were decided by the votes of the latter-day PLP on its own, rather than by the tripartite college.

The third reason is well articulated by Kinnock: 'I haven't given up the remnants of my youth to pass the party to any coup-mongerers, real or imagined.'

So, despite the existence of enemies on both wings of the party, Kinnock seems secure in his job, certainly if he were to win the election and probably, too, in the event of defeat. Through a series of deliberate manoeuvres he has established a firm grip on the party. He has not been able to eradicate all of its more florid excesses but he has marginalized them and shown that they will not be allowed to influence him if he becomes Prime Minister. His record makes it hard for Labour's opponents to sustain the thesis that a vote for Kinnock is a vote for Hatton/Scargill/Knight although, as the Greenwich by-election showed, that does not deter them from trying.

He has also trimmed away some of the policies that derived from ancient prejudices and were patently harming the party's electoral chances – such as the insistence on full renationalization, with minimal compensation, of industries privatized by the Conservatives; and the dogmatic refusal to consider any sales of council houses. He knows that the biggest threat to a Labour victory comes from the party's being perceived as exclusively concerned with the poorest members of society. Although their interests will always be central in determining his and the party's policies, the under-class are statistically a minority. To win an election, Labour needs the support of a significant section of the middle class, willing to share its social priorities but wishing to be assured that in doing so they are not harming their interests. He wrote in *The Times* in 1983: 'We need "haves" and "haven't-got-enoughs" if we are to help the "have-nots".'

For instance, holders of small quantities of British Telecom, British Gas, British Airways and Trustee Savings Bank shares would be foolish to vote Labour if doing so meant a substantial drop in the real value of their savings. That is why the policy stops short of full renationalization. Similarly, council tenants hoping to buy their house will not support a party that would prevent them from doing so.

Kinnock's sensitivity to those considerations became apparent in April 1985, in a significant quarrel over tax relief on mortgage interest payments. For some months a joint policy committee of the NEC had been working on a plan to amalgamate mortgage interest tax relief with the housing benefit scheme, so that home owners and tenants should get assistance with housing expenses more closely related to their needs. The inequity in using tax relief as a means of financial assistance is that by its nature it is of greatest value to the highest earners who pay the highest taxes. Couples buying their first home, who most need help, often do not earn enough to benefit from the tax relief to any significant extent, and as house owners they do not qualify for housing benefit at all; so they lose out in all respects.

Michael Meacher, the shadow spokesman for the social services, let slip at a press conference that such a review of Labour policy was under way. Next morning *The Times* and the *Daily Express* interpreted it as a firm commitment to abolish all tax relief on mortgage interest payments, implying that it was part of Labour's generalized attack on the property-owning class. Meacher denied it, but because the details of the new policy had not been worked out he was unable to refute the charge in the detail needed to make the denial convincing. It was an object lesson in the dangers of jumping the gun by offering hints about policy developments before they have been properly formulated.

Kinnock was in Brussels when the controversy broke, and Roy Hattersley was going to chair that Wednesday's meeting of the Shadow Cabinet. He summoned Meacher and said a further clarifying statement must be issued. The draft proposed by Hattersley made the point that there was no question of abolishing the tax relief, but the whole question of housing aid was being reviewed.

Gerald Kaufman, the shadow Home Secretary, thought the potential damage to the party's election prospects so great that he wanted a still stronger statement, amounting almost to a repudiation of Meacher, containing an unequivocal pledge to continue mortgage tax relief in its present form. After some acrimonious discussion, the Shadow Cabinet rejected the Kaufman amendment, but the incident highlighted the continuing tension between the left and the right wings of the leadership, and its tendency to manifest itself when Kinnock's guiding hand was temporarily absent.

When Kinnock returned, Meacher asked to see him, to apologize for the damage the incident had caused. Kinnock said he should put it down to experience. In practical terms, the result of Meacher's indiscretion was to make it even harder to devise a new policy on housing aid, and by the end of 1986 none had been announced, save for a general commitment as part of that year's Freedom and Fairness Campaign to introduce 'a new scheme to help first time buyers'. Tactically, it illustrated the importance of sensible public relations, of launching policies in a way which does not allow the opposition to seize on one aspect of them and imbue it with menace.

*   *   *

The Freedom and Fairness Campaign, launched in April 1986, was the first product of Labour's new emphasis on presentation, and the first campaign masterminded by Peter Mandelson after his arrival at

Walworth Road. The subjects covered and the manner in which they were presented owed a lot to the party's private polling, which showed that housing, health, education and personal safety were the issues most likely to influence people's votes at the next election. So a press pack had been prepared with a set of powerfully designed leaflets on those topics, supported by a television party political broadcast on the same themes.

Reporting the launch next morning, the press placed as much emphasis on the slickness and staging of the presentation as on the content of the campaign material. Some commentators poked fun, but it produced a positive response in terms of poll ratings. The same approach was used for the launch of two more policy documents later in the year; the defence policy and *Investing in People*, a full-colour booklet attractively setting out Labour's stance on social and some economic issues. When *The Guardian*'s James Naughtie questioned Kinnock on this new approach to presentation, Kinnock quoted George Bernard Shaw on the subject of the Fabian Society:

> I think it was by no means the least of our merits that we always, as far as our means permitted, tried to make our printed documents as handsome as possible, and did our best to destroy the association between revolutionary literature and slovenly printing on paper that is nasty without being cheap.

The stress now being laid on appearances was soon vested with a catchy name by the fashion-conscious sections of the media: designer socialism. It was the socialism of snappy suits and dresses, international conferences at glossy venues, the soft emblem of the rose, appearances on TV chat shows, endorsements from actors and pop stars. It was not the socialism of the working men's club, the meetings in draughty trade halls, the horny hands and the grimy finger-nails. Kinnock's active support of this new image did not spring directly from the fuss a few years earlier when Michael Foot, as Leader of the Opposition, attended the November memorial service at the Whitehall cenotaph in a donkey jacket. Kinnock had always been a man for neat clothes and shiny shoes, because in the community from which he sprang it was a social obligation to keep up appearances. The cultivated shabbiness of intellectuals is alien to him.

Only diehards, of the stamp of Dennis Skinner and Eric Heffer, thought there was something inherently wrong with Labour's new glossy character. They believed it symbolized a compromise with the values of a consumer society and was incompatible with the pure socialist creed. Kinnock had a message for them in *Making Our Way*.

He wrote that the attitude was 'the result of a narrowness of perception reminiscent of theocrats' and went on:

> In others it seems to come from shallowness of conviction; they seem to lack the confidence that democratic socialism is a creed and a commitment which draws life from realities and is not threatened or defiled by being matched to social and economic change . . . There is a criticism that an 'upwardly mobile' appeal has no place in the armoury of socialism. That is profoundly wrong and defeatist . . . If we are not directly engaged in the upward economic, social and political mobility of people, they face a fate of downward mobility or, at best, stagnation.

The roses thrown at Blackpool in 1986 represented the flowering of that philosophy. But is a new sense of style enough? Patently not, neither as a qualification for office nor a reliable means of achieving it. Kinnock knows that his paramount need is to convince the electorate that he is a credible leader who can be trusted and relied upon to do what is best for the country. To do that he must hold in check those elements in his party who too combatively pursue what they perceive to be the interests of the class or faction they represent, to the disadvantage of the rest of the populace. He put it concisely in his new year message to the party at the beginning of 1985:

> Power can only be won at the polls and that rests on the public understanding the party, understanding its motives and having confidence in its commitment to democracy.

In his 1986 book *Labour's Future*, Eric Heffer maintained that ejecting or watering-down socialist policies was turning the party into an 'SDP Mark Two'. He wrote:

> There are two ways of dropping Labour's socialism. There is the Gaitskell way, open and honest like the man himself, and there is the other way, killing it off by kindness, paying lip service to it but in reality ignoring it. That, I fear, is the danger today . . . If the party does not renew itself in a socialist direction, if it adopts SDP concepts, it may gain some short term advantages, but in the longer term it will fade into history as it is forced into competition with the Alliance for votes . . . We need a socialist future, not a half-baked capitalist one.

Labour leaders show a natural reluctance to acknowledge how great a change has been effected on the British political landscape by the formation of the SDP and its alliance with the Liberals. Its implications for

Labour are not all adverse. Many Alliance voters are disaffected Conservatives, and students of political statistics affirm that an Alliance vote of some 25% would help Labour secure an electoral majority. But the new party does present Labour with a serious problem over presentation – how to distinguish itself sharply from the Alliance without frightening away its moderate supporters.

Heffer and his allies have no doubts that the way forward is to increase the socialist content of the party's policies, abandoning the centre to the Alliance. But the arithmetic argues against this course. For all their talk of 'the masses', the reality is that the policies of the hard left attract nowhere near enough support to return a government that espouses them. The path Kinnock has chosen is to persuade the party to adopt moderate policies, presenting Labour not only as the authentic party of social democracy but also as the only one with a hope of defeating the Conservatives.

To distance himself further from the Alliance, Kinnock has consistently refused to contemplate any deal or coalition with them if the election should result in a hung Parliament. If he were to find himself leader of the largest party in the Commons, but without an overall majority, he says he would form a government, write a Queen's Speech and challenge the Alliance parties to vote against it and force another election.

The Alliance leaders have said that they would not vote for any legislative programme that did not include a commitment to introduce proportional representation, a cause held dear by both the Liberals and the SDP, whose electoral prospects it would transform. In a letter to Kinnock in May, 1985, David Steel, the Liberal leader, wrote:

> If you are not prepared to contemplate power sharing and dusting down the Labour Party's pre-war commitments to electoral reform, then you must not be surprised if the Conservative Party moves fast in these directions post-election and if you find yourself continuing as leader of the official Opposition.

Kinnock's plans for his first Queen's Speech include no such pledge. He would concentrate initially on tackling what he sees as the chief legacy of the Thatcher years – unemployment, deprivation and the destruction of Britain's manufacturing base. His inaugural programme would mainly consist of emergency measures in these fields, which the Alliance would find it hard to oppose on policy grounds. He would bank on David Owen and David Steel being unwilling to risk the opprobrium likely to fall upon them if they were to force a second quick election. He said as much in a speech responding to Steel's letter:

We will get on with the job of creating jobs and investment, and anyone who did not think that was a matter of national urgency and would prefer for reasons of political prejudice or personal ambition to vote against us – well, let them. Frankly, I don't think they'd have the guts.

Even if they did, the chances are that a new Government, with a small majority or no majority, would improve its electoral performance at a subsequent early election, as Harold Wilson's did in 1974.

Those exchanges in May, 1985, came at a time when the Alliance had enjoyed a surge of support in the opinion polls. Kinnock responded with an unbridled attack on David Owen and the SDP, in a speech at the Welsh Labour Party conference in Llandudno. Owen, he declared, had 'an ego fat with arrogance and drunk with ambition'. The Alliance was 'liquid grease that slips and slides to the lowest level of responsibility'. The SDP was a party without policy, principle or purpose.

All they have is a sort of movable *Question Time* programme where the answers are determined by the latest fad and current fashion, where only inconsistency is consistent and equivocation is firm.

And he recalled some words of Bevan:

Political renegades always start their career of treachery as the 'best men of all parties' and end up in the Tory knackery.

Politicians are notorious for their pragmatism, for going back on the very firmest of undertakings in the light of changing circumstances. They are also largely insensitive to personal abuse. Yet even given those provisos, it is hard to imagine any formal understanding between Kinnock and someone he describes in those terms, especially while the bitter memories of the 1981 breakaway are still quite fresh. To do a separate deal with the Liberals, as Callaghan did, would involve splitting the Alliance, an unlikely prospect. Steel has said he would not do it because it would be a 'betrayal of the platform on which the election was fought'.

If Kinnock needed to continue relying on Alliance support to govern, even without a formal coalition he would have to shelve those parts of the manifesto most dear to the left, including the abandonment of nuclear weapons and the renationalization – or taking back into social ownership – of privatized industries. He insists that he would make no such compromise. If he changed his mind it could provoke a backbench revolt, although it would be a bold Labour MP who would risk being held responsible for bringing down a new Labour government.

Steel and Owen maintain that Britain is ready for coalition government, like many countries of western Europe. That argument ignores the fact that the two major parties are themselves coalitions of groups with differing views, united only by a broad philosophy – exceptionally broad in the case of Labour.

* * *

In nearly four years as leader, Kinnock had done enough to leave no doubt about his ability to control the Labour Party and its factions. In doing so he had revealed a streak of ruthlessness previously hidden, a willingness to alienate many who had, in the 1970s, counted themselves his allies. Could the Neil Kinnock of those years have looked forward a decade he might scarcely have believed the transformation himself. In advance of the general election it had still to be shown whether voters were satisfied that these new-found political and manipulative skills were applicable to running the country in a better and fairer way than Thatcher's Conservative administration. The evidence of the fluctuating opinion polls was unclear.

The role of Opposition Leader has many frustrating aspects, among them the inescapable truth that the voters' decision is loaded by the power of the incumbent Prime Minister to choose the date of the election. By the judicious exercise of that power she can also, to an extent, determine the issues on which the campaign is fought. Kinnock would find it hard to bear if, having spent four years cleaning out the stables, he were to be out-jockeyed in the actual race.

And assuming he did win it? Prime Minister Kinnock would, at least to begin with, be reluctant to delegate any portion of his hard-won authority. Because he has more than once been let down by the incautious remarks and actions of colleagues, he would want to keep a close eye on the detail of all controversial legislation – and in the first months of a Labour government most legislation would be controversial. As far as possible, he would deal himself with representatives of those vested interests most likely to oppose the party's programme, especially emissaries from industry and the City.

His shortage of experience in heading a government department and in negotiating with foreign statesmen will be stressed by his electoral opponents. Anticipating that, he has made more overseas trips in the last four years than is usual for an Opposition leader. In 1986, as well as his visits to America and Europe, he fitted in India and Jamaica. Through the Socialist International he has met many overseas Labour leaders, although most are out of government.

From the popular, non-expert standpoint the acid tests for a Prime Minister in the field of foreign affairs are the abilities to 'get on with' the

Americans and 'stand up to' the Russians. Labour's defence policy will leave Kinnock exposed to criticism on both fronts – and would have done, no matter how much previous experience he could boast. Here, he could expect stout support from his Shadow Foreign Secretary, Denis Healey, one of the most experienced men in any party at negotiating with Americans and Russians. Despite the uneasy relationship between the two men in earlier years, Healey, with no realistic hope of becoming leader himself, would have no motive for treachery and no inclination to kick over the traces. On the home side, the same would be true of the other two senior men on his team, Roy Hattersley and Peter Shore. Kinnock has shown in his handling of the Shadow Cabinet that he will not be dominated or cowed by his more experienced colleagues, any more than he is by the self-righteous rhetoricians of the hard left.

A Kinnock administration would be as much a reflection of the views and style of its leader as the Thatcher administration has been. The pressures of those early months, as he laid the foundations for his personal concept of the new socialist Britain, would be great. But he has deep reserves of adrenalin – enough to project him across the obstacles and disappointments that would undoubtedly crop up. After the impotent years of opposition, he would cherish power. Early on, he would discover which senior colleagues he could trust, and would gradually interfere less in their departments. Those he found seriously inadequate would be dismissed or sidelined without ceremony. Although his personal manner is accommodating and affable, he is impatient with incompetence, particularly if it interferes with his larger objectives.

His family would enjoy life at Downing Street. Glenys, with her involvement in politics dating back to childhood, would relish being hostess to politicians and statesmen. Neil would find her a valuable inspiration and sounding-board – more so than any Prime Ministerial spouse of recent memory – although the suggestion that she would be at the centre of a powerful 'kitchen cabinet' is a fantasy of Labour's opponents. She has no such inclination and, even if she had, Neil would not allow it. They would miss the minor domestic pleasures, such as the chance to slip out late at night for an impromptu meal, but in any case as opposition leader those opportunities have occurred less and less. As the Indian restaurant incident confirmed in December 1986, such forays into the real world are scarcely feasible nowadays for anyone with a high public profile.

But will any of it happen? He has won previous political battles with apparent ease. Can he win the final one? Kinnock would find it difficult to accept that he could not, or to adjust to it. The Greenwich by-election of February 1987 was an undoubted setback, and there would be others.

But, on balance, an assessment of the man and the recent national mood, combined with a searching look into the crystal ball, suggest that it is more likely than not that Labour's youngest and most attractive leader for years will one day become Prime Minister, and an effective one.

Chronology

28 March 1942	Neil Kinnock born at Tredegar, South Wales
1961	Enters University College, Cardiff, to study history and industrial relations
1965	President of Students' Union
1965	Graduated BA
1966	Awarded teaching diploma, joins WEA
1967	Marries Glenys Parry in her native Anglesey
1969	Selected as Labour candidate for Bedwellty
January 1970	First child Stephen born
June 1970	Elected to Parliament. Labour lose general election
December 1971	Daughter Rachel born
1972	Family move from Wales to London
March 1974	Labour win election. Kinnock becomes PPS to Michael Foot
1975	Resigns as PPS
April 1976	Harold Wilson resigns as Prime Minister, replaced by James Callaghan. Kinnock rejects Callaghan's offer of junior ministerial post
April 1979	Labour defeated in general election
June 1979	Kinnock becomes front-bench spokesman on education
November 1980	Callaghan resigns. Michael Foot elected Labour leader
September 1981	Denis Healey beats Tony Benn in election for deputy leader after Kinnock abstains
June 1982	Britain wins Falklands war

1983

June	Conservatives win general election. Labour share of vote only 28% Foot announces resignation
15 September	Gallup poll puts Labour support at 24½%
2 October	Kinnock elected leader
31 October	Launches campaign on health services
October	Miners begin overtime ban
11 November	Eric Varley resigns from Shadow Cabinet
November	Cruise missiles arrive at Greenham Common

1984

January	Visit to Greece
February	Visit to Washington
1 March	Coal Board announce closure of Cortonwood colliery, Yorks.
1 March	Tony Benn wins Chesterfield by-election
6 March	Miners' strike begins
28 March	NEC passes unanimous resolution supporting miners
21 May	European election campaign launched
23 May	Stan Orme gets two sides in coal dispute together for first time, with Kinnock also present

29 May	Series of violent confrontations begins outside Orgreave coking plant
4 June	After meeting Liverpool city councillors, Kinnock calls on Government to find extra funds for the city
14 June	Elections to European Parliament. Labour share of poll up to 36.4% and number of seats almost doubled
15 July	Kinnock and Arthur Scargill share platform at Durham Miners' Gala
1 October	Defeated at Blackpool party conference on one-member-one-vote plan for reselecting Parliamentary candidates
28 October	*Sunday Times* reveals negotiations for Libyan support for miners
2 November	Kinnock turns down Scargill's invitation to address four NUM rallies
21 November	Visit to Moscow
30 November	Welsh taxi driver killed while he drives a miner to work. Kinnock and Scargill at Labour Party rally at Stoke
12 December	NEC decide not to commit Labour government to reimbursing the NUM for fines incurred in the strike

1985

3 January	Kinnock visits picket line in his constituency
8 January	Begins four-day visit to Nicaragua
17 January	Left-wingers force suspension of Commons to press for debate on miners' strike. Kinnock sharply critical
30 January	Larry Whitty elected general secretary of Labour Party, with Kinnock's support
1 February	In 'dented shield' speech, Kinnock urges local councils not to break the law in campaign against ratecapping
9 February	Glenys joins anti-Cruise demonstration at Molesworth
12 February	In Commons, Kinnock accuses Thatcher of lying about the Clive Ponting affair
26 February	Glenys on teachers' picket line
5 March	Coal strike ends after weeks of gradual drift back to work
10 March	GLC sets rate, breaking ranks with councils fighting ratecapping
27 March	NEC defeats left-wing move to commit party to quit NATO
31 March	On TV, Kinnock rules out coalition with Alliance in a hung Parliament
2 April	Jobs and Industry Campaign launched
14 April	Six constituency parties defy leadership and decide to affiliate black sections
16 April	Labour launches education document with a commitment to abolish private education 'very quickly'
28 April	Ken Livingstone selected as candidate for Brent East
2 May	Shire county elections show Labour starting to recover from 1983 low point
22 May	Clash with Benn at NEC. Benn's resolution to commit party to more radical policies defeated by 14 to 12
6 June	Black sections delegation visit Kinnock, find him 'very intransigent'
24 June	Kinnock attacks Militant at TGWU conference
26 June	NEC warns it will not bail rebel councils out of legal trouble. Also approves Walworth Road reorganization
2 July	Kinnock repudiates call by Scargill for more industrial action by miners

4 July	Labour lose Brecon and Radnor by-election by 559 votes after opinion polls had put them well in the lead
7 July	Bernie Grant selected as Labour candidate for Edmonton
8 July	NEC Home Policy Committee votes for council house sales
13 July	At Durham Miners' Gala, Kinnock says: 'We do not want glorious historic defeats'
23 July	Visit to East Africa
6 August	Launch of *A New Partnership, a New Britain*, advocating greater co-operation between unions and management
5 September	Compromise prevents TUC split over Government money for ballots
17 September	In Paris, Kinnock meets President Alfonsin of Argentina and talks about Falklands. Thatcher criticizes him
1 October	Kinnock attacks Militant at Bournemouth party conference. Heffer walks off platform
6 October	Rioting on Broadwater Estate, Tottenham, PC Keith Blakelock killed
20 October	Kinnock's visit to Liverpool ends row with councillors
21 November	After Liverpool councillors reject report on finances, Kinnock warns of expulsion of some Militant leaders
21 November	Launch of Red Wedge, pop stars supporting Labour
27 November	NEC suspends Liverpool district party
30 November	Liverpool gets £3m loan from Swiss banks
2 December	Labour win Tyne Bridge by-election with marginally increased share of the poll
18 December	Kinnock and Benn clash at NEC over Militant expulsions

1986

January	Dispute over future of Westland Helicopters leads to resignation of two Cabinet ministers
30 January	Kinnock says he will boycott Rupert Murdoch's newspapers after their move to Wapping without the print unions
26 February	NEC accept report of inquiry into Liverpool party, recommending expulsion of Militant leaders
19 March	In Budget debate, Roy Hattersley promises that Labour will produce 1,117,000 jobs in three years
24 March	Kinnock angrily rejects Walworth Road proposal to remove all legal restrictions on strike action
26 March	Seven NEC members walk out of meeting to prevent action to expel Liverpool Militants
26 March	NEC decide not to withdraw party membership from supporters of breakaway miners' union, the UDM
10 April	Labour score convincing win in Fulham by-election
15 April	Kinnock criticizes use of British bases for US bombing raid on Libya
22 April	Freedom and Fairness campaign launched
8 May	In by-elections, Alliance win Ryedale from Conservatives and lose by only 100 votes in West Derbyshire
21 May	Start of hearing into expulsion of Liverpool Militants
22 May	After two days only three expulsions completed, including Tony Mulhearn
26 May	Starts nine-day visit to India, where he promises a new look at immigration legislation

9 June	Candidate reselections end with only six MPs ousted
12 June	Derek Hatton expelled from party *in absentia*
17 July	Llin Golding wins Newcastle-under-Lyme by-election for Labour, but by only 799 from Liberal
22 July	Hard left groups form Campaign Forum at Hampstead meeting
30 July	Robert Kilroy-Silk resigns seat at Knowsley North, claiming he has been hounded out by Militant
1 September	TUC approve Labour policies of legislating for pre-strike ballots and national minimum wage
17 September	Starts three-day visit to Jamaica
24 September	NEC halt candidate selection for Knowsley North by-election, preventing nomination of Leslie Huckfield
28 September	New rose symbol introduced at party conference
29 September	On BBC *Panorama*, Caspar Weinberger, US Defence Secretary, attacks Labour's non-nuclear defence policy
30 September	Left-wingers Eric Heffer and Margaret Beckett voted off NEC
2 October	Conference reaffirms non-nuclear defence policy and commitment to NATO
14 October	Launch of *Investing in People*, new domestic policy document
15 October	Visit to Germany
6 November	Kinnock's first book, *Making Our Way*, published
13 November	Moderate George Howarth easily wins Knowsley North by-election despite non-co-operation of local party
28 November	Conservatives criticize Kinnock's discussions with defence lawyer in Government secrets case in Australia
29 November	Visit to United States to explain defence policy
10 December	Launch of defence policy document, *A Power for Good*
12 December	In fracas in Indian restaurant in Ealing

1987

22 January	Criticizes Thatcher for ineffective bid to block *New Statesman* article on Zircon spy satellite
26 February	Labour lose Greenwich by-election
6 March	Patricia Hewitt criticizes 'Loony Left' in letter to Frank Dobson
10 March	New defence row as James Callaghan calls for Trident missiles to be retained

Glossary of Initials

AEU	Amalgamated Engineering Union (formerly AUEW)
AGR	Advanced Gas-cooled Reactor
ASTMS	Association of Scientific, Technical and Managerial Staffs
AUEW	Amalgamated Union of Engineering Workers (later AEU)
BAAC	Black and Asian Advisory Committee (of NEC)
BBC	British Broadcasting Corporation
CBI	Confederation of British Industry
CLP	Constituency Labour Party
CND	Campaign for Nuclear Disarmament
CP	Communist Party
CPSA	Civil and Public Services Association
EEC	European Economic Community
EETPU	Electrical, Electronic, Telecommunications and Plumbing Union
GC	General Committee (of a CLP – formerly GMC)
GCHQ	Government Communications Headquarters
GLC	Greater London Council
GMBATU	General, Municipal, Boilermakers and Allied Trade Union
GMC	General Management Committee (of a CLP – now known as GC)
ILP	Independent Labour Party
IMF	International Monetary Fund
ITN	Independent Television News
ITV	Independent Television
LCC	Labour Co-ordinating Committee
LPYS	Labour Party Young Socialists
LWAC	Labour Women's Action Committee
MEP	Member of the European Parliament
NACODS	National Association of Colliery Overmen, Deputies and Shotfirers
NATO	North Atlantic Treaty Organization
NCB	National Coal Board
NCCL	National Council for Civil Liberties
NEC	National Executive Committee (of the Labour Party)
NGA	National Graphical Association
NHS	National Health Service
NS	*New Statesman*
NUJ	National Union of Journalists
NUM	National Union of Mineworkers
NUPE	National Union of Public Employees
NUR	National Union of Railwaymen
NUS	National Union of Students
PLP	Parliamentary Labour Party
PPS	Parliamentary Private Secretary
PWR	Pressurized Water Reactor
RSL	Revolutionary Socialist League (Militant tendency)
SDP	Social Democratic Party (Britain)

SI	Socialist International
SOGAT	Society of Graphical and Allied Trades
THORP	Thermal Oxide Reprocessing Plant
TUC	Trades Union Congress
TUFL	Trade Unions for Labour
TGWU	Transport and General Workers Union
UDM	Union of Democratic Mineworkers
USDAW	Union of Shop, Distributive and Allied Workers
WEA	Workers' Educational Association
YS	Young Socialists
YTURC	Youth Trade Union Rights Campaign

Bibliography

Crick, Michael, *The March of Militant*; Faber 1986.

Crick, Michael, *Scargill and the Miners*; Penguin 1985.

Drower, G. M. F., *Neil Kinnock – the Path to Leadership*; Weidenfeld 1984.

Durbin, Elizabeth, *New Jerusalems: The Labour Party and the Economics of Democratic Socialism*; Routledge 1985.

Foot, Michael, *Another Heart and Other Pulses*; Collins 1984.

Goodhart, David and Wintour, Patrick, *Eddie Shah and the Newspaper Revolution*; Coronet 1986

Goodman, Geoffrey, *The Miners' Strike*; Pluto 1985.

Harris, Robert, *The Making of Neil Kinnock*; Faber 1984.

Hattersley, Roy, *Choose Freedom*; Michael Joseph 1987.

Heffer, Eric, *Labour's Future – Socialist or SDP Mark 2?* Verso 1986.

Hoggart, Simon and Leigh, David, *Michael Foot: a Portrait*; Hodder & Stoughton 1981.

Kellner, Peter and Hitchens, Christopher, *Callaghan: the Road to Number Ten*; Cassell 1976.

Kilroy-Silk, Robert, *Hard Labour*; Chatto and Windus 1986.

Kinnock, Neil, *Making Our Way*; Blackwell 1986.

Lloyd, John and Wintour, Patrick, *The Miners' Strike*; Routledge 1986.

MacGregor, Ian, *The Enemies Within: The Story of the Miners' Strike 1984–5*; Collins 1986.

Mann, John and Woolas, Phil, *Labour and Youth: the Missing Generation*; Fabian Society 1986.

Pelling, Henry, *A Short History of the Labour Party*; Macmillan 1961 (eighth edition 1985).

Wilsher, Peter, MacIntyre, Donald and Jones, Michael, *Strike: Thatcher, Scargill and the Miners*; Deutsch 1985.

Index